Object Lessons

Object Lessons

*How Nineteenth-Century Americans
Learned to Make Sense of the Material World*

SARAH ANNE CARTER

OXFORD
UNIVERSITY PRESS

OXFORD

UNIVERSITY PRESS

Oxford University Press is a department of the University of Oxford. It furthers
the University's objective of excellence in research, scholarship, and education
by publishing worldwide. Oxford is a registered trade mark of Oxford University
Press in the UK and certain other countries.

Published in the United States of America by Oxford University Press
198 Madison Avenue, New York, NY 10016, United States of America.

Library of Congress Cataloging-in-Publication Data
Names: Carter, Sarah Anne, author.
Title: Object lessons : how nineteenth-century Americans learned to make
sense of the material world / Sarah Anne Carter.
Description: New York, NY, United States of America : Oxford University
Press, 2018. | Includes bibliographical references and index.
Identifiers: LCCN 2018006686 (print) | LCCN 2018022541 (ebook) |
ISBN 9780190225049 (updf) | ISBN 9780190225056 (epub) |
ISBN 9780190908317 (online component) | ISBN 9780190225032 (hardback : alk. paper)
Subjects: LCSH: Education—United States—History—19th century. |
Perceptual learning. | Material culture—Study and teaching—
United States—History—19th century.
Classification: LCC LA216 (ebook) | LCC LA216 .C37 2018 (print) |
DDC 370.97309034—dc23
LC record available at https://lccn.loc.gov/2018006686

1 3 5 7 9 8 6 4 2
Printed by Sheridan Books, Inc., United States of America

For my loving parents, Constance Daniele Carter and Paul Carter, who serve as object lessons in what parents should be.
And for my son, Paul.

CONTENTS

ACKNOWLEDGMENTS

In the decade that I have been working on this project I have acquired an archive of academic and personal kindnesses much longer than my endnotes.

This project started as a dissertation on object lessons, which I completed as part of the History of American Civilization program (now American Studies) at Harvard University. I was fortunate to have had Laurel Thatcher Ulrich and Jennifer Roberts coadvise this project. Laurel was my mentor long before I began work on my dissertation. Her faith in me led me to pursue a research topic that did not initially appear to register in secondary historical sources and to explore questions that crossed and redefined disciplinary boundaries. Jennifer challenged me to think through the aesthetic implications of my project, dramatically expanding the interpretative potential of object lessons. I could not have done this work without them. Committee members John Stauffer, Jill Lepore, and Ivan Gaskell guided my work with transformative questions and thoughtful suggestions. This research was funded by an ACLS/ Mellon Dissertation Completion fellowship, a yearlong fellowship for work at the Smithsonian American Art Museum, as well as short-term fellowships to conduct research at the Winterthur Museum, the Huntington Library, a Patricia Klingenstein Research Fellowship at the New-York Historical Society, a Cotsen Children's Library Research Fellowship at Princeton University, and a Jay and Deborah Last Fellowship for work at the American Antiquarian Society. Additional support from the Charles Warren Center, the History of American Civilization, and the Harvard Graduate Student Council allowed me to take shorter research trips and to share my work at academic conferences. From 2010 to 2013, support from Harvard's History and Literature program and since 2013 the Chipstone Foundation have allowed me to continue to develop and present my research at conferences in the United States and abroad. I gratefully acknowledge all of this support.

Several archivists, curators, and researchers deserve special thanks. This project would have been impossible without their daily efforts. At the American Antiquarian Society, Gigi Barnhill and Laura Wasowicz produced amazing things (as if by magic) from the stacks. Elizabeth Pope, Jackie Penny, Caroline Sloat, and Paul Erickson made it such a pleasant place to work. At Cotsen, Andrea Immell and Aaron Pickett did not flinch when I took over part of their office with my boxes full of rather odd things and kindly offered me their time and good humor for the whole month of my fellowship. At Winterthur, Rosemary Krill, Jeanne Solensky, Helena Richardson, and Emily Guthrie went above and beyond their duties to help me find sources. At the Smithsonian, Amelia Goerlitz and the late Cindy Mills created a wonderful academic home (a scholar's paradise), the library staff graciously handled my endless interlibrary loan requests, and curator Peggy Kidwell helped me think about the pedagogical items in their collections. At the National Museum of the American Indian, curator Emil Her Many Horses thoughtfully spent an entire afternoon with me helping me understand a single photograph. Reference librarians at the New-York Historical Society; staff at the Penfield Library Special Collections, State University of New York–Oswego; Julio Hernandez-Delgado at the Hunter College Archives; Edward Copenhagen at Gutman Library Special Collections; and Diana Carey at the Schlesinger Library all provided invaluable assistance. Additional research at the British Library and the Victoria and Albert Museum have fleshed out my project. Expert research support first at Harvard by Marina Magilore and later at the University of Wisconsin–Madison by the tenacious and smart Ann Glasscock helped me bring this project to its completion.

I look back with fondness on my years in the History of American Civilization program at Harvard. I am grateful to program staff Christine McFadden and Arthur Patton-Hock. My cohort, Jamie Jones, Eve Mayer, and Christina Adkins, were and are wonderful scholars. Jamie read my whole manuscript and has always been there when I have needed her. Phyllis Thompson provided a crucial reading of a chapter at an early stage in the project, as did Clinton Williams. Lauren Brandt, Noam Maggor, Katherine Stevens, George Blaustein, Mark Hanna, Judy Kertesz, and Katie Rieder all helped. Beyond the History of American Civilization program, Amber Moulton has read and improved many parts of this project. Ellery Foutch, Robin Veder, and Sarah Gould—all friends from my time at the Smithsonian—have collaborated with me on conference panels and commented on my work. Jennifer Black and Mary Beth Zundo frequently share object lesson references with me. Robin Bernstein, Mary Malloy, and Betsy More have cheered me on with references and suggestions. Jules Prown kindly discussed the history of his method with me and its relationships to object lessons. Generous friends Emily Jones, Daniela Jodorkovsky, Margaret Healey-Varley, Pam and Nick Schonberger, Andrea Tao, and Erica Westenberg have offered me their homes and their company during research trips. I have been privileged to present drafts of my writing to many audiences at conferences and universities. I am deeply thankful for these opportunities, though there is no space to detail each of them here.

In 2013, I started working at the Chipstone Foundation in Milwaukee as the curator and director of research. Jonathan Prown has been a fantastic and supportive mentor and colleague who gave me the space and resources I needed to finish this project, even when it took longer than expected. Chipstone also provided an important subvention in support of the color images in this book. The whole Chipstone team—Claudia Arzeno, Elizabeth Dunn, Brent Budsberg, David Knox, Shana McCaw, Ted McCoy, Melissa Hartley Omholt, Jackie Sarich, Tina Shinabeck, Steve Wallschlaeger, and Natalie Wright—has supported and encouraged me as I have worked on various parts of this project.

When my son, Paul, was born in 2014, Milwaukee became home. Since then, my dear friends Carolyn Lee, Katie Vater, and Kay Wells have walked with me though many joys and challenges. Jodi and John Eastberg have modeled intellectual and personal generosity and have brought many kind and interesting new people into my life. Kelsey Weaver's Urban Om yoga studio has been a welcoming second home. I am grateful for the good friends I have made there. My writing group of wonderful women academics (Kay, Katie, Jodi, Tara Daly, and Sarah Schaefer) have kept me intellectually grounded and inspired. Milwaukee and Chicago friends Allison Efford, Katie Hemple, Caitlin Rafaelidys, and Bess Williamson Stiles, all professionals and moms to awesome boys, have encouraged me through their examples. I have found hospitable communities in both the UW–Milwaukee's Art History and at UW–Madison's Art History and Material Culture programs. My son's caregiver, Jennifer Wills, has provided Paul and me with so much love and support.

This book has been a long time coming. As I revised my manuscript I had the privilege of working on the Tangible Things exhibition, book, and course with Laurel Ulrich, Ivan Gaskell, Sara Schechner, and Sammie Van Gerbrig. That project helped me think through the process of teaching with objects in new ways. Nancy Toff has been a patient, brilliant, and always wryly funny editor, even as she kindly pushed me to get stuff done. The anonymous readers she commissioned for my draft provided excellent feedback and helped me dial into the core of my argument. I am grateful for their thoughtful responses to my work. Nancy's able assistants, most recently Elizabeth Vaziri, and project manager Julia Turner have shepherded this book to completion. My editorial collaborators and friends Ivan Gaskell and Ellery Foutch supported me when my life got in the way of our projects, displaying a true generosity of spirit. Jamie Jones never stopped asking me questions about my book and reminding me that it would get done and be worthwhile. JoJo Bahnam, Daniela Jodorkovsky, and Erica Foley Hanson Pietricola have always understood what this project means to me. My little sister, Allison, has encouraged me and made me laugh whenever I have needed it.

Most important, my amazing parents, Paul and Constance Carter, again and again have flown out to Milwaukee to provide care and unwavering support. They have visited museums with me, read endless drafts, and listened to me talk about object-based learning more than is reasonable. From the moment I conceptualized this project—and many years earlier when they decided to send me to Montessori school so I would not be kept back in first grade for a slow start in reading—they have validated and nurtured my intellectual choices and abilities. This book is dedicated to them for good reason.

Paul's birth made this topic a mystery again and made this book better. He showed me how object lessons work, how a young mind unfolds and considers the ideas embedded in everything around it. Like so many object teachers before me, I hope that my son's curiosity, fueled by his excellent little school, New World Montessori, and our own object lessons, can help inspire him to "wander truant-like among so many good things." This has reinforced for me the vital power of observation and the potential of interdisciplinary learning to teach reasoning skills, if deployed equitably. These are and always have been the real stakes of my project. And so, this book is also for him.

PROLOGUE: A BOX OF IDEAS

I would like this book to arrive packed away at the bottom of a heavy box of carefully selected things. Each item piled on top of this narrow volume would be individually packed in its own small compartment. There would be no labels. On the way to the buried title page, you would be challenged to differentiate flax from hemp, whalebone from India rubber, slate from granite, and mace from fragrant ginger. Perhaps you might stop to unwrap an oyster shell, a pair of scissors, or a hunk of porcelain. A particular item might force you to pause and to wonder.

To the curious reader, this box would be filled with both things and questions. Why was this item included? What is it? Where did it come from? Is it familiar? How is it used? These queries would not simply be about the material world, the physical qualities of the items, or their potential functions. The items in the box might also provoke inquiries into the nature of knowing and perceiving. Are there patterns? Absences? How does one know what an item may be? What is assumed and what is sensed? Maybe something draws one back to a nature walk, a dusty mineral collection, a display in a museum, a grandparent's trunk, a yard sale, or a kindergarten round of Show and Tell. Some might just wish to look closely and try to tell a compelling story.

As a material prologue to this study of object lessons, this box of varied things would not be a metaphor but an orientation or, better yet, a medium for disorientation. Nearly any material thing, placed at the center of one's sustained analysis, may become surprisingly foreign, complex, and confusing. Upon close examination, one may discover the limits, the assumptions, and the unexamined associations that undergird what most think they know about the material world. More significantly, the words used to identify and explain those things may be imprecise, or misleading. An observer is often unable to express what he or she does not know.

Object lessons were designed to address this intellectual gap by attempting to teach children how to find and express the ideas in the things around them.

Notions of this material and linguistic disconnect—the relationship between reality and its description—are key to the origins of object lessons and to the debates and transformations that surrounded this practice in the nineteenth-century United States. To take this historic practice seriously one must consider the potential of this interpretative unsteadiness to structure classroom pedagogy, daily life, and intellectual culture. Starting in the early 1860s, object lessons shaped the ways Americans reasoned from the material world and have impacted how scholars have worked to find meaning in that world ever since. To learn how to study things was considered the best way to learn how to think, leading from close looking to critical thinking. As you begin this book, pause and mull over the possibility that a box of things may be a box of ideas.

Introduction: Reason from Things

For most twenty-first-century readers, an "object lesson" is an unexceptional metaphor used to describe any sort of reasoning from a concrete example to an abstract concept. Everything from the children's TV character Elmo and Ebola survivors to subpoenaed text messages and the latest financial crisis has been dubbed an object lesson.[1] In academic circles, the phrase has appeared as the title or subtitle of numerous scholarly books, articles, columns, features, and museum exhibitions, typically capitalizing on a potential reader's familiarity with the term to introduce a key piece of evidence, to offer a history of a specific object or topic, or to indicate a material culture approach.[2] These familiar understandings of the term capture just one aspect of its meaning and history. According to the *Oxford English Dictionary*, "a striking practical example of a principle or ideal" is only the secondary definition of this phrase. The primary definition of object lesson, "(now chiefly *hist.*) a lesson in which a pupil's examination of a material object forms the basis for instruction," merely hints at the complex mode of reasoning at the center of this nineteenth-century practice. It is the *examination*, the process of learning to perceive, and not simply the material object under examination that matters.

By the 1860s, most students, their parents, and their teachers were quite familiar with this primary definition of object lesson. It was the newest trend in pedagogy and was implemented in schools across the United States from Boston to San Francisco. There were many variations on the object lesson. The most formal variation had originated in England three decades earlier and comprised a five-step method that was applied to the study of a carefully selected series of objects and pictures. It sometimes even included lessons on the human body and the senses, the physical vehicles that gave one access to the material world. Teachers might begin a lesson with a pair of scissors, a penknife, loafsugar, a chair, a match, a butterfly, or a picture of a happy family. In an ideal lesson, their aim would be to lead a classroom of students from examining an object or image to writing a composition about it. Along the way, they worked to develop students' perceptive skills, reasoning ability, and vocabulary. The first step was a close study of a carefully selected object. Next, students were led to examine the object for its determinative qualities. Then, students were to consider the information that was not evident solely through sensory engagement with a material thing. In the fourth step students learned to categorize the objects they studied, perhaps as minerals or spices. Finally, students were to write a composition about the selected object. Another way to describe this process is the gradual movement from training children's perceptive abilities through observation, to developing their "conceptive powers" by moving from perceptions to ideas and the development of new information, next to the process of organizing and categorizing that information, to finally employing "reason and judgment" to write a narrative composition about the object.

These lessons were intended to unfold slowly, over a child's entire primary school career, with the early steps intended for younger children. A class of six-year-olds might each be given a ladybug and asked to describe the insect's shape and color; eight-year-old children would later learn to find and describe the specific aspects of the insect's wings, legs, and antennae before eventually learning about the creature's habitat and use to man. Similarly, young children might each be handed a needle and asked to determine the function of this common object and its parts. Slightly older children would examine it to consider the qualities of the object that allow it to function as a needle. Later on they might examine it to determine evidence of its manufacture and to learn about how many hands touched it as it was transferred from an iron mine to a sewing bag, before comparing it to other metals and finally writing a composition on it. Children from ages six to fourteen could all learn from this simple thing.[3] In this way, "object lesson" often referred to a highly developed pedagogical method, as opposed to a single lesson.

The term also referred to more general, less formal ways of teaching that involved objects. For example, a description of a simple "object lesson" to be used in a primary school began with a teacher holding up a book, asking children to identify the object and then following up with, "How do you know it is a book?" The lesson continued to examine the book for its parts, to consider how paper was made, and perhaps to discuss the things—other than books—that were made from paper like a bandbox, a letter, or a kite.[4] The object lesson referred not to the book, but to the entire classroom conversation organized around the book. Sometimes, the more general phrase "object teaching" could be used to refer to this type of lesson, though there was not always a sharp difference between the two terms.

The classroom practice of object lessons was premised on the notion that children needed to be taught to experience the objects and images around them more fully. This book examines the intellectual, cultural, and material history of this forgotten nineteenth-century classroom practice. Educators hoped that through object lessons children would learn to derive meaning from the material world and to reason both critically and morally based on this knowledge. During the Civil War these lessons were a particularly appealing way of addressing anxiety about the nation's failed reasoning skills. Americans had not been able to think their way through the crises of slavery, succession, and war. The hope was that students trained in this method would approach the world with curiosity and the confidence of making their own rational and moral judgments. The goal was to teach children to think for themselves and to avoid the lazy, simplistic thinking brought about by memorization and rote learning. This was the ideal of the object lesson and the goal of object-based teaching. But something else happened. The pedagogy that was designed to teach expansive thinking often ended up teaching a specific, object-based way of looking at the world. Instead of replacing rote learning with a new expansive pedagogy, material evidence sometimes became a receptacle for already held concepts, serving as mere illustrations.

As the practice gradually fell out of favor in the classroom, "object lesson" emerged as a useful metaphor to describe a way of reasoning from a concrete object or example to an abstract idea. It became a way to talk about objects, pictures, and even people. At the Hampton Normal and Agricultural School, for example, the phrase "object lesson" simultaneously referred to both a way of teaching and to the African American and Native American students taught there. Politicians such as Grover Cleveland used the idea of the object lesson to argue about tariff reform and the meanings of goods. Authors, advertisers, and museum curators employed the metaphor to tell stories, to sell their products, and to explain their exhibitions. The pedagogy grew up alongside and shaped the materialism that came to define the post–Civil War United States. As both practice and metaphor, object lessons were the mechanism through which things in classrooms and parlors, in department stores and on individuals' bodies came to communicate much more information than modern viewers may be able to discern from those same things today. The object lesson had been intended to solve the nation's reasoning problem. Instead, it became a tool that allowed one to move quickly from object to idea. In the process, material things became shorthand signs for widely held ideas about American life, defining the ways images, commodities, labor, and citizenship were understood in the decades after the Civil War.

But the object lesson idea did not begin that way.

1

Windows and Ladders

As a student of object lessons, I am at a great disadvantage. Trained instructors typically passed on their techniques through demonstration, relayed from one teacher to another. Like learning a craft, it had to be experienced. I cannot turn up at the Home and Colonial Schools at Gray's Inn Road, London, on a Tuesday afternoon. There, in 1848, curious visitors would witness students (who ranged in age from two to twenty) develop the idea of four, the parts of a watch, the concept of friability, or the work of a refiner. I simply have to accept that five- or six-year-old children watched their teacher rub a loaf of stale bread to pieces to teach the abstract notion that a category of things crumbles. Or that older children, when presented with silver ore and a specimen of the bright, shiny refined metal, learned how one became the other and, more boldly, how the process reflected Christ's role as a refiner and purifier of people. I have to imagine the headmaster leading his pupil-teachers through a dissection of these Tuesday afternoon model lessons, asking, "How will a child, taught in this way, regard words in reference to objects?" And their eager reply, "As the signs of ideas." On a Tuesday afternoon in 1848, objects—a hunk of silver or a block of salt—were understood as ideas; for the pupil-teachers the many model lessons were the idea of the method. I know from these lessons that simply reading and studying the detailed transcript of the event will always be inadequate.[1]

I cannot observe and assess whether objects became, perhaps simply were, ideas in the hands of trained teachers. Published accounts show clearly that object teachers believed the process of finding these ideas in things exercised children's senses and minds. They believed that through heightened faculties children could better reason based on what they observed and perceived, as opposed to passively accepting what they were told. As Elizabeth Mayo, the foremost nineteenth-century British writer on object lessons, explained in an 1838 manual, the observation of things under children's direct purview "promotes habits of truth and veracity, it involves the necessity of clear and distinct ideas and prevents the practice so common to all of slurring over our impressions and contenting ourselves with vague and ill-defined notions."[2] The hope was that children would learn to think more rigorously and have solid evidence for their conclusions. For the evangelical Home and Colonial Schools this reasoning was explicitly moral and religious. In the fall of 1848, the society published a new journal in which editors suggested that this pedagogy could even stave off the revolutions then rocking Europe by teaching the common person to reason, both intellectually and morally.[3]

In the first half of the nineteenth century, European and American educators came to believe that the observation of a loaf of stale bread could help children learn to think. Nineteenth-century educators liked to imagine the origin of object-lesson pedagogy in Johann Heinrich Pestalozzi's makeshift convent schoolroom in a war-torn Swiss canton—a romantic setting far removed from an orderly classroom like that of the Home and Colonial Schools. In this environment, lessons drawn from actual things became a way to make ideas clear to children and to develop their mental capacity. This mode of pedagogy replaced both textual descriptions and "counterfeits," like pictorial representations, with the observation of and encounter with actual things. While Pestalozzi's system was never fully developed in his schools or definitively outlined in his own convoluted letters, lectures, and manuals on method, teachers who worked along with him in his many educational endeavors adopted and modified some of the key aspects of his pedagogy for their own schools and their own needs. In some ways, Pestalozzi's biography and pedagogy served as a fickle prism through which later educators were able to shape and project their own visions for object-based classroom teaching.

Transplanted to England, lessons on objects were transformed into orderly, systematic, and moral exercises that keyed into the intellectual and moral goals of the Scottish Enlightenment, particularly as read through the work of John Locke and Adam Smith. Though often overlooked in reductive studies of empiricism, sensory engagement and experience are central to the writing of these thinkers and their continental counterparts.[4] In this context, lessons on objects and common things affected both parenting and teaching in Europe and—of central importance to this study—the new United States, where the sensory, sentimental, and intellectual capacity of a young citizen to observe, feel, and think was of increasing moral and political importance.

Pestalozzi did not invent the notion that children could learn through their interaction with and experience of the material world. John Locke's theories about understanding and perception, exemplified in his famous description of the human mind as a sheet of blank paper imprinted on by experiences, made Pestalozzi's pedagogy possible. In his "Essay Concerning Human Understanding," Locke explains that all ideas come from sensation or reflection, from one's actual experience of the external, physical material world or from consideration of the "internal workings of the mind."[5] According to Locke, these experiences are then the foundation for ideas and form the basis of knowledge. Locke links this development to education, noting in "Thoughts Concerning Education" that "the difference to be found in the manners and abilities of men, is owing more to their education than anything else."[6] Locke, writing for the wealthy father of his students, is talking about the education of a gentleman, but the same process, the mental "seasoning" of children, had a broader application.

A key part of this seasoning was stocking the mind with ideas. The perception of things like color or sound were "simple ideas" that had to come to an individual through the senses and were one's foundational knowledge. To illustrate this principle, he offered an anecdote:

> A studious blind man, who had mightily beat his head about visible objects, and made use of the explication of his books and friends, to understand those names of light and colours which often came in his way, bragged one day, That he now understood what scarlet signified. Upon which, his friend demanding what scarlet was? The blind man answered, It was like the sound of a trumpet. Just such an understanding of the name of any other simple idea will he have, who hopes to get it only from a definition, or other words made use of to explain it.[7]

In this case, the blind man only grasps the idea of the color, the possibility of a verbal definition, as opposed to the reality behind it. He only has words. In a way, this is a problem that lessons on objects sought to address. All knowledge for Locke was developed through either sensation or reflection, but the sensory input was necessary. More complex ideas were built from these perceptions. As Locke explained, a blind man cannot understand a rainbow without the simple concept of color. Similarly, how can one represent in mere words the taste of a pineapple or an oyster? Sensory engagement and experience are required.

In *Emile, or Education* (1762), Jean-Jacques Rousseau offered his vision of learning through the interactions between a tutor and his charge. Emile is encouraged to learn by following the "course of nature." Rousseau advocated a child-centered system in which a child would learn by experiencing the world around him and acquiring skills—like reading and writing—only as he needed them.[8] As with Locke, the emphasis is on giving a child experiences, and in some cases carefully orchestrating those experiences, in order to shape him into a reasoning being. With these basic concepts in mind, let's meet Pestalozzi.

Pestalozzi's Lessons

The image, ideals, and ambitions of Johann Heinrich Pestalozzi may be more appealing than the man himself, as is the case with most Romantic heroes.[9] Upon first meeting him, visitors were immediately struck by his disheveled appearance. One new assistant noted that the pedagogue's stockings, ungartered, hung loose around his ankles, and his coat was covered in dust. He continued, "His whole appearance was so miserable that I was inclined to pity him, and yet there was in his expression something so great, that I viewed him with astonishment and veneration."[10] Shown in an 1804 chalk drawing, the thinker's face is incised with pronounced wrinkles and his chin-length hair is unkempt. Pestalozzi stares off into the distance, with an intensely piercing gaze, his lips pursed.[11] A terracotta mask from around 1808 highlights his wide, deep-set eyes and his furrowed brow.[12] Posthumous representations of him as a teacher depict him actively looking at his students, with his head angled toward them. He always stares into the faces of his young charges, typically represented as a mixed group of boys and girls, of all ages and states of dress and cleanliness, actively buzzing around him. Typically, he encircles them with his arms or reaches out to touch them. Instead of an orderly stepped gallery or rows of forms and tables, these classroom scenes are full of movement embodying the active learning experiences he described in his many letters.[13] As Pestalozzi wrote of his time as a teacher in Stans, in Unterwalden,

> The tediousness of the ordinary school tone vanished like a ghost from my rooms. They wished,—tried,—persevered,—succeeded: and they laughed. Their tone was not that of learners, it was the tone of unknown powers awakened from sleep, of a heart and mind exalted with the feeling of what these powers could and would lead them to do.[14]

It was in this kind of almost magical environment later teachers liked to imagine the birth of object lessons.

It is no coincidence that Pestalozzi's aversion to the "tediousness of the ordinary school tone" may resonate with Rousseau's *Emile*. Pestalozzi read *Emile* as a young man and used the book as his guide for educating his only child, Jean-Jacques. Pestalozzi kept a journal of his son's early education in which he described his son's observation of a bubbling brook, the boy's confusion over the meaning of numbers and ways of interacting with his family, as well as his father's worries about balancing liberty with obedience—often at odds with

Figure 1.1. H. Bendel, "Pestalozzi in His School," *Howitt's Journal* 3, no. 77 (June 17, 1848): 383. Pestalozzi was often portrayed gazing intently at his students, modeling the close looking that would come to define his pedagogy.

Rousseau's ideas. A reader sympathizes with the well-intentioned, frustrated Pestalozzi who implored, "O God! who art my Father and the Father of my child, teach me to understand the holy natural laws by which Thou preparest us slowly by means of an innumerable variety of impressions for conceiving exact and complete ideas, of which words are but the signs."[15] Pestalozzi was clearly discouraged that he could not be as dispassionate, patient, and successful a tutor as the fictionalized Rousseau. Rousseau's natural method did not account for family ties, particularly the role of the mother, the need for moral order and more direct lessons, and in this case, a total lack of comprehension on the part of the young pupil. In spite of Pestalozzi's efforts to teach his only child according to nature's directions, the experiment did not improve his son's painful life. Jacobli, as his family called him, did not learn to read until age twelve and never mastered a trade or his moods. The young man married and fathered one son, Pestalozzi's only grandchild. Jacobli suffered from ill health, including a combination of seizures and paralysis. He died at the age of thirty-one.[16] Pestalozzi's journal of his parenting experience echoes the concerns his teaching would suggest decades later in Stans (1798–99) and in his subsequent schools in Bergdorf (1799–1804) and Yverdon (1805–25). How can one teach children through experience and simultaneously control the learning process—something he was unable to do?

In the spring of 1798 the French Revolution arrived in Swiss territories, leading to the demise of the aristocratic regime that long dominated the Swiss cantons. Pestalozzi supported the new, short-lived Helvetian Republic, led by a Directory of five members. Citizen Pestalozzi produced government pamphlets and worked to ease the political transition from ancien régime toward the ideal of brotherly equality. His earlier writing projects and attempts at serving the poor prepared him for the task of communicating with and about a range of people.[17]

In the decades prior to the Revolution, Pestalozzi, accompanied by his wife, had purchased land for a farm. This venture fell apart after the European crop failure of 1771–72. Undaunted, he installed looms in his farmhouse and tried to teach the poor children in his community to weave cotton. This early industrial school also failed because the children were not self-supporting. However, this experiment inspired Pestalozzi to think about how basic education linked to manual training could serve the poor. His popular novel and work of social criticism *Leonard and Gertrude* (1781) was based on his observations of village life. In it, he offered descriptions of the importance of the mother's role in the family and village as a moral and educational hub, even in the face of corruption. It is his emphasis on the role of the mother in children's education and the importance of early childhood education in the home for which Pestalozzi is best known, especially because of later developments in the kindergarten movement through the work of one of his assistants, Friedrich Fröebel.[18] In *Leonard and Gertrude*, a book of country life, he also theorized about the importance of education for the poor, by creating a village school organized along the lines of mother Gertrude's home instruction.[19] The vignettes Pestalozzi created for his readers offered a sentimental education through example, like other novels of the eighteenth century.[20] With the support of the Helvetian government he would have a new chance to serve the poor. They promised him a school in which he could attempt the reform of the new republic through education.[21]

In fall of 1798 the new republic was rocked with violence. French forces, possibly reacting to protests from devout Catholics roiling under the secular influence of the Directory, killed hundreds of people near the market town of Stans. The massacre left many children without one or both parents. The children needed care and the Helvetian government had promised Citizen Pestalozzi a school. Against the advice of his long-suffering wife, the fifty-three-year-old teacher arrived in Stans in December of 1798. In January he opened his school on the grounds of an Ursuline convent. Around fifty students ranging in age from five to fifteen arrived; more followed. According to contemporary descriptions, they were covered in vermin; some had been beggars and most were barely able to recite their letters. The school survived for only five months, but Pestalozzi's encounters with these children would make a lasting imprint on his pedagogy and legacy.[22]

In his letters—which were intended for publication—Pestalozzi described the importance of learning from and through his students. Pestalozzi modeled his approach on his ideas about motherhood. A mother, he noted, "must be able to judge daily, nay hourly from the child's eyes, lips and face of the slightest change in his soul."[23] The most striking thing Pestalozzi saw in children's faces was their ability to observe. He described the suffering children, "I saw in this combination of unschooled ignorance a power of seeing (*Anschauung*), and a firm conception of the known and the seen of which our ABC puppets have no notion." (These "ABC puppets" were students able to recite letters and memorize texts, as opposed to obtaining what he referred to as "real knowledge" through observation of the material world.) Pestalozzi continued,

> I learned from them—I must have been blind if I had not learned—to know the natural relation in which real knowledge stands to book-knowledge. I learned from them what a disadvantage this one-sided letter knowledge and entire reliance on words (which are only sound and noise when there is nothing behind them) must be. I saw what a hindrance this may be to the real power of observation (*Anschauung*), and the firm conception of the objects that surround us.[24]

Pestalozzi discovered the importance of adapting his system of learning to the students' "faculties or circumstances" in order to produce real learning.[25]

Lessons on objects were one way to approach this goal. Though it is impossible to re-create the first moment Pestalozzi and his teachers made the intellectual move to teaching with things, his followers record the memory of the event with a focus on two objects: a glass window and a ladder. Charles Mayo, arguably the best-known English student of Pestalozzi, placed the first lesson in Stans, to the "brutalized children" of the massacre; Hermann Krüsi, a teacher closer to Pestalozzi and the lesson, remembered it in Bergdorf, the master's next teaching appointment the following year. Regardless of the details, the story is the same.

Because the children were unable to think abstractly, the master decided to instruct the students with engravings, presenting them with pictures for discussion. As Charles Mayo described in his preface to his sister Elizabeth's *Lessons on Objects*, one day, a teacher began his lesson with an engraving of a simple ladder, likely asking students to look closely and to describe what they saw. Later lessons on such objects often noted the geometrics of the item, the color, the materials, its use, or the parts. The engravings were probably those made by an assistant to Pestalozzi, Johannes Buss, and likely similar to later published *Anschauungunterricht* available with both French and German text to help children learn to talk about objects and spaces. A boy of about six challenged the teacher explaining, "But there is a real ladder in the court-yard, why not talk about it rather than the picture?" According to Mayo, the teacher quickly dismissed the suggestion, noting, "The engraving is here . . . and it is more convenient to talk about what is before your eyes than to go into the court-yard to talk about the other." As the lesson continued, the teacher produced an engraving of a window, not unlike the windows in the classroom. The same boy protested again, "But why . . . why talk of this picture of a window when there is a real window in the room, and there is no need to go into the courtyard for it." When the teacher shared this story with Pestalozzi that evening, the thinker replied, "The boy is right." He continued, "The reality is better than the counterfeit: put away the engravings and let the class be instructed by means of real objects."[26] Krüsi also recalled the incident in his memoirs, noting that it was he who worked with the six-year-old boy who made the astute observation about the window and the ladder. He recalled that Pestalozzi replied, "When I repeated this childlike re-mark to Pestalozzi he exclaimed 'The boy is right; the real object is better than any picture since every drawing incompletely represents nature.' "[27]

Both items—a window and a ladder—were not simply things with innate qualities that could be described. Rather, they were also tools for accessing other experiences. Looking through the window, traveling up or across the ladder presented the lesson not as an end, but as the beginning of a sensory process. When Charles Mayo's younger sister Elizabeth created her *Lessons on Objects*, appropriately, "Glass" was the first lesson. Yet, in memories of one of Pestalozzi's students at Bergdorf, the lessons on items in the schoolroom take on a different cast and seem less symbolic. John Ramsauer, who would go on to teach with Pestalozzi through his schools in Yverdon, recalled that Pestalozzi led the students in an exercise on the paper-hangings in the schoolroom, on old, torn wallpaper. Looking back on his childhood, Ramsauer recalled what seemed like two- and three-hour sessions spent staring at the figures in the paper while Pestalozzi asked them what they saw among the shapes and colors and then, would form sentences for them to repeat: "I see a hole in the wainscoat [sic]" or "I see round-black figures on the paper hanging."[28] Such lessons may have trained children in observation and expression, helping the ten-year-old John and his younger classmates link descriptions with concrete realities. But how could this simple description help children learn to think?

Looking closely at material things, like the figure in the wallpaper, and making observations was one part of Pestalozzi's pedagogical philosophy, which encompassed all aspects of children's intellectual, moral, and physical develop-ment. Two key texts, the oddly named book *How Gertrude Teaches Her Children* (1801) and *Method* (1800), offer the general qualities of the thinker's approach.[29] Pestalozzi's writings on method are confusing and inconsistent. Many of his metaphors are impenetrable. Much of this comes from the thinker's inability to distill his classroom observations into straightforward ideas conveyed through language, a mode of expression in opposition to his ideals of learning through individual experience. Perhaps his classroom focus on experience and learning through observation and personal understanding was related to this difficulty of stating his method, as opposed to illustrating it through personal anecdotes or fictional vignettes.[30] Examples of his teaching sometimes contradict his theories and his theories sometimes contradict themselves. One critic quoted Pestalozzi confessing, "We announced publicly things which we had neither the strength nor the means to accomplish."[31] He apologized for his writing, explaining, "Since my twentieth year, I have been incapable of philosophic thought, in the true sense of the word."[32] One of his assistants noted that Pestalozzi "had great difficulties in finding always the precise term which would convey his meaning."[33] This problem has rankled both his pedagogue followers and translators, who have struggled with his key terms, such as *Anschauung,* which can at various times mean sense perception, sense impression, observation, or intuition, and sometimes, it seems, all of those things at once. Throughout, he wanted pupils and assistant teachers to help students move from concrete to abstract, from observation to understanding. He states and restates these ideas in different forms, with different applications and various goals.

At the core of his philosophy is a basic principle: "Sense-impression of Nature is the only true foundation of human instruction, because it is the only true foundation of Human knowledge."[34] From this foundation, Pestalozzi teaches children about God's and mother's love and their connection to each other, numbers and geometry, material observations of nature, people or things as the foundation of language, drawing, mathematics, and geography as well as moral training. He developed a number of flexible principles that were glossed in memorable sayings like moving from the "near to the far" or "from the simple to the complex."[35] Pestalozzi's ideas are often expressed as "drawing information out of students as opposed to cramming it into them" or "moving from familiar to unfamiliar." With these confusing, vague, and varied interpretations and applications for his own ideas, the thinker left himself open for critique, revision, and derision. The imprecision also offered ample opportunities for the next generation of educators to put his ideas into action in a range of ways.

Given the nature of Pestalozzi's expansive philosophy, his schools needed and attracted many assistants to help develop and implement his ideas. He started his serious engagement with teaching in his fifties, and ill health frequently slowed him down. He was sickly, and in addition to lung complaints, he was once trampled by a horse, and in 1812, according to an early biographer, nearly died after accidentally running a knitting needle through his ear.[36] He was dependent on his assistants to spread and publish his ideas. Some followers applied his methods to mathematics, reading, music, geography, and drawing. For example, one of Pestalozzi's followers, Johannes Buss, put together *ABC der Aschauung* (1803). The book taught observation through drawing, breaking forms into lines and shapes that children could learn to draw through observation. The same idea was used for mathematics founded on counting and comparing and units and images as opposed to abstract figures.[37] Nineteenth-century works both by and about Pestalozzi frequently contain the biographies of these men, particularly his first assistant, Hermann Krüsi.

Pestalozzi's own writings and those of his followers point to his eccentricities. *How Gertrude Teaches Her Children* reveals the emotional ups and downs of Pestalozzi's endeavors and suggests what it must have been like to work with him. In some ways, what his biographers and students referred to as the "imperfections of his character" were a way to argue for the value of his ideas while condemning his implementation of them.[38] His writing suggests that he was not an even-tempered man, describing extreme joy and extreme despair that he experienced as a result of his teaching, claiming that he would succeed or die. He was not very organized and was not good with money. Apocryphal accounts mention that he was always giving needed cash away to the poor instead of using it for his family or schools; at one point he supposedly offered a beggar his silver shoe buckles and tied his shoes with straw. The student from Bergdorf, John Ramsauer, recalled that when he first met Pestalozzi, he was giving the children a lesson on a monkey.

> As I did not understand a bit of what was going on when I heard the word "monkey, monkey," come every time at the end of a sentence, and as Pestalozzi, who was very ugly ran about the room as though he was wild, without a coat and without a neck-cloth, his long shirt sleeves hanging down over his arms and hands, which swung negligently about, I was seized with real terror and might soon have believed that he himself was a monkey.[39]

Pestalozzi's schools worked insofar as they replicated a family structure, bound with true affection between him and his assistants and students. Ramsauer coupled the description of the crazed monkey teacher with his memory of his master's kiss, a tender moment he never forgot. But a familial school environment did not mean the pedagogue knew how to run a school.

When he opened his next school in the castle at Yverdon in 1804–1805 it quickly grew to more than 250 people in residence, including many assistants, and later included a school for girls as well as for boys.[40] Unlike his earlier schools, this institution primarily served children who were able to pay some tuition. The students were kept constantly active, and all lessons—ten a day—revolved around experience and observation, different aspects of *Anschauung*.

Classes were taught in both French and German. Teachers were specialists in subjects like mathematics, music, natural science, history, and geography, and they used the school to develop innovative teaching techniques in these areas.[41] In the early years of Yverdon, student-teachers from Prussia were particularly influenced by the methods. They would go on to make the international reputation of Pestalozzi on the success of their renowned and reorganized school system.[42] Years later, the American educator Horace Mann would remark favorably on aspects of the Prussian system derived from Pestalozzi's, such as classroom exercises in observation and thinking.[43]

As Yverdon expanded, the laissez-faire educational model was strained. An American visitor to the school in 1819, John Griscom, remarked in a memoir of his European trip that for Pestalozzi, it was "all mind and feeling." Griscom, a New York City school manager, worried, "It is quite unfortunate for the progress of his system on the Continent, that he pays so little attention to exteriors, regarding dress, furniture etc as of no moment whatever, provided the mind and heart be right."[44] To an outside observer the material realities of Pestalozzi's school offered their own kind of lessons. Griscom knew that it took more than good intentions to manage a school. With few books, and instruction conducted via conversation and observation, it was difficult to maintain order. While initially successful, the school was bogged down with infighting among his teachers and debt that eventually closed the institution in 1825. The thinker died insolvent and despondent in 1827.

Even as the school continued its decline, up through 1825 the Yverdon castle was a destination for visitors from around Europe and the United States. For some it was simply a stop on their Grand Tour. Others, like Charles Mayo, hoping to learn about education focused on real knowledge that was acquired through observation and conversation instead of mere signs, came to teach with and learn from Pestalozzi.

In through the Senses

Charles Mayo studied Classics at St. John's College, Oxford, with the intention of going into law. After being admitted to the bar at Gray's Inn Road, he realized that his increasing deafness would prevent him from hearing the proceedings. After considering this sensory failure, he became a headmaster at a local grammar school and an Anglican priest—likely positions in which he expected to speak more than listen. In 1819, Mayo learned about Pestalozzi's experiment in Yverdon from John Synge, an Irish landowner who shared Mayo's evangelical approach to their faith. Synge had stopped at Yverdon for what he intended to be a brief visit on his way home from Italy during his Grand Tour. Mayo noted that Synge had intended to visit for just a few hours and ended up staying with Pestalozzi for three months. Though Synge could not even understand the language of the first class he observed, Mayo explained that he was "much struck with the intelligence and vivacity portrayed in the features of the pupils."[45] The words did not matter; the Irish traveler believed he saw learning.

In the summer of 1819, Mayo traveled to Yverdon with a group of English boys. In addition to learning innovative pedagogical methods, he planned to teach Classics and English and to serve as Anglican chaplain. Upon arrival, Mayo worried about how the school was run, and he had concerns about religious training and the application of Pestalozzi's methods. As opposed to instructing students in religious doctrine, teachers taught morality and religion through example. Furthermore, as many critics noted, the ideals and the reality of the pedagogy were often at odds. A critical former teacher contrasted Pestalozzi's claim that "the instruction, as a whole, does not proceed from any theory, but from the very life and expression of nature" with Pestalozzi's descriptions of geography lessons, outlined though detailed instructions.[46] Instead of dismissing the ideas along with the problems he observed, Pestalozzi told the Englishman, "Examine my method, adopt what you find to be good and reject what you cannot approve."[47] Mayo took this advice and became a close ally and friend of the thinker. Pestalozzi even suggested that Mayo might one day run his school and continue his legacy.[48]

After studying these methods for three years, Mayo went home to England in 1822. He was convinced of the value of Pestalozzi's methods, but not the form they took at Yverdon. Though he had promised Pestalozzi he would return, he decided instead to transplant these ideas to England. Mayo took it on himself to explain that Pestalozzi's failings as an administrator and not his methods led to the ruin of the school, noting that "the elastic, imperishable nature of that truth" that was the foundation of his teachings was why the methods were continually reinterpreted, while his various ventures crumbled.[49] In his *Memoir of Pestalozzi*, Mayo explained what he viewed as being at the core of Pestalozzi's teaching. He wrote, "Education should be essentially *organic*. A stone increases in size by mechanical deposition of matter on its external surface; a plant on the other hand, grows by continual expansion of those organs which lie folded up in its germ." Instead of simply adding knowledge—cramming it in as some might say—students' "human faculties," whether moral, intellectual, or physical, were to be developed though activities and experiences. The process demanded a clear system of teaching, not simply foundational principles. Back in England, Mayo immediately started teaching and invited his younger sister, Elizabeth to join him in his labors.

Elizabeth Mayo was only one year and ten days younger than her brother, but her recorded biography begins with his return from Switzerland in 1822 when she was twenty-nine years old.[50] Though she did not have the benefit of his Oxford training or a personal relationship with Pestalozzi, she became his most important pedagogical collaborator. She continued to write about object lessons and to work as one of the "first practical teachers" in England for two decades after his death. It is her work that would shape ideas about object lessons in the United States.

First in Epsom and starting in 1826 at Cheam in Surrey, the pair worked to integrate Pestalozzi's principles into classes for boys. Unlike Pestalozzi's schools that had been initially geared toward the poor and the development of universal education, the Mayos first applied the methods to the education of the privileged few. Some wealthy families even placed their sons' names on their enrollment list at birth, seven years before they could have been admitted. These children were bound for Oxford and Cambridge and the curriculum reflected this intention. From 1822 to 1834 (the year in which Charles married and Elizabeth moved to another position), she worked closely with him and published *Lessons on Objects* (1830) and *Lessons on Shells* (1832). These texts were based on their regimented and replicable interpretation of Pestalozzi's principles. Elizabeth Mayo noted that all lessons were tried out in her classes. A student's recollection of her cabinet of minerals suggests she was well prepared.[51]

As Charles explained in his introduction to *Lessons on Objects*, Pestalozzi's versions of object-based teaching had been "too miscellaneous in their character, so devoid of systematic arrangement," while his sister's lessons were organized in such a way as to leave the students with a feeling of progress.[52] Her lessons on objects—like glass, India rubber, and leather—offered teachers a set list of objects to study in a set order and through a series of five steps moving from observation to composition. Eventually, she would make available entire collections of these objects, ready-made for teachers' classroom use. As if answering the worry Pestalozzi had voiced as a frustrated young father who tried to teach his son how to move from an "innumerable variety of impressions" to "conceiving exact and complete ideas," the books offered a workable system that could be employed and repeated in the classroom.

The Mayos' system led students through five stages of learning, with the eventual goal of working from material things toward an understanding of the natural and metaphysical meanings of the world. The first step involved the use of the senses to identify the physical qualities of objects. Observation of those objects was supposed to lead to new vocabulary (i.e., using whalebone to understand "elastic") and to an understanding of the material world through observation of its qualities. Moving from those observations, the second series of exercises was designed to help children identify the abstract ideas of qualities shared among objects—for example, understanding that candles and pencils had the same shape. This realization was supposed to highlight the senses that had enabled them to come to these conclusions (in this case, touch and sight). The third series of lessons helped children learn how to draw nonsensory conclusions from objects. These ideas, which were often answers to questions not solely derived from observation, led children to understand things as natural or artificial or animal, vegetable, or mineral. The fourth series helped children learn how to classify and connect objects. The final series focused on helping students write about and talk about the things they observed. The Mayos' object-lesson methods were designed for children of different ages, with texts intended to instruct children aged two to ten.

A full set of items arranged to follow Elizabeth Mayo's course—likely what Mayo advertised at the back of *Lessons on Objects* as "Cabinets containing substances referred to in this work"—survives in the collections of the Victoria and Albert Museum (Plate 1).[53] The mahogany box contains four trays of labeled specimens. The surviving cabinet or specimen box is an important material reminder of the knowledge developed through and required for study of these materials by both students and teachers. For example, linen, sackcloth, sailcloth, cotton velvet, calico, flannel, satin silk, and sarsnet silk are all fabrics and quite different. Cloves, allspice, and pepper may look similar, but they do not smell or taste the same or have the same accidental qualities or origins. What of gypsum and marble? India rubber and whalebone?[54]

Starting with glass and the items required to complete Mayo's First Series, the levels of the cabinet move through her whole curriculum. Each object in the first tray, linked to Series One, has a "distinguishing quality" that may be discerned solely through observation. There is no other means by which a pine cone, a watch glass, a mustard seed, a key, and a cube of wood may be linked other than the qualities they allow pupils to develop. There is method to the lesson that allows students to understand what it means for a piece of wax to be a piece of wax and a jar of camphor to be what it purports to be.[55] Similarly the lessons of the Second Series could be applied to whole objects like a thimble or a pair of scissors, to isolate and identify qualities shared among objects. The Third Series focuses on qualities that cannot be observed—for example, studying the needle to determine the process by which steel is created, or examining a stone to decide that it is "inorganized" or inorganic.[56] The fourth allowed students to classify objects, focusing on spices in the text, but also offering other categories like cloths, treads, or papers in the cabinet. All of the items offered possibilities for the compositions suggested in the Fifth Series and beyond. Teachers could also develop their own boxes (Plate 2).

These pedagogical ideas and texts were useful beyond private schools like Cheam. The Mayo siblings became involved in the wider movement to train teachers who would staff the growing number of infant schools in England.[57] In 1836, John Stuckey Reynolds, a civil servant involved in finance and an evangelical Christian, helped to found the Home and Colonial Infant School Society to train teachers in Pestalozzian principles to meet this need.[58] The school consisted of three model schools: an infant school for children under the age of eight, which focused almost exclusively on topics could be taught through object lessons; a juvenile school for children from eight to fifteen, which gradually introduced knowledge from books; and a mixed-age school, intended to offer training in the style of the ungraded country school. A practice or model school and a training school for teachers completed the institute.[59] In addition to church history, natural history, geography, and arithmetic, teachers in training studied the theory and practice of education and worked as practice teachers in the model schools. Elizabeth Mayo led the education department. The Mayos were involved from the beginning, and starting around 1843, Elizabeth Mayo devoted all of her energies to the school, writing model lessons and leading teachers in those lessons.[60]

The Home and Colonial Schools (HCS), like David Stow's Glasgow Infant School Society, was a key training institute for the infant school movement in Great Britain and the British colonies. The evangelically oriented HCS trained teachers for a number of different situations—ranging from schools for the urban poor to private families—in England, Ireland, Scotland, Canada, and India. The secretary of the society boasted in 1847 that the school's teachers served from "the frozen snows of Canada" to the "burning suns of India."[61] As early as 1852, an edition of Mayo's *Lessons on Objects* was translated into Bengali. When adapted for Indian schools, object lessons aimed to secularize Hindu students' approaches to their sacred—and sometimes "living"—religious objects.[62] In this situation and others, lessons on objects were intended to shape students' ways of thinking by linking empiricism and observation to a Christian way of interpreting material things. They were not simply about educating students but creating a particular material worldview.[63]

Some of Mayo's lessons—designed for both the metropolis and the colonies—explicitly instructed students in how to view the substances associated with distant places. Part of her lessons distinguished between objects' "essential" material qualities that physically defined them and other information about objects' production that should be associated with them, like the "accidental" nature of their foreign origin in relation to their domestic consumption.[64] Spices were the ideal vehicles through which to teach these lessons. They had distinct, discernible qualities that could only be determined through the sense of taste or smell. A child could chew on a clove and have a memorable physical sensation, something one could not do with the subjects of all lessons. This information could then be used to help students isolate and identify a unique taste, an essential quality of cloves, as opposed to what they were told about the item's origin. Mayo explained that foreignness was "accidental," not "essential" to the definition of cloves, mace, cinnamon, or nutmeg, which were to be defined by qualities gained through the senses like aroma, texture, and color. Even with these distinctions clearly laid out, the lessons worked to embed nonsensual information about an object's perceived "foreignness" into the studied spices.[65] One could not smell that cinnamon was grown in Ceylon or Malabar, but to Mayo and her students, that accidental foreignness was as much a part of the substance of the spice as its brittleness, opacity, or sweetness.[66] In the classroom, such lessons could help to create a material and somatic geography of the British Empire.

After *Lessons on Objects*, Elizabeth Mayo created other practical manuals designed to help teachers at home and abroad approach and prepare their classroom lessons. Instead of conveying knowledge to students about objects, these manuals were intended to help teachers in training draw information out of their students. Although an HCS reference guide for teachers, *Information on Common Objects for the Use of Infant and Juvenile Schools and Nursery Governesses*, included information about subjects from a watch spring to an oyster, from barley to a tortoise shell, the goal was not to help students acquire information. Rather the reference was intended to give teachers just enough to "satisfy the desire for information which an examination of any objects may awaken in the minds of their pupils."[67]

Mayo's emphasis on method reinforces the importance of not simply cramming children's brains but developing their minds like germinating flowers. Her model lessons, like those published in *Model Lessons for Infant School Teachers and Nursery Governess Prepared for the Home and Colonial School Society*, were designed to demonstrate this process. She complained that untrained teachers were simply "repeating the names of the books of the Old and New Testaments" or asking students to memorize the names of mountains or capital cities. Through her methods, teachers should realize that "the daily transactions of the school-room and play-ground should furnish the subjects for moral training and the material objects around the children the subjects for intellectual development."[68]

Furthermore, student-teachers were instructed to help their students understand where information came from, how the senses formed and shaped the conceptions each individual developed about not only color, sound, smell, and size but also right and wrong and what it meant to be a Christian. Mayo's *Lessons on Objects* included clear discussion of the senses, and how these were avenues for the development of ideas. For example, in a model lesson on the senses, Mayo imagines or possibly records the following lesson, which includes the previously mentioned example of a blind man explaining color:

TEACHER: How do you know when a thing is red or blue?

CHILDREN: By sight.

TEACHER: How if you were blind could you form a correct idea of colour? What other means is there of gaining this knowledge?

CHILDREN: None.

TEACHER: True and to ascertain this point a blind man was once questioned as to what notion he had of scarlet he said he thought that it must be like the sound of a trumpet. It is obvious that he had no correct idea of a quality discoverable by the sight and he could only compare it with one that he had acquired through the medium of another sense. Can you tell me the reason why persons born deaf cannot speak?

CHILDREN: They cannot imitate sounds because they never heard any.

TEACHER: Since deaf persons have no correct ideas of sound nor blind persons of colour how did we acquire our ideas of sound and colour?

CHILDREN: By the means of the senses of seeing and hearing.

TEACHER: How then do we suppose our minds become stored with ideas?

CHILDREN: By the exercise of our senses.[69]

The experienced teacher warned her pupil-teachers that children might not come to this conclusion right away. The teacher must slowly lead the children to this understanding through careful questions. For Mayo, it was not possible for the blind man to have the correct idea of color, though this Lockean description may be synesthetically appealing to modern readers. Only through the proper sensory channels could one form correct ideas about the world.

Mayo's story of the blind man who "sees" the color scarlet as the sound of a trumpet is her direct classroom interpretation of Locke's anecdote from his *Essay Concerning Human Understanding*. Her regimented lessons on material things, the carefully choreographed sets of experiences teachers hoped to provide to children, would have been understood as stocking a child's mind with true ideas. Only when schooling was based on the foundation of such sense-based ideas, she suggested, could a child learn to reason. This approach could even be applied to the development of the moral sense through the study of pictures.

While Locke may be known for his writings on education, Adam Smith's ideas about sentiment and sympathy also certainly influenced the reception of the Mayos' methods in 1830s England. A Home and Colonial Schools advertisement for teachers noted that those who would apply to be teachers must realize "the power of sympathy is felt by all, but its effect on young children is almost incalculable."[70] In *The Theory of Moral Sentiment* (1759) Smith offers a theory of morals that explains why it is that individuals feel sympathy for those they observe suffering, describing the development of "fellow feeling" among others. This sympathy was key to the society's moral and religious teachings. The concept of fellow feeling, of being in sympathy with an observed individual, required a sensory input, like the sensory foundations of Locke's simple ideas. Object teachers worked to actually demonstrate moral examples and biblical stories to children so they could observe and feel sympathy for the characters, learning right feelings through sympathy.[71] Teachers stocked children's minds with these feelings as well as sensory perceptions.

The opportunity to observe or to sense, whether in the infant school classroom or as one walked down the street or tasted an apple, was linked to the power to think, to feel, and to act. On both sides of the Atlantic these notions affected the ways parents understood themselves and their children and the ways those children learned about the world. In 1831, just a year after Elizabeth Mayo's *Lessons on Objects* was published in England, American teacher John Frost edited a version of it in the United States under the name *Lessons on Common Things*. In his second edition of Mayo's text, published in 1835, Frost added illustrations to Mayo's object-based lessons. Instead of assuming that teachers would circulate a piece of bark among their students, Frost included a picture of a tree; for the study of ivory he added a picture of an elephant; and he included a dazzling large greenhouse to illustrate glass.

As if willfully ignoring the scene in the Swiss schoolroom that inspired Pestalozzi to teach with objects, Frost's text encouraged children to look at pictures of windows instead of the actual windows that surrounded them. In an advertisement that prefaced the third edition he encouraged teachers to put the book into the hands of students, allowing them to look at the pictures and to read. These changes were at odds with the Mayos' stated philosophy and did not serve to unfold children's perceptive powers; rather the goal was to convey information, and (if placed in the hands of every child) to sell more books.[72] But Frost's *Lessons on Common Things*, explicitly advertised as "on the system of Pestalozzi," was part of a larger movement in the United States to improve education, both at home and at school.[73]

Common Things across the Atlantic

When she died in the late nineteenth century, Dorothea Lynde Dix was lauded as a crusader for the mentally ill, the injured, and the imprisoned. The suffering she sympathetically observed visiting asylums, prisons, and hospitals motivated her to reform institutional life in the United States. Twenty years before she set down this path, Dix taught school in Boston, teaching on her own and in the well-known Boston Female Monitorial School. She also published a number of children's books. Her most popular book, *Conversations on Common Things or, Guide to Knowledge: With Questions* (1824), remained in print for more than four decades.[74] She began the book with an epigraph from John Locke. She quoted, "The taking a taste of every sort of knowledge is necessary to form the mind, and is the only way to give the Understanding its due improvement to the full extent of its capacity." This line, taken slightly out of context from section 19, "universality," of Locke's 1697 essay "On the Conduct of the Understanding," was sometimes quoted in educational texts of the period as an argument for the benefit of a student's broad exposure to a diverse array of subjects and experiences.[75] As students could form simple ideas through sensory engagement that could lead to complex thought, individuals could learn to think expansively if they were not limited in the fields they chose to study. While universal understanding might be difficult to achieve, the development of common knowledge was a worthy goal.

Informed by her reading of Locke, Dix suggested that knowledge came from the first-hand observation and interrogation of common things found in the material world. Children, in this approach to learning, needed to have experiences that could lead to knowledge, the access to intellectual or material opportunities to "taste" it, to question it, in order to fully develop their potential as thinkers. Dix organized her book as a series of conversations between a mother and her daughter. The text opens with an instructive anecdote. The daughter, Sarah, questions her mother as to why the older woman apparently spent so much time watching the whirring spools and spindles in a local textile mill. After acknowledging that she would be "mortified" if she could not explain how the machinery worked after visiting the manufactory, the mother gave her daughter a better reason: "Does not the acquirement of any thing new to your understanding contribute to your lasting enjoyment in a higher degree, than mere superficial observation or any pleasure you receive from the gratification of your appetite, or mere transient amusements?" The fictional mother warned, "Observe and remember every thing that will inform your mind and enlarge your understanding."[76]

For Dix, whose later activism would be driven by observation, accurate observation was a responsibility, a joy, and a tool to develop one's mind. Her goal was to teach children how to draw conclusions from their observations and to make decisions—both rational and moral—based on what they perceived. Dix's own reform work on behalf of prisoners and the mentally ill would rely on her active observation. In a concrete way, her observations created new knowledge as well as new categories of thinking about the world.

Dix's popular book joined a number of British and American texts on common things and the natural world. Many of these texts were published as conversations between mothers and teachers and their children and pupils. In the late eighteenth and early nineteenth centuries, Sarah Trimmer, Mrs. Marcet, Maria Edgeworth, and other authors offered models for leading children to experience the natural world. Some of Elizabeth Mayo's books for teachers may fall into this category. The desire to learn from this directed experience grew out of a new Romantic approach to child-rearing, directly influenced by Locke's theories, which had gained sway in the mid-eighteenth century. These ideas affected how Americans during the early Republic thought about their children. For example, Sarah Trimmer's book *Knowledge of Nature* (first published in the United States in 1796) begins with a walk through the garden with two children; they observe the world around them, gather plants, and possibly look up information on their collected specimens when they return home. The idea was to encourage curiosity and introduce children to the study of the world.[77] In the process, parents and teachers came to think of children not as fully formed beings but as the products of deliberate educational choices.[78] Empirical observation became central to children's intellectual development. Just as Locke had advocated in *Thoughts Concerning Education* and *An Essay Concerning Human Understanding*, individuals were shaped by their exposure to the sensible, physical world. This approach emphasized children's hands-on encounters with material things as key to developing their minds and teaching them how to think.

These "lessons on common things" could be quite different from the lessons on objects at the Home and Colonial Schools and later popularized in the 1860s in the United States. Instead of being designed solely to teach children how to approach the world, "lessons on common things" also intended to "give a certain amount of practical information about the things and processes of everyday life."[79] They form an important foundation for understanding how object-based study shaped American schools and culture more broadly. Lessons on common things did not necessarily depend on actual material things for instruction; they could consider common themes like passage of time or faraway labor. In some ways these two categories of lessons relate to Locke's distinction between the two ways individuals can gain knowledge: sensation or reflection. Object lessons start with sensation and move to reflection, while lessons on common things more explicitly seem to embrace both parts of Locke's theory of understanding. These lessons encouraged parents and teachers to lead children's experience of the material world as well as to shape children's reflections on this world.

The urban Northeast and particularly eastern Massachusetts were hotbeds of educational and literary innovation throughout the first half of the nineteenth century, leading to experimental schools and a range of texts for children that shaped the reading culture of the entire nation's young. Children's educational experiences were changing dramatically in the early years of the nineteenth century. Through common school reforms and an array of state and local funding schemes, education was becoming viewed as a citizen's right, even as some children were laboring more than ever outside the protective family farms that had long benefited from their work. At the same time, apprenticeship as a structured personal and professional relationship was falling out of favor. New ways of shaping children's engagement with the material world began to characterize how parents viewed their children's earliest experiences.[80]

This new approach to learning emerged as part of broader patterns of change regarding children and child-rearing in the mid-eighteenth century. Though Locke had written about understanding and education in the final years of the seventeenth century, these texts did not begin to greatly affect American life until the mid-eighteenth century.[81] Parents in America began to read Locke and, more important, many books and newspaper articles affected by Locke's theories that suggested the importance of experience over misperceptions created by children's innate notions.[82] Locke's writings were such a vital intellectual force (along with those of Newton) that he is a central lens through which to view American culture in this period.[83]

The correspondence of one enlightened eighteenth-century mother provides an excellent case study of how Locke's ideas transformed the thinking of American parents. Eliza Lucas Pinckney of South Carolina, who managed several plantations, was well read and studied the writings of Locke. She noted in one letter that his writings helped her see "wherein personal identity consisted." But she also engaged in a transatlantic conversation about the efficacy of Locke's teachings through Richardson's detailed exegesis of *Some Thoughts Concerning Education* in *Pamela* (1740), a book Pinckney mentions in her letters, noting the fictional character's critique of Locke's theories in an undated letter (ca. 1741).[84] In May 1745, Pinckney wrote to a friend, then in England, requesting that she acquire blocks for Pinckney's four-month-old son made on the Lockean plan. She politely asked, "Shall I give you the trouble my dear Madam to buy him [her son] the new toy (a description of which I inclose) to teach him according to Mr. Lock[e]'s method which I have carefully studied to play himself into learning."[85]

Pinckney is referring to Locke's recommendation that parents employ ivory dice modified by gluing letters onto the faces of the block the same size as those in a folio Bible. In *Thoughts Concerning Education* (section 150) he detailed how this toy might help a child learn. Unlike Richardson's Pamela, who cautiously writes to Mr. B that she feared such training might lead to gambling, Pinckney was thrilled by the possibility that her son would quickly learn to read. After first identifying letters, according to this theory, motivated by competitive play for apples and cherries, children were to learn the sounds letters make together and possibly to read. Pinckney offers a rough quotation of Locke in her letter, who described a boy who "played himself into spelling, with great eagerness."[86] It appears that Pinckney's Lockean precursor to Boggle worked. She proudly reported that her precocious son, at twenty-two months, knew his letters and had started to spell.[87]

Locke's ideas affected child-rearing experts in both England and the American colonies. The writings of authors like physician William Cadogan, reprinted by Benjamin Franklin in the *Pennsylvania Gazette*, and later through the work of physician William Buchan ensured that scenes like the one suggested by

Pinckney's letters took place in homes throughout the colonies and later the United States.[88] Parents read Locke's works, writings about the thinker in novels and newspapers, and texts inspired by his philosophies. By the time Dix published her *Conversations* in the 1820s, Locke's ideas about education inflected educational theory as much as his ideas about natural rights had impacted the founding documents of the United States.[89] Historians of education have credited Locke's emphasis on the transformative power of education with the importance of charity schooling in the early Republic.[90] Unfortunately, many of Locke's ideas about pedagogy, particularly his recommendations against physical punishment and excessive memorization, were not always practical. District schools, which served many students of different ages, emphasized recitation and keeping order, with a focus on basic skills like reading, writing, and arithmetic.[91] It was through the efforts of educational reformers, teachers, and authors that new interpretations of Locke's theories came to shape the start of the common school movement in the United States—as the ideas of both European and American thinkers came to be applied to broad educational challenges. These reformers emphasized different aspects of the thinker's theories that were developed by later writers and teachers, used to justify everything from blackboards to object lessons.

Perhaps the broadest understanding of Locke's educational theories may be read in his *Essay on Human Understanding*. Here Locke elaborated on some of the specific suggestions in *Thoughts Concerning Education* by explaining that all understanding originated from two key paths: sensation or reflection. Although Dix does not specify which of Locke's essays she was reading in an undated letter likely from the early 1820s to her good friend Ann Heath, she was probably reading the *Essay on Human Understanding*.[92] In the same letter, she mentions her appreciation for the life of Elizabeth Smith, the British writer and translator. *Fragments in Prose and Verse* was published after the scholar's untimely death in 1806. Dix remarks to her friend that she read this book twice.[93] In it, Smith offers a reasoned critique of the *Essay on Human Understanding*, challenging the validity of sensation as a source of knowledge and argues for the centrality of scripture and revelation.[94] The material world, Smith suggests was not as useful a teacher as Locke suggested. Though Dix clearly admired this book, she seems taken with Locke's ideas about the important link between sensation and reflection—recognizing both the value of experiences and things and knowledge about those things.

Dix's *Conversations* was part of a genre of educational books that were not direct antecedents to the object lessons that would animate American schools in the 1860s. They are important to acknowledge and understand because they suggest the broader cultural interest in lessons on material things and the perceived value of observation to children's intellectual and moral development.

Several educators in the young United States were deeply invested in the work of Pestalozzi and aimed to transplant his ideas to American soil in a range of small, organized schools prior to the widespread adoption of object lessons. Through their efforts, many educators learned about Pestalozzi's methods. The first of these pedagogues was Joseph Neef, a student and assistant of Pestalozzi, who immigrated to Philadelphia in 1806. Instead of the Mayos' lessons on objects, his work focused on Pestalozzi's general philosophy, which Neef interpreted in the following way: "According to my humble opinion, education is nothing else than the gradual unfolding of the faculties and powers which Providence chuses to bestow on the noblest work of this sublunary creature, man."[95] William McClure, a wealthy businessman, geologist, and educational reformer, sponsored Neef's immigration and set him up in a school on the Schuylkill River. Neef published an adaptation of Pestalozzi's system for the American context. His *Sketch of a Plan and Method of Education* is said to be the first book on education to be published in English in America. In the 1820s, Neef worked with Robert Owen and McClure to establish their workers' utopia in New Harmony, Indiana.[96]

The transcendentalist writer and teacher Bronson Alcott was also deeply affected by Pestalozzi's writings and philosophy, which he viewed as in sympathy with his own ideas. Alcott was sometimes called the American Pestalozzi for his work in Temple School in Boston. Alcott's conversations with children, transcribed in Elizabeth Peabody's *Record of a School* (1835), revealed how through questions and self-reflection children's minds could be unfolded and imaginations developed. A group of English Pestalozzians even called their school Alcott House in honor of the transcendentalist.[97]

Alcott and Neef were both well known to their contemporaries, but neither dramatically changed American education, though many educators followed their experiments closely. For both men, their lessons were less about observation and sensory training than about the development of children's innate faculties.[98] It would be through the success of the common school movement that Pestalozzi's ideas became increasingly familiar to teachers, parents, and children in the United States. While most white children in the northeastern United States had access to some schooling prior to this movement, it was inconsistently funded, teachers were not regularly trained, the academic calendar was often linked to harvest, and attendance was sporadic. Most children sat with a mix of students of diverse ages and intellectual attainments and learned reading, memorized texts, wrote on slates and with pens, and acquired basic arithmetic skills. Starting in the late 1830s, Horace Mann, noted educational reformer, was instrumental in creating not only the Massachusetts Board of Education, of which he became secretary, but also the country's first normal school to train teachers as well as short teachers' institutes for ongoing professional development. The goal was to improve common schooling for children by extending the school year, professionalizing teachers, standardizing textbooks, and ensuring that children had access to school materials.

From the 1830s through the 1850s many American educators learned about Pestalozzi and variations of his ideas through textbooks, as authors in every discipline invoked Pestalozzi's name and principles. Typically, these approaches are consistent with the notion that children should be learning through their senses and experiences, as opposed to memorizing or passively accepting information from external sources. Lowell Mason developed a system of musical instruction based on Pestalozzi's ideas, explaining, "It always pleases scholars *to find out things themselves*; and what is thus learned is not only remembered but understood" (italics in original). In his system, the students are supposed to learn by their own ear and through their own abilities, not from the teacher.[99] In mathematics, the work of Warren Colburn on "intellectual arithmetic" emphasized observation and real-world examples as opposed to working out all problems on a slate.[100] The Swiss Arnold Guyot—about whom later educators would note, "The mountains and glaciers of his native land were his School Room"—created geography texts.[101] Hermann Krüsi, the son of Pestalozzi's first assistant, became known for his Pestalozzian drawing manuals. Through his "inventive system" he taught students how to draw objects from observation, focusing on outlines and the lines, shapes, and forms visible in the subjects of their composition. In teaching drawing, he applied the method learned from his father to teach drawing as a process of observation moving between object and outline to understand the many visual components of any image.

Several of these men knew each other and worked together in teachers' institutes and training classes. At these institutes, scholars, such as the Harvard naturalist Louis Agassiz, and members of local boards of education gave lectures to the public in addition to presentations by well-known educators like Mason, Krüsi, or Guyot.[102] For example, in 1847 Agassiz and Mann conducted a teachers' institute in Newton, Massachusetts. There, instead of simply lecturing on insects, Agassiz, whose childhood in pastoral Switzerland included an observation-based education similar to that generally associated with Pestalozzi, distributed hundreds of grasshoppers to the crowd. Each teacher could hold and observe an insect and, over the course of the lecture, would learn to see it differently.[103]

Krüsi was first welcomed into this dynamic pedagogical world of midcentury Massachusetts in 1852, when he was invited to join a new normal school in Lancaster, Massachusetts. He spent the first five years of his life in Yverdon, and Pestalozzi was one of his godfathers. In spite of this early childhood, Krüsi learned his teaching methods from his own father, Pestalozzi's first assistant, and later in London at the Home and Colonial Schools. From 1847 through 1852 he had worked at the Home and Colonial Schools teaching mathematics and drawing and learning the basics of teacher training. It is likely that he attended the Tuesday afternoon sessions for pupil-teachers offered at the Home and Colonial Schools. He recalled in his memoir, "I profited, myself, a great deal by being forced to consider all the exercises of instruction with regard to their capability of developing a power of the mind. . . . The children, as a whole, did well and proved the excellence of Pestalozzian instruction,—whenever they were well taught,—which, of course, was not always the case."

In 1853 he immigrated to the United States and began applying these lessons. Upon arrival, Krüsi met Agassiz and Guyot, fellow Swiss, and quickly joined with them and other educators in training teachers. In 1853, Krüsi was invited to give a lecture at the American Teacher's Institute in New Haven, Connecticut, on Pestalozzi's theories, which he described as his "debut."[104] For the next several years Krüsi taught in training schools and teachers' institutes throughout New England and in New Jersey, perfecting his methods and learning about life in America. In the winter of 1859–1860, Krüsi taught in a normal school in Salem and took on private students, including African American educator and writer Charlotte Forten (later Grimké).[105] Two years later, in 1862, a Mr. Sheldon from Oswego, New York, invited Krüsi to take part in a new educational experiment.

2

Thinking with Things

Edward Austin Sheldon did not read about object lessons in a book. Rather, performing the methods he came to champion, he always maintained that he had experienced the pedagogy. By 1859, Sheldon had spent six years as the superintendent of the Oswego Board of Education in upstate New York. In the years before his appointment, abysmal attendance, poor teacher training, and the lack of a shared curriculum made it difficult for students to make progress. In an attempt to standardize what had been an unregulated group of ungraded primary schools, Sheldon had started a Saturday school for teachers. There, he planned every hour of their teaching time. Known as "Pope Sheldon" for his strict ways, he developed a "straight-jacketed system" of exhaustive public examinations for students and their teachers. In 1859, his class-by-class exams included a total of more than sixteen thousand questions of which the students answered 92 percent correctly. This was the easiest way to prove the success of his newly organized school district; the percentage was up from only 74 percent in 1856.[1] But even with the improvement in funding, space, attendance, and discipline brought about by his reforms, he felt something was missing. As he would write years later, "As a machine it was perfect, but it lacked vitality."[2]

In October 1859, as the United States reacted to news of abolitionist John Brown's raid on Harpers Ferry, Sheldon made a trip to Toronto, Canada. Toronto was just a day's steam ferry ride away from the small industrial city of Oswego, sited on the opposite side of Lake Ontario.[3] There, in the Educational Museum in Saint James Square on the grounds of the Toronto Normal School, Sheldon found the solution to his problem. On the first floor of the Educational Depository, a special shop for teachers, Sheldon came upon pedagogical exhibitions put together by Egerton Ryerson, the founder of the Canadian normal school's museum. Sheldon recalled, "Here I found, greatly to my surprise, what I did not know existed anywhere—collections of objects, pictures, charts of colors, form, reading charts, books for teachers, giving full directions as to the use of this material."[4]

Egerton Ryerson had spent fourteen months traveling through Britain and the continental Europe gathering pedagogical materials that could be used in Upper Canada's classrooms. Clearly modeled on the South Kensington Museum in London (the plan of which he even included in his 1858 report on the Canadian museum), Ryerson's museum contained galleries of casts, paintings, and prints as well as an array of educational "specimens" from maps and plans to philosophical apparatus and taxidermy.[5] In addition to presenting art and information about current teaching methods, he offered various pedagogical items for sale in the depository. A visitor could purchase an *omnium gatherum*, a sturdy box that contained everyday items such as "silk, muslin, flannel, linen, oil-cloth, felt, drugget, brick, pottery, china, glass, iron, steel, copper, lead, tin, brass, pewter, a type, a ring, a needle, a pin, a button, a steel pen, paper, parchment, leather, morocco, kid, buckskin, cocoon, hair, wool, hemp, flax, wax, gum, bean, pea, clove, coffee, cinnamon, wheat, oats, barley, buckwheat, sponge, shell &c" arranged for classroom use. Charts, pictures of animals, plants, and moral scenes as well as the pedagogical publications of the Home and Colonial Schools (HCS), Charles and Elizabeth Mayo's organization, were also available for a fee. Sheldon invested $300 in objects, pictures, and books. He returned home to Oswego to begin implementing these new object-based pedagogical techniques.[6]

Sheldon's interpretation of object-based pedagogy marked a turning point in primary school instruction in the United States. Pestalozzi's Romanticism had made an impact on domestic, infant, and common school education in the early Republic and in the antebellum period. In the 1860s, under the leadership of Sheldon and others, Pestalozzi's ideas about drawing information out of children, treating them as individuals, and training their senses were substantially reworked. The curriculum Sheldon implemented in Oswego was a highly systemized version of the Swiss pedagogue's philosophy newly ordered around particular objects and pictures. Explicitly building on the methods of the Mayos and Home and Colonial Schools in England, he showed teachers precisely how objects and objective methods could be incorporated into their curricula. Sheldon's translations of these theories crystallized the definition of an "object lesson" for Americans as a specific pedagogical approach to the study of the external, material world.[7]

Sheldon had certainly known about object lessons as a concept before he visited Toronto, but he had no idea what such a lesson looked like or how to teach one. Like most teachers in the antebellum period, he had not intended to be an educator. He grew up in New York State and attended Hamilton College for a few years, planning to pursue a career in law. In the summer of 1847, after an embarrassing failure in his class's junior exhibition, he spent the summer working with the Downing brothers, Andrew Jackson, the well-known writer on domestic architecture and landscape, and his brother Charles, in their horticulture business.[8] Through the Downing brothers, he met a man who was looking for a new business partner. Sheldon dropped out of school and moved with him to Oswego to open a gardening business. After the business failed, he transferred his attention from the cultivation of plants to the cultivation of children.

Oswego was then an active port and had a large of number of poor Irish immigrants who worked in the city's shipping industry. Surprised at what he considered to be high illiteracy rates among the children of Oswego's workers, Sheldon decided to do something about the problem. He helped to found the Orphan and Free School Association and served as its first teacher. His diary from these early years describes his job as being as much social worker as primary school teacher for his 120 students: he spent his free time conducting home visits, stopping fights, and finding clothes and shoes for the students in his school. After a year in his "ragged school," he married Frances A. B. Stiles of a prominent Syracuse family. Her father, a Yale graduate and in turn a minister, teacher, and businessman, had been a strong abolitionist.[9] She had worked as a teacher before marriage and assisted Sheldon in a private school he tried to open in Oswego in 1849.[10] When this attempt also failed, they moved together to Syracuse. There, Sheldon served as the superintendent of the city school system before returning to Oswego to head the Oswego School District.[11] It was after six years of effort in this school system that Sheldon began attempting to include the lessons he learned in Toronto in his schools. A teacher recalled, "I well remember one Saturday morning after our weekly teachers' conference, that we saw through the glass partition doors, Mr. Sheldon and a half dozen other teachers busy with an armful of plants, blossoms and twigs, a scene about which, we the uninitiated were very curious."[12] Soon, it became clear.

The materials that Sheldon had discovered in Toronto and that he and his teachers were likely working through had been created by Elizabeth Mayo and her team at the HCS. Mayo's straightforward writing for parents and teachers, particularly her *Lessons on Objects* and *Lessons on Shells*, offered a series of graduated exercises organized around lessons on objects that were intended to train children's senses according to Pestalozzi's theories.[13] Convinced of the value of the Mayos' methods, Sheldon dramatically altered the curriculum of the Oswego public schools. Not only did he quickly adapt the HCS's methods for children through the age of fourteen, he also modified Mayo's primer *Lessons on Objects* to suit his classroom, translating the series of lessons into a heavily regimented six-hour school day that ran from 8:30 to 4:30, minus two hours for lunch; later, class time was reduced to five hours. Sheldon's detailed curriculum plans reveal just how his new understanding of object lessons shaped his curriculum from 1860 onward. Sheldon's curriculum contained very general lists of subjects covered, including spelling, object lessons (which were neither defined nor described in any way), picture lessons, printing lessons for drawing on slates, and physical exercises. It also included provisions for "oral teaching," which he considered to be a form of object teaching, but specified no specific method for employing this pedagogy.[14] Sheldon included specific step-by-step curricular guides based on HCS methods in his next annual report. School timetables from 1860 record Sheldon's detailed interpretation of the HCS methods (see Table 2.1).[15]

Table 2.1 **Daily Schedules for the Oswego Public Schools, 1860**

Programme for Class C	*Programme for A and B Classes*	
Friday	Monday	Tuesday
8:30 to 8:45, opening exercises	8:30 to 8:45, opening exercises	8:30 to 8:45, opening exercises
8:45 to 8:55, C sub. 5 class, words	8:45 to 8:55, moral instruction	8:45 to 9:00, lesson on Form, B, sub. 2
8:55 to 9:05, C sub. 4 class, phonetics	8:55 to 9:15, reading, B, sub. 1	9:00 to 9:15, lesson on Weight, B, sub. 1
9:05 to 9:25, C sub. 3 class, primer	9:15 to 9:20, gymnastics	9:15 to 9:20, gymnastics
9:25 to 9:35, lesson on color	9:20 to 9:35, lesson on Number, B, sub. 2	9:20 to 9:35, spelling, A class
9:35 to 9:45, 1st recess	9:35 to 9:45, recess	9:35 to 9:45, recess
9:45 to 9:55, C sub. 5 class, words	9:45 to 10:00, lesson on Place, A class	9:45 to 10:10, reading, B, sub. 2
9:55 to 10:05, C sub. 4 class, phonetics	10:00 to 10:25, reading, B, sub. 2	10:10 to 10:20, B, sub. 1, drawing
10:05 to 10:25, C sub. 3 class, primer	10:25 to 10:30, gymnastics	10:20 to 10:25, gymnastics
10:25 to 10:35, physical exercises	10:30 to 10:50, lesson on Number, B, sub. 1	10:25 to 10.50, lesson on Number, B, sub. 1
10:35 to 10:45, lesson on objects	10:50 to 11:00, recess	10:50 to 11:00, recess
10:45 to 10:50, little children dismissed	11:00 to 11:20, reading, A class	11:00 to 11:15, lesson on objects, A class
10:50 to 11:00, 2d recess	11:20 to 11:40, writing on slates, B, sub. 1	11:15 to 11:35, reading, B, sub. 1

Table 2.1 **Continued**

Programme for Class C	Programme for A and B Classes	
11:00 to 11:20, C sub. 2 class, primer	11:40 to 12:00, lesson on Number, A class	11:35 to 12:00, lesson on Number, A class
11:20 to 11:35, lesson on Number	12:00 to 2:00, intermission	12:00 to 2:00, intermission
11:35 to 12:00, C sub. 1 class, primer	2:00 to 2:20, lesson on Number, A class	2:00 to 2:15, lesson on Number, B, sub. 2
12:00 to 2:00, intermission	2:20 to 2:30, lesson on Animals, A and B	2:15 to 2:30, drawing, A class
2:00 to 2:05, singing	2:30 to 2:35, gymnastics	2:30 to 2:35, gymnastics
2:05 to 2:20, C sub. 5 class, words	2:35 to 2:55, reading, B sub. 2	2:35 to 2:55, reading, B, sub. 1
2:20 to 2:35, C sub. 4 class, phonetics	2:55 to 3:10, lesson on Number, B, sub. 1	2:55 to 3:10, lesson on Weight, B, sub. 2
2:35 to 2:40, physical exercises	3:10 to 3:15, calling roll	3:10 to 3:15, calling roll
2:40 to 3:00, C sub. 3 class, primer	3:15 to 3:30, recess	3:15 to 3:30, recess
3:00 to 3:05, roll called	3:30 to 3:45, spelling, A class	3:30 to 3:45, lesson on Number, A class
3:05 to 3:10, singing	3:45 to 4:10, reading, B, sub. 1	3:45 to 4:00, lesson on Form, B, sub. 1
3:10 to 3:15, little children dismissed	4:10 to 4:30, reading, A class	4:00 to 4:10, spelling, A class
3:15 to 3:30, recess		4:10 to 4:30, lesson on Number, B, sub. 1
3:30 to 3:55, C sub. 2 class, primer		
3:55 to 4:10, lesson on Number		
4:10 to 4:30, C sub. 1 class, primer		

Oswego students would begin in Class C around age five or six and then move on to Classes B and A as they grew older.

Source: Seventh Annual Report of the Board of Education of the City of Oswego for the Year Ending March 31, 1860 (Oswego: Tarbell, 1860), 15–16.

Though rote memorization and written examinations had been replaced by object lessons, Pope Sheldon, who had once proudly noted that "by looking at my watch, I could tell exactly what every teacher in the city was doing," was still very much in control of his schools.[16] For example, in the first year after the discovery of the HCS methods, the overzealous Sheldon organized a curriculum that accounted for every moment of class time, down to five-minute intervals. A typical Friday for students in Class C included twenty-nine short units ranging from five-minute breaks to twenty-minute lessons, each lesson planned around a specific small pedagogical goal, such as lessons on phonetics, color, form, or number or on specific objects that were supposed to provoke the learning of a specific concept. Only a small percentage of these lessons focused explicitly on common objects, but many were variations on object lessons on weight, place, or form. A plan for a Tuesday in Class B and A was similar.[17] The schedule for slightly older students included twenty-six separate units, with lessons on form, weight, objects, number, and drawing. Each of these lessons had to be prepared in advance, requiring teachers to think through over a hundred separate lessons a week.[18] The method may have been intended to draw more information out of children, but it also certainly demanded far more from their teachers as well. When Sheldon became president of the New York State Teachers' Association in 1861, he challenged his unhappy teachers, most of whom were women, "Those who are unwilling to devote the time and effort necessary to such preparation, may as well put the seal to their marriage contracts" and leave the profession.[19] Sheldon liked to think he was professionalizing the occupation, but he did not quite know what he was doing—yet.

For example, for Friday morning in Class C, a teacher was expected to prepare a ten-minute lesson on an object, perhaps a lesson on loaf sugar. This lesson required the teacher to have the children taste the sugar to learn that it is sweet, be able to explain the geographic location and labor conditions of this commodity's production, offer a scientific explanation of why sugar dissolves in water, but is fusible and melts in fire (she was to employ a burning candle), and a description of its appearance (sparkling, hard, and white). Much of this was common knowledge, but extracting this information in fewer than ten minutes from a group of six- to eight-year-old children who were also handling and tasting the sugar themselves seems impossible.[20] Plus, it required much more work and preparation than simply teaching a lesson from a book. It was made doubly difficult because teachers were operating without any more training than a half a day weekly—and that from a man who had never witnessed an object lesson. Sheldon and his teachers recognized after a year of classroom time that they needed better training.

After trying to figure it out for himself for several months, working with the materials he had found in Toronto and reading all the books he could find, Sheldon wrote to the HCS to request an instructor who could serve as a model, "for the purpose of introducing this system into our public schools." To tempt the teacher, Miss M. E. M. Jones, to leave her regular post at the Home and Colonial Training Institution in England and to spend a year instructing the "pupil-teachers" of Oswego, New York, he offered her a salary of a $1,000. Sheldon noted that many of the teachers even contributed half of their annual salaries to defray the cost of her instruction.[21] Prior to her appointment, she had spent fifteen years at the HCS working with Elizabeth Mayo. Her teaching involved both clear lecturing on the matter and method of education and providing model lessons, advertised by Sheldon as "fully illustrated and worked out in the schoolroom."[22]

A few months after Jones arrived, Sheldon hired Hermann Krüsi to assist in his school, further cementing Oswego's ties to both HCS and Pestalozzi. Sheldon was so aware of the centrality of experience that he enrolled and is listed as a graduate from the school's first class taught by Jones. Jones even instructed her pupils in the creation of their own textbooks, based on their individual experiences as pupil-teachers.[23] This requirement emphasized the problems of relying on established texts as opposed to experience in training teachers. These books were supposed to include information gathered from secondary texts, observations of objects, oral lessons, and questions. They were organized into two sections, *matter* and *method*, highlighting the importance of considering the way a topic was to be taught in addition to the actual substance to be presented, a central tenet of Jones's philosophy. Jones's lessons as well were bifurcated into *matter* and *method*, so that pupil-teachers could take notes on the matter of the lesson, the information to be conveyed, and separately on the method through which it would be explicated. In order to gather certain ideas from objects and substances, children were to engage with them in specific ways. At the same time, the different modes of engagement trained their perceptive abilities.

Sheldon's own in-class notebooks are very close to *A Manual of Elementary Instruction for the Use of Public and Private Schools and Normal Classes*, first published in August 1862, months after he left Jones's classroom. In his preface, Sheldon explained that much of the book was based on Jones's original manuscripts from the HCS and Elizabeth Mayo's published writings. Though Sheldon notes in the preface that he had the "kind consent" of Mayo to adapt her ideas for his *Manual*, she is not credited on the title page. Sheldon, Jones, and Krüsi changed the objects selected, added more information about those objects, more model lessons, and more detail about the way the lessons were to unfold over time, but large sections are simply copied from Mayo's work. When

Students in training construct a sketch of a Lesson on "Mercury," or "Air," modelled after the "Lesson on Water."

5. *Sketch of a Lesson on Loaf Sugar.*

Points.—Qualities as discovered by the senses. Less obvious qualities.

MATTER.	METHOD.
1. Sugar is white, sparkling, opaque.	1. Present a piece of loaf sugar, and ask the children to give the name, and tell what they can discover by looking at it. Compare it with a piece of crystal. Points of difference—one translucent, the other opaque. Points of resemblance—hard, white, bright. Compare the brightness of both objects—one is bright all over, the other full of little bright points. A thing clear, bright all over, is said to be *lucid.* A thing full of little bright points, is said to be *sparkling.* Children name other objects that sparkle, and find by comparison that things that sparkle have usually a rough surface.
2. Sugar is rough and hard.	2. Bring out *rough* and *hard*, by asking children what they can say after feeling of it.
3. Sugar is sweet.	3. By taste.
4. Sugar is fusible, brittle, granulous, and crystallized.	4. Bring out *fusible, soluble, brittle,* and *granulous,* by direct observation and experiment. *Crystallized* developed by putting threads into strong solutions of salt or alum, which, after a few hours, will be covered with crystals. (*a*) Children compare the grains with each other, and find that they are all of the same shape. (*b*) Children notice that they are solid, by reference to the broken grains. Whether they find anything inside? (*c*) Produce some of the simplest solids, and some amorphous stones. Which do the grains most resemble? Why? Because they are all of the same shape. Show one part of a solid concealing the other part. What children expect to find on the other side—corresponding faces and edges. Will know that crystals are alike. Give the term *regular.* Tell children that

Figure 2.1. "Sketch of a Lesson on Loaf Sugar" from E. A. Sheldon, Margaret E. M. Jones, and Hermann Krüsi, *A Manual of Elementary Instruction, for the Use of Public and Private Schools and Normal Classes: Containing a Graduated Course of Object Lessons for Training the Senses and Developing the Faculties of Children* (New York: C. Scribner, 1862), 112–113. Object lessons were divided into "Matter" and "Method" to help

substances formed in little grains, all of which are regular solids, are said to be crystallized. Refer to sugar as juice of a plant. Children state the origin and original form of sugar (liquid). Produce various specimens of crystals, and after drawing attention to them as such (being regular), tell them that every one of these was once a liquid, and has now become a regular solid. Examples found by children of a liquid that crystallizes (snow). Might be followed by lesson on the forms, into which many objects crystallize.

5. Sugar is vegetable, and manufactured. | 5. Bring out *vegetable*, by reference to the sugar cane, of which show a specimen. *Manufactured*, by comparison of the cane with its product (sugar). Some information given as to the processes the article undergoes in the course of manufacture.

Points, as worked out, written on the board.

Summary.—Erase "Matter." Children say which of the qualities they have considered have been discovered by sight; which by feeling; by taste; by experiment; and by reference to previous knowledge. Write the qualities, as the children shall dictate, in separate columns.

Qualities discovered by more than one sense, may be written in separate columns, thus:—

Sense of Sight.	Sense of Feeling.	Sense of Taste.	Experiment.	Previous Knowledge.
White.	Rough(^{2}).	Sweet.	Fusible.	Cultivated.
Sparkling.	Hard.		Soluble.	Manufactured.
Opaque.			Brittle.	Vegetable.
Rough(^{1}).			Granulous.	
			Crystallized.	

Students in training construct a sketch of a lesson on "Bread," after the model of the one on "Sugar."

teachers link the material qualities of the items they were using to the strategies or methods intended to sort the sensations developed through study of those qualities. In this case, sugar and its physical qualities—sparkling, rough and hard, sweet, fusible, etc.—are the "Matter." The "Method" is the teacher's approach through which those qualities are discovered.

Figure 2.2. "First Step" from Elizabeth Mayo and E. A. Sheldon, *Lessons on Objects, Graduated Series: Designed for Children Between the Ages of Six and Fourteen Years: Containing Also Information on Common Objects* (New York: Charles Scribner, 1863), 8. Lists of objects to be used in object lessons contained a range of natural and man-made materials from baskets and scissors to feathers and oranges.

Jones returned to England, after bringing the HCS's methods to the United States, she faced censure from her former colleagues. An Oswego teacher who visited Jones in 1881 wrote to Sheldon,

> When Mrs. Jones returned to England, she found Miss Mayo in great indignation over the manual, and she would never listen to an explanation regarding it. Many sympathized with Miss Mayo as shown by the fact that a Home and Colonial teacher returned to Miss J. a manual which she presented him. Within the last two years, Mrs. Jones was informed, soon after Miss Mayo's niece became a member of the board of education, that the lessons that she had been giving (which were not finished) as a member of the same board would no longer be required.[24]

There appears to have been some kind of miscommunication. Perhaps Mayo was upset over a lack of appropriate credit or even Sheldon's claim that his volume corrected "errors in principles and practice." The same Oswego teacher asked Sheldon, "I am sure a short letter from you to Mrs. J stating that Miss Mayo gave her consent to the use of her book would be very gladly received in as much as it would be a quick and convenient method of refuting any charge. If Miss M's letter could be found, it would be a boon."[25] Nearly two decades later, Sheldon's adaptation of the method was still an issue in English pedagogical circles.

The classroom study of objects and images was certainly not new in the 1860s, but object lessons as presented by Jones and Sheldon at Oswego projected a different aspect of object-based learning. Peering into a well-funded antebellum classroom, one would expect to see maps, globes, wall charts, blackboards, and perhaps even a microscope or a camera obscura, all tools of objective or inductive learning, broadly defined. By the 1850s, various kinds of instructional apparatus were common in primary schools. A drawing of a classroom made as a gift to a teacher from her student in 1856, highlights a map of Africa and a globe.[26] Assistant superintendent of New York City schools S. W. Seton detailed the apparatus available in the primary school classrooms of New York City public schools in 1856. He carefully described the use of a numerical frame, a syllabarium (similar to a printer's composing stick), collections of rocks, minerals, and specimens as well as a box of objects, "natural and artificial, viz.: Cloth, Leather, Metals, Wood, Cotton, &c. for teaching common things."[27] He described how these materials were to be used in his report, suggesting the origin of that favorite axiom "show not tell," by calling on teachers to challenge their students, "If you know, show." Seton argued that "illustrations by sensible objects would secure knowledge as a possession." Even in his articulate cry for object-based study in the classroom, his interest was less in training the senses than in imparting knowledge that could be assessed and tested. A clear example of his kind of object-based study was to teach children multiplication as "three the root and nine the fruit" and "twelve the root and one hundred and forty-four the fruit" linking a math fact with a mental picture of the fact.[28] A midcentury Multiplication Table Tree in which the equations are on the trunk and the answers are depicted in the fruit suggests the kind of visual learning Seton might have had in mind.[29] A numerical frame (like an abacus) might allow children to count out and understand the meaning behind the tables they were memorizing, an extremely useful connection and certainly objective teaching, but it was not training them to understand sensory differences.

At Oswego, instead of using objects and pictures as telling examples or as metonyms for set stories, the objects were intended to develop students' senses. This is the crucial difference between formal object lessons and simply teaching with objects. Sheldon and his team endeavored to train their pupils' perceptive abilities and to help them acquire a vocabulary to express their new knowledge about the material world. Though it often fell short of these goals, as gauged by considering the results that the teachers hoped to achieve via object teaching, sense training emerges as a sincere intellectual and moral aim.

A lesson published in Sheldon's book that was based on his notes from his class with Jones suggests how a lesson might work. Starting with a familiar

material object or substance, the students were explicitly instructed to consider
the object's physical qualities, form, color, size, and function and to organize
those sensations. Slowly circulating a bolt of fine silk around the classroom,
an instructor was supposed to draw the words "lightness, luster, strength, and
beauty" out of her students, using these words to help them understand what
they were feeling in the fabric. Teasing apart the threads of the fabric, she
could lead her students to understand how the fibers might be manipulated or
how to perceive the differences between velvet and bombazine. In addition to
instructing her students on the qualities of silkiness, the teacher would use the
fabric swatch as an opportunity to convey information about the natural history
of silkworms, geography, trade, and industry, offering a biography of the thing
described.[30] The silk, to the trained pupil-teacher, contained all of this information (i.e., Matter) and the careful questioning by the instructor (i.e., Method)
was intended to use the object to draw it out of the students. This lesson engaged the sense of touch. Other lessons encouraged a student to smell, to hear,
to observe minute details, or even to taste the objects and substances under
consideration. Instead of allowing the object to stand in for already memorized
information or merely to aid in memorization, the object lesson intended to
create that information through the student's sensory experience and to categorize that sensual information.

Jones's first cohort of students, which would become the first class of the
Oswego Normal School, consisted of Oswego teachers and two other students
who were keen to learn how to apply the new object teaching methods. Jones
led classes after school, three afternoons a week including Friday afternoons,
when the pupil-teachers were instructed in lessons they could give to a special Saturday "Practice School" that consisted of primary school students. Her
lessons allowed pupil-teachers to learn a new lesson and then, immediately
practice it, learning from their own experience of interacting with children.

A student in that first normal class detailed one of Jones's most memorable lessons in a letter she wrote to the school years after graduating.
Louisa Plumb (later Andrews) had already been teaching in the Oswego
Public Schools for several years when, in 1861, she entered Miss Jones's
classroom as a pupil-teacher. Plumb described the scene Jones created for a
lesson on vinegar. On a low table in the basement of a local Catholic church,
Jones had arranged small glass vials of water, vinegar, and two other colored
liquids, along with sugar, bread, and cake. Jones "made the objects the textbooks," Plumb recalled. By instructing the six ten-year-old children in her
care to taste, mix, and arrange the substances in different ways, her students
came to understand the color, flavor, origin, and function of the quotidian
substances. Plumb believed this mode of teaching, from familiar object to
new abstract concept, immediately improved her classroom presentation.

She recalled, "Some of us [the pupil-teachers] repeated [the lesson] the next morning before our own classes. We knew them, they knew us and understood our every word. We were surprised at our own success." Writing to the school decades after graduation, Plumb exclaimed, "Forget that lesson, the cruet on my table forbids." Years later, a simple cruet of vinegar still had the power to conjure up Jones's lesson.[31]

The following February, when Sheldon decided to display his new methodology to the teachers of the United States in a public exhibition, he chose Louisa Plumb to present her variation on this lesson as part of the three days of activities. A local newspaper described her demonstration in detail, as did the *Proceedings of the Educational Convention*. Standing on the stage of Doolittle Hall with her students, before a large audience of invited educational experts, she first asked her students to organize a variety of acid and alkaline substances in some way. A boy arranged them into two groups: liquids and solids. She asked them to try tasting the various items—which in her lesson included cream of tartar, tartaric acid, oxalic acid, and sal soda, lye, pearlash and soda, in addition to vinegar—and challenged them to organize the items according to taste and smell. The sour, bitter, and burning "texts" were then arranged under newly conceptualized categories of "acid" and "alkaline." Plumb then produced vegetable dye and soapy water, into which the children were instructed to mix certain acidic and alkaline substances and to observe their relationships to each other, creating new colors and fizzing effects. Through these simple experiments, the students concluded that the acid and the alkaline neutralized each other. This object lesson first presented the substances to the children and helped them categorize the sensations created by the substances. The teacher then gave the students tools to further describe and understand what they had observed by asking and answering questions, leading to new understanding of abstract concepts. For Plumb, recalling it decades later, the cruet of vinegar was a key to comprehending how an entire lesson of complex concepts could be embedded in a simple everyday thing.[32] To the distinguished guests who had traveled from all over New England and the Mid-Atlantic states to see Sheldon's new method, it was an object lesson in object lessons.

The Oswego Method

In February 1862, after more than a year of pedagogical experimentation in what would become the Oswego State Normal School, Sheldon made a risky move. As the president of the New York State Teachers' Association, he decided to invite a number of leading educators, including the editor of the *New York Teacher*, to a three-day program held in downtown Oswego. There, he put some of his best pupil-teachers, like Louisa Plumb, with her vinegar and pearlash, on display to demonstrate the pedagogical techniques employed in his school district. His school was not yet funded by the state government, and his own community was fairly skeptical about this methodology. Object teaching was poorly understood, often poorly executed, and a topic of debate in the pedagogical press. Sheldon wanted to show what could be done if a clear system of organization and structure were applied to Pestalozzi's Romantic, child-centered ideas about intellectual development. In his presidential address to the New York Teachers' Association the previous summer, he had emphasized the importance of a system of education, not simply a philosophy.[33]

Though he would often be praised as the founder of this mode of pedagogy, Sheldon was aware that he had adapted an explicitly English rendering of Pestalozzi's ideas for an American audience already familiar with the thinker and his methods. Sheldon's contribution was to transform those Romantic ideas about child-centered learning, formalized in the English classroom of Elizabeth Mayo, into a concrete method that might produce consistent and true results. The educators he invited to survey his methods understood this, explaining in their report, "We do not claim that the principles of this system are new in this country. For years they have been quietly and almost imperceptibly creeping into our educational theories, and in an isolated and disjointed way. . . . Good teachers everywhere are working more or less in accordance with some one or more of these principles . . . thus they have been preparing the way for the introduction of these principles, embodied into a system of primary education of which they constitute the very web and woof. It is this feature which we claim as new in this country."[34]

In a way Sheldon simply expanded on what Mayo had done in her work and included more specific instructions about how these lessons could be used. As nineteenth-century Anglo-American educators had said of Pestalozzi for decades, his ideas may have been sound but were rarely properly applied. Sheldon's system offered what he argued was an explicit Americanization of those ideas, complete with a school timetable. Sheldon's convention turned out to be a shrewd act of public relations, presenting what had been an accepted set of educational principles in the form of a rigorous regimen, which quickly acquired passionate champions and detractors.

Sheldon and his committee of educational leaders—most of whom were from the northeastern United States (not surprising since the Civil War was well under way)—spelled out their interpretation of object lessons and object teaching very clearly in the *Proceedings* that recorded the speeches made at the convention. At the foundation of his interpretation of object teaching is his belief, derived from Pestalozzi, that the training of children's senses leads almost directly to the ability to reason morally. He summed it up succinctly:

> The Committee believe it to be the generally received opinion that, in childhood, all positive knowledge comes through sensation and perception. Sensation arises from the contact of our senses with the outer material world. Perception is the reference of a sensation to its cause. Sensations lead, through observations, to conceptions. Conceptions form the basis of our reasoning, and, through reason, we are led to discover our relations to the material world, to our fellow-men, and to the Creator; and, finally, the will, as the executive power, enables us to act according to the dictates of reason, of conscience, and of duty.[35]

The steps were as follows: sensation leads to perception, through observations to conceptions, which allow one to reason and act based on volition, "according to the conclusion reached by reason, acting in harmony with the conscience and the nobler emotions and impulses of our nature."[36] In this model, one does not learn how to observe purely to acquire knowledge or language, though those are crucial ancillary goals. Rather, one learns through the senses in order to learn to reason and to think for one's self. Sheldon represented this process of learning graphically in his *Manual of Elementary Instruction*, published six months after the convention. He represented learning as a tree, with sensation at the roots and an understanding of cause and effect and power of judgment as branches that grow out of its foundation.[37] For example, Louisa Plumb's lesson on acid and alkaline revealed that there were many facets to every substance, that form, taste, smell, and other more abstract properties could variously define an object or help frame a problem. The goal of Sheldon's Educational Convention was to show children thinking, providing an object lesson for guests and the community. The schedule of events circulated prior to the meeting explained that the goal was to show methods, not results.[38] Just as his rigorous written examinations had earned him needed public funds to develop his schools during his early years as the superintendent, perhaps he hoped a public exhibition would serve as similar proof of the pedagogy's success.

Sheldon demonstrated his system through a series of twenty lessons on objects, number, form, color, animals, and place. Each of these lessons was prefaced with information about the background of the children on stage, including their ages, class in school, and in some cases specific information about their training. For example, in a lesson on "size" a group of children from Class C, who were between the ages of five and seven, were asked to show the guests how long an inch was using their fingers, and to use that measurement

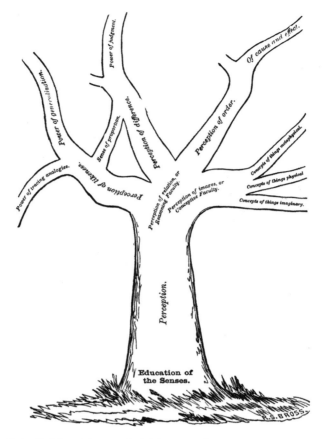

Figure 2.3. E. A. Sheldon, Margaret E. M. Jones, and Hermann Krüsi, *Manual of
Elementary Instruction* (New York: C. Scribner, 1862), frontispiece. By representing
object-lesson pedagogy as a tree, Sheldon emphasized the ways all forms of thinking
and learning developed not only through perception but also grew out of the
"education of the senses."

to draw lines and rip paper into a variety of sizes, reflecting their understanding
of the relationship between different units of measurements. In order to develop this skill, the children had studied "size" for twenty minutes a day for
eight weeks.[39] A group of older children, average age of nine, presented a lesson
on place in which they used a map of Oswego to measure distances around
the community and presented a scale drawing of the schoolroom that they had
created. Other lessons examined pepper, lead, the ibis, and other vegetables,
minerals, and animals for the information that could be drawn out of them, like
the pungency of the pepper, the malleability of the lead, and the likely habitat
of the ibis based on its morphology. These public examinations went on for
three days.

The examining committee requested what could be considered a control group, students who had not benefited from Jones's methods and Sheldon's system. Sheldon imported a group of children from outside of Oswego and had an instructor teach them according to the Oswego method. Putting a group of solids, spheres, cubes, cones, and other forms in front of the children the first teacher led them to observe the connections between the various shapes of the objects. Later, a different teacher came on stage to teach the concept of "vegetable" through the display of a small rose plant. The out-of-town children were then given a leaf and a picture of a leaf and challenged to explain the difference between the two. Unfortunately, the limited English of the students, who turned out to be from German-speaking families, curtailed the lesson on object and representation. Sheldon's choice to include non-English-speaking children certainly would have highlighted the difference between his trained students and the new group from out of the city, but surely it also suggested that anyone could learn via his method. Even the German-speaking children were able to grasp the concept of "vegetable," suggesting cabbage as analogous to the rose plant presented by the teacher.[40]

The convention included lectures on object teaching given by N. A. Calkins, who had recently published a book on his own version of object teaching and would serve as superintendent of the New York City primary schools from 1863 to 1895, and a paper written by Jones (read by a colleague), in which she outlined the "Laws of Childhood." Jones's outline of the system of object teaching was broad reaching and featured lofty platitudes about the nature of childhood and the goals of object lessons, claiming that this method could move children from "Color to Chromatography . . . Objects to Mineralogy . . . Chemistry . . . Actions to Art and Manufacture," arguing that the careful training of children's senses would lead to the development of more complex modes of reasoning.

In addition to object-teachers Calkins and Jones, Sheldon cited the work of a contemporary, the Reverend Thomas Hill. Hill's pamphlet, *The True Order of Studies,* had initially been given as Phi Beta Kappa lectures at Harvard in 1858. Hill had recently replaced Horace Mann as president of Antioch College and would soon become the twentieth president of Harvard. A close friend of Louis Agassiz, Hill was extremely interested in the role sense perception had in the development of what he called "noetics" or the "training of the mind." He divided noetics into three parts, the development of perceptive, imaginative, and reflective abilities. Hill's carefully organized system of learning began with the senses and sense perception, which appealed to Sheldon and his followers, in spite of important differences between the two systems.[41] The conference served the purpose Sheldon had hoped it would. Not only did he give educators a concrete idea of how object lessons could be employed, but he also started a renewed discussion about the methodology that tore through the educational press of his day. How might sense education and the study of the external, material world fit into the education of children?

The sharpest attack on Sheldon's methodology came from Syracuse, not thirty miles from Oswego. H. B. Wilbur was the founder and superintendent of the New York Asylum for Idiots, an experimental school for the treatment of people who would now be described as living with developmental and intellectual disabilities or differences. He did not see the applicability of object teaching for the average child. He also critiqued the specific ways in which Sheldon's methods attempted to teach children language and to access complex subjects, particularly in the sciences. In his controversial 1862 address to the annual meeting of the New York State Teachers Association, Wilbur emphasized that humans—who were not in some way disabled—had a unique ability to learn and retain knowledge that had not been shown to them simply through their senses. He made this claim based on his success with object teaching in his work with the mentally disabled.[42]

At the New York Asylum for Idiots, Wilbur engaged in a form of sensory education to develop what he called the "deficiency of Will in Idiocy." Wilbur's definition of idiocy came directly from the ideas of M. Seguin, a French doctor who believed that "intelligence and sensitivity are not absolutely wanting in an idiocy, but dormant and undeveloped."[43] In Wilbur's classrooms, which were often opened to visitors, the senses of his pupils were considered the only avenues through which one could reach these variously disabled individuals. Often gruesome in practice, his theory reflected optimism that idiocy could be "cured." Wilbur's descriptions of the techniques he employed will make a twenty-first-century reader cringe—he described repeatedly touching the eyeballs of his students, manipulating their bodies into painful positions to encourage willful response, or confining children to dark rooms in order to heighten the effects of bright lights—but to a nineteenth-century reader they likely sounded like an extreme form of the sense education advocated in object lessons. For example, Wilbur described his interaction with an eight-year-old girl who had no control over her body. He was able to teach her to use her hand by placing various kinds of substances into it, things that were hard and soft, smooth and rough, hot and cold. This stimulation engaged her sense of touch and she eventually learned to grasp and drop the things she was holding, exerting will. Similar exercises were performed using color, light, noise, and motion, depending on the perceived needs of a specific child. Wilbur advocated this kind of education for the students he encountered in his asylum and whom he considered to be closer to "savage life," but he did not see it as necessary for all children. He noted, "In higher social states, by means of superior instruction and earlier habits of inference there is less necessity for that active, sharpened use of sense." Children can simply be told what they need to know, he explained; they do not need to discover everything for themselves. For average pupils, he argued, that ability was simply part of being human and was developed easily outside of school.[44] Wilbur's critique suggested that Sheldon's methods were infantilizing, or fit only for those he called "idiots."

Sheldon was not alone, however, in his emphasis on sense training. In the 1850s, authors of children's books explicitly addressed the development of the senses. Paralleling the growth of objective forms of teaching, the sense education of children was of serious concern to parents of young children. Elizabeth Prentiss's book *Little Susy's Little Servants*, published in 1857, detailed the discovery of a little girl's senses, her five servants. Little Susy's early education echoes the methods Wilbur advocated for the education of the mentally disabled girl he described in his address. The frontispiece of *Little Susy* illustrates the moment she discovered touch, with her doting parents handing her objects. "At last they did learn to hold her rattle for her, and then an orange and then a bunch of keys." "They" refers to "her servants," her hands.[45] The text details each of her senses from "her two black servants," her eyes, to her grasping hands, highlighting the ways she needed to learn about her body in order to control it and use it well. Considering sense education in this context, it is not simply an abstract goal but a topic that related to one's ability to will control over one's body and by analogy over one's mind. Wilbur believed most children should be able to develop these skills independently at an early age, outside of school.

Wilbur did not simply criticize object teaching for not recognizing the developmental needs of most children; he saw the system as overemphasizing language acquisition through observation. Wilbur attacked the notion that observation led to expression and understanding of complex concepts. Without this link, he believed that it was a waste for children to spend limited school time engaging in observational training. The kinds of words that children were instructed to discover were also often words that were far too complex for a seven- or eight-year-old child, although according to Elizabeth Mayo's publication, they could be explained through analysis of their Latin or Greek roots. Wilbur mocked Mayo's practice, musing on the possible use the definition of a "rhombic dodecahedron" might be to a child, or what comfort a seven-year-old pupil would find in knowing the word cylinder came from the "Greek *Kulindo*, I roll." In a later version of his speech to the New York State Teachers Association, which he published in the *American Journal of Education* in 1865, he claimed,

> Looking at the real object of a public school system such as our own, supported from the public treasury, designed to obviate the accidents of birth or fortune, by placing the keys of knowledge in every youthful hand, is such chaff a substitute for a thorough grounding in the elementary branches? . . . Perceptions of form and color are quite distinct from geometry and chromatography.[46]

Wilbur did not view object teaching as conducive to learning, nor did he find clear links between sense perception and useful fields of academic study. He emphasized this theme by comparing Sheldon to Mr. Gradgrind in Dickens's *Hard Times* (1854) to make this point. He described the classroom scene in which Mr. Gradgrind insisted that his pupils define material things in the most precise way possible. A boy answered his teacher's query to define a horse in the following way:

> Quadruped. Graminivorous. Forty teeth, namely twenty-four grinders, four eye-teeth, and twelve incisive. Sheds coat in the spring; in marshy countries, sheds hoofs, too. Hoofs hard, but requiring to be shod with iron. Age known by marks in mouth.[47]

The specialized vocabulary parroted by the boy was not dissimilar, Wilbur argued, to a lesson in a textbook advocated by Sheldon that defined a Lady Bird as "hemispherical, fragile and jointed." Sheldon's methods, to Wilbur, were merely the "thin gruel of utilitarianism," producing only a useless repetition of information and no measurable effect on his pupils.[48]

Another basic criticism of Sheldon's method as a specific pedagogical strategy within the common schools was that there was no way to know that the exercises children went through would actually lead to higher reasoning. Wilbur homed in on Jones's claim that the lower branches of study pursued in object lessons might lead directly to disciplinary studies of geometry or chromatography, and other sciences. He implicitly argued against the logic behind Louis Agassiz's fish lesson, in which the Harvard naturalist suggested his students could learn everything about zoological classification from the close study of a single object, understood solely through the senses.[49] Higher branches of learning, Wilbur's writings suggested, were simultaneously too general, too dependent on large systems, and too detailed and complex to be understood in any single moment of observation.

Another writer raised a similar concern. In "Education to Be," published in 1862, the anonymous author claimed that the practice of object teaching encouraged children "to wander truant-like among all sorts of good things— exploiting now a color, then milk and in good time gratitude and the pyramids, then leather . . . then sponge, duty to parents, lying and the points of the compass." This joyous, even promiscuous exploration of the world might be good for children in some ways, but it lacked "consecution" and did not prepare children for higher studies as readily as it should—not moving from a study of common things to the study of specific domains of knowledge.[50]

Sheldon and an anonymous advocate responded to Wilbur in print. Wilbur, they contended, did not understand that object lessons were a system to be unfolded over many years of education, not simply contained in any one lesson or to meet any one specific sense-based goal. M. E. M. Jones and Elizabeth Mayo echoed these sentiments in correspondence with Sheldon. Jones explained that the goal was to develop "habits of thought," not scientific knowledge.[51] Sheldon continued that he recognized that true science was for higher learning, but that children could be trained to "examine carefully and critically all objects brought under their observation," leading over time from form to geometry and color to chromatography. Elizabeth Mayo wrote that Wilbur confused "Practice with Principles." In terms of the language employed in her lessons, she explained that Wilbur did not understand that her method was developed for her brother's school in Cheam. Unlike Sheldon's school system in Oswego, it instructed children in Latin and Greek along with object lessons to directly prepare them for entrance to Cambridge and Oxford.[52] An anonymous author writing in the *New York Teacher* published a detailed response to Wilbur, attacking his emphasis on language. The writer argued, "The process does not depend chiefly upon the memory of words for retaining the knowledge, but upon the memory of the thing itself which will readily call up all facts associated with it. This process puts the child in possession of real knowledge, and also enables it to remember the needful words more easily."[53] The writer believed that memory of the concrete would obviously lead to a memory of the abstract.

The ongoing debate in the *New York Teacher* and other educational journals did not settle the question of whether object teaching was the best pedagogical approach. In 1865, a committee of prominent educators led by Samuel Stillman Greene, professor at Brown University and then president of the National Teachers Association, decided to examine the practice.[54] The committee investigated the intellectual meaning of object teaching, starting with the question, "What place do external objects hold in the acquisition of Knowledge?" It went on to consider the specifics of the Oswego Method. The committee was ambivalent in its assessment of the philosophical problem of whether external objects contained knowledge, noting that there is a difference between "rational" and "experimental" knowledge. Greene and his colleagues were pointed in their arguments about object teaching in general and the Oswego Method in particular. They defined object teaching not as any of the various concrete methods to which the name had been applied (i.e., a teacher pulling out some blocks in class or asking students to memorize a specimen lesson) but as "that which develops the abstract from the concrete,—which develops the idea, then gives the term." The committee argued that in this natural chain of associations a student would then later be able to travel from the word or concept back to the thing itself, with the ability to also move from abstract to concrete. Regardless of the kind of knowledge contained in the material world, object teaching could link the external with the internal.[55]

Another direct benefit noted by the committee was that object teaching was the best way to teach teachers how to give any sort of lesson. Greene wrote,

> The chief and highest advantage of giving these lessons lies . . . in its direct influence upon the *teacher himself.* . . . He who can give an object lesson well is capable of giving any lesson well, because he has learned that it is the *reality* and not the expression of it that is the chief object to be gained. . . . He must know the present capacity and attainment of the child and what *realities* are suited to them.[56]

With teaching rooted in material things, it was clear that the relationship between matter and method posed by M. E. M. Jones had to be direct. As opposed to lecturing on abstract concepts, the object teacher would discover immediately whether he or she was able to draw information out of his or her students and would need to know how to respond to that information to the best effect. The teacher had to have not only clear, flexible pedagogical goals in mind but also several possible ways of arriving at those goals in an appropriate sequence. The committee praised the decision to have object teaching as the foundation of the normal school curriculum at Oswego. After observing several classrooms at Oswego, Professor Greene offered his approval of the system for elementary education but warned of the danger of replacing books with object lessons for older students. He tempered his praise by noting that not all of the teachers he observed were equal in their ability to give object lessons.[57]

Greene's conditional endorsement of object teaching highlights a major problem with the methodology: assessment. Unlike the rigorous tests Sheldon had given in the late 1850s to prove the progress of his schools, learning by object teaching could not be so easily measured. The door remained open for critics like Wilbur. For example, an examiner, likely Sheldon, visited Louisa Plumb's class in 1859 and asked her students a total of 539 questions, of which her students answered 479 correctly. She received a grade of 89 percent. In 1863, after two years of object-teaching training, an examiner measured her performance and that of her students through skill-based exercises in writing, then geography, in which they were instructed to look at maps drawn on the board and discuss boundaries, the natural resources and occupations and character of the people from different lands. Next they read aloud and completed arithmetic exercises, before being given an object lesson on beeswax. Without numbers or a rank, it was not always clear how her class might compare to that of another pupil-teacher.[58] Though Oswego teachers proudly exclaimed that with object teaching, "we no longer have any dull pupils," it was a difficult claim to prove.[59]

Certainly some of their lessons went wrong. A criticism lesson, or model lesson, on bats, published in Sheldon's *Manual of Elementary Education*, found fault with a teacher for pouring information into children instead of drawing it out through observation. The headmaster challenged his pupil-teachers' choice to tell their students instead of showing them how the physical details of the bat specimen related to bats' function.[60] A trained teacher could transform these sensations into knowledge through clear questioning and simultaneously giving the student crucial observational skills. Louisa Plumb remembered what had happened when a little Irish boy gave an answer that displeased his teacher (in this case Jones). Jones simply sent him home. Another pupil-teacher recounted an episode in which a child responded to a lesson on doves. When asked why doves were more peaceful than birds of prey and treated their mates sweetly, he responded by saying, "Doves don't know any better." All of the observers laughed at his comment.[61] Certainly neither response was what object teachers claimed they hoped to elicit from students, whose developing young minds were to be treated with gravity and dignity. A student in the mid-1860s, Lill Salmon, described a failed object lesson in a letter to a classmate; a chemical fire brought about by the accidental mixture of iodine and phosphorous produced a dangerous smoke that nearly asphyxiated the pupil-teachers in attendance.[62] For advocates of object lessons, however, moments like these were minor details. The Greene Report had endorsed object teaching, at least for the youngest children. Five years after his trip to Toronto, Sheldon was at the helm of what became a state-funded normal school that was spreading a new way of thinking with things at school throughout the United States.[63]

Object Lessons in the Classroom

In the early 1860s, progressive educators in schools across the continent employed object lessons. The pedagogy was popular in primary schools. It was taught alongside reading, mathematics, moral lessons, geography, and other subjects, all of which could be presented objectively. Training in object teaching was soon offered in most normal schools.[64] New York City began offering special instruction in object teaching in the public schools.[65] The California state teachers' exam for 1863 asked, "Have you had any practice in giving 'Object Lessons?'"[66] In 1862, the *Chicago Tribune* offered a basic, layman's understanding of the practice for its readers: "The new feature in teaching being now rapidly introduced everywhere is 'Object Lessons.' The idea, simply, is to present an object for a lesson instead of a picture or a description of some object, this real object being theoretically a neuclus [*sic*] around which is to be grouped the facts and relations pertaining to that object."[67] With the object as a nucleus there was little danger of abstract concepts disappearing into the ether or, worse, being misunderstood by a generation of children. However, the *Chicago Tribune* only described one aspect of object lessons. Material things certainly served as nuclei around which all kinds of information might orbit. The concreteness of the thing at the center of the lesson continued to be of the utmost importance. The stuff of object lessons, their materiality, the hardness of glass, the smell of beeswax, the ductility of lead, the translucence of a porcelain cup, and the form of a stuffed owl shaped students and teachers.

One common critique of object lessons was that teachers did not always understand the importance of including objects or pictures in their lessons. Writers complained that they merely included descriptions of objects or even asked children to memorize qualities associated with certain objects. A newspaper commentator described the real problems inherent with object lessons without an object. A New Jersey visitor to the Cincinnati schools described a situation in which "properties of substances and things were placed on the board, copied by the pupils, stupidly memorized, and hopelessly parroted." The students would associate the wrong substance with the wrong quality and learn nothing.[68] Object lesson in this case was code for memorization and rote learning about objects, something the visitor was pleased to see replaced with more appropriate lessons on actual objects. The Lady Teachers' Association of Cincinnati debated this question in 1873, asking if it was ever acceptable to give an object lesson without an object or a reproduction of it in the classroom. This question evoked "considerable mirth" as they weighed the merits of lessons on butter and cheese in the classroom.[69] But what did a successful lesson look like in the classroom?

It is difficult to trace the on-the-ground implementation of classroom practices in the 1860s, 1870s, and 1880s. There are few, if any, classroom photographs, few descriptions of actual as opposed to ideal practices, and seemingly infinite classroom contexts. For example, in 1863 teachers in the newly freed regions of the South brought object lessons with them as a strategy that could be employed without books. Twenty-five-year-old African American educator and author Charlotte Forten Grimké, who had studied with Hermann Krüsi in Salem, Massachusetts, described lessons she gave to a large group of recently freed African American children in South Carolina. In what was likely a kind of object lesson on the body and senses, she discussed the function of the ears. The children explained that ears were "to put rings in," while they told another teacher that they were "to put cotton in." After a lesson on metals, in which they learned that iron came from the ground, a little boy proclaimed to her that gold, another metal, came "from the sky." Forten noted, "They listen with eager attention, and seem to understand and remember very well what I tell them," but her examples do not support that assertion.[70] Were these students resisting the lessons, being imaginative, noting their own experiences, or just missing the point?

School leaders in the 1860s struggled over these same questions. A close look at one progressive school department, that of Boston. Massachusetts, and its superintendent for nearly twenty years, John Dudley Philbrick, suggests how one community engaged with the practice over time. In 1862, Philbrick reported that some teachers were attempting object teaching on their own by reading books in the library on the topic.[71] The following year the lessons were first incorporated into the prescribed primary school curriculum. While Philbrick acknowledged that "object teaching has always been practiced more or less by our best teachers," teachers were now to include a "systematic and progressive mode of developing the observing faculties by means of lessons on objects."[72] In 1865, Philbrick encouraged teachers to visit the Training Department of the Girls High and Normal School (actually led by Miss Jennie Stickney, who studied at Oswego) to watch model lessons. Philbrick adopted the belief of the HCS and Sheldon that the pedagogy must be experienced. He explained, "No mere printed page can convey an adequate conception of an Object Teaching School. The school itself must be visited."[73]

After these early years of eager adoption, Philbrick developed two specific concerns about the practice. First, he feared that object lessons often became too formal and were a new kind of rote learning. He wanted teachers to appreciate the goal of the object teaching idea: "to excite curiosity of a desire of knowledge." That is "not a curiosity to know what is said, but a curiosity to know what is true . . . with a view to moral improvement and the promotion of the happiness of society." He knew the pedagogy was about learning to think, even if it was not always presented in that way. Philbrick's second concern was that teachers were not actually incorporating short oral object lessons—lessons on size, form, and color, objects in the schoolroom, plants and animals, trades and occupations, and so on—into their daily schedules because visiting committees were not paying attention to these lessons. He noted, "Hence the mode of examination adopted by the Committees has a powerful influence in determining the kind of instruction imparted." He called for those examining to "bestow the highest commendation for that kind of service which really does the most good to the pupils, and not that which merely makes the best show in a recitation." Philbrick seemed to earnestly believe in the power of this method. As he explained the goal, "When our children have been taught according to the true spirit of this system (object lessons), both morally and intellectually, they will be found on their holidays crowding the galleries of our noble Museum of Natural History, instead of crowding as they are now too much inclined to do, the halls and galleries of negro mistrals." This challenge of inadequate assessment continued into the 1870s, when Philbrick again and again called on visiting committees to focus on the practice.[74]

In 1877—fifteen years after they were first introduced—object lessons and oral lessons were still part of the curriculum but were used more sparingly than they had been previously. Object lessons appeared as part of science instruction for older students in grammar school and for writing exercises for younger students. Philbrick went on a whirlwind tour of schools throughout the Midwest to study their methods. He cited examples from other midwestern schools that completely used object lessons as the focus on their curriculum and forbade teachers from giving these lessons without appropriate physical objects present in the classroom, rules created because teachers were actually "cramming" students for examinations on object teaching. He finally came to a startling conclusion that changed the way object lessons were used in his schools. Because object lessons are "an application of the intuitive method" they may be applied to all areas of study. They do not require a special section in the curriculum. In Boston after early eager adoption, the method fundamentally changed the way teachers interacted with their students and moved away from rote learning to a more intuitive approach. Object lessons had changed classroom teaching so thoroughly that they were no longer needed. This is one case in one progressive school system. School department records document object lessons in schools throughout the United States through the end of the century, well after their heyday in the 1860s and 1870s. This case study suggests that the ambition of object-lesson pedagogy was limited by practical concerns like assessment, even while these lessons were taught in thousands of classrooms.[75]

It may be impossible to assess children's learning through time. However, close examination of one type of common lesson demonstrates both the variation and core goals of object lessons, as advocated by reformers and educational entrepreneurs, represented in the media and understood by classroom teachers. Lessons on forms—like spheres, cubes, and pyramids—were often the first object lessons given to young children.[76] Pestalozzi and his assistants had advocated these lessons from the beginning and nearly every teacher or school board that suggested a course of object lessons included this type. Photographs from the end of the century document these forms in classrooms across the country, in children's hands, on teachers' desks, or sitting on a windowsill. In the 1860s and 1870s, teachers believed these blocks of wood could be used to develop children's abilities to perceive and to think. At a basic level, school reports and class schedules show how these lessons were supposed to be integrated into the curriculum for young children—in short blocks of time from ten to twenty minutes. These short lessons were intended to keep the students' attention and develop skills of observation through repetition.[77] Each of these short blocks of time may be linked to specific lessons suggested in teacher training manuals, like N. A. Calkins's *Primary Object Lessons*, which rivaled Sheldon's in popularity. First published in 1861, it went through at least forty editions. According to the manual, a teacher is to show students forms of wood carved into spheres, cones, and cubes and allow students to handle them. The students are supposed to sketch them on slates and gradually learn to categorize the objects.

Illustrations of lessons on form offer more details. "Colored School—Object Teaching," published in *Harper's Weekly* in February 1870, shows a teacher with a class of nineteen African American students. The ages of these students are not given, but they appear older than the six- to eight-year-old children to whom these lessons were often directed. The wooden forms may not have been handed around the room as directed in prescriptive materials, but they are the center of this lesson. The teacher is asking the students, arranged so that all may see her desk in a modified gallery, to call out the names of the forms she is showing the class—she holds up a sphere in her left hand. The sphere, her body, and the globe on the floor, captured within her shadow, create a triangle that seems to link the globe to the sphere in her hand. This visual rhetoric supports the suggestion in pedagogical sources that teachers should make connections between forms and classroom objects, developing categories like "sphere."[78]

Surviving objects suggest how these might have been used. J. W. Schermerhorn of New York City marketed a set of forms and solids in 1870 quite similar to the teacher's models in the picture.[79] These small, smooth wooden forms had been around for decades by 1870 and had been developed before object lessons took off in the United States (Plate 3).[80] The forms are proportional to each other, allowing for the study of geometry. As a user handles them, one is drawn to compare their shapes and sizes: cones, conoids, and spheres, cubes, and pyramids. Each form is numbered and keyed to a chart that lists its proper name. This potential lesson could have led to the study of geometry, appreciation of symmetry and beauty, or offered students' new vocabulary and an understanding of how to see these shapes in daily life.

But how might these lessons have unfolded? The notebooks of pupil-teachers suggest how lessons were actually translated from textbooks into actionable plans for pupil-teachers in normal schools and high schools. Fanny Rothkopf's notebooks record lessons on forms likely dating to 1879 when she was fifteen and a third-year student at the New York City Normal School, later Hunter College (Plate 4). In the notebook for her methods course, Rothkopf includes her synthesis of Calkins's *Primary Object Lessons* as well as her teacher's gloss on the subject and her own questions about how to apply these lessons in the classroom. She re-creates the lessons as they are supposed to be given to students, finding ways to represent the shapes and coming up with possible objects that might be similar in form to the lessons described. In her notes, a sphere became a barbell, a soap bubble, a pill, a currant, or a plum. A parallelogram became a rubber eraser,

COLORED SCHOOL—OBJECT TEACHING.

Figure 2.4. "Colored School—Object Teaching" in "Our Common Schools," *Harper's Weekly* 14, no. 687 (February 26, 1870): 141. In New York City, object lessons were used in segregated schools even for slightly older children, as this image of "Colored School—Object Teaching" suggests.

a candy, and a cake. Her notebook reveals an approach likely modified from Calkins to teach some of the concepts aimed at in the lessons. Her illustrations document the use of a folding penknife to teach different kinds of angles that are important to the study of geometry. She describes these angles as square, blunt, and sharp in simple descriptive words—rather than as right, obtuse, and acute. The common penknife might have been used in other lessons to teach students about the natural and industrial history of metals or ivory. Rothkopf's critic's report for her work in the model school suggests that she did fairly well in her application of these methods. She earned a grade of 8/10 that semester.[81]

State teachers' examinations tested the variety of object lessons teachers would be able to offer as a way to separate the "pretenders" from the serious students like Rothkopf. The questions often linked object lessons to lessons in thinking and moral reasoning, aligning the study of an object with the study of a moral precept. For example, a California exam from 1863 included the following questions, "19. Write an outline of questions in a primary object lesson, on 'Glass.' 20. Outline of a brief moral lesson, on 'Lying.'"[82] In this case the study of a substance, such as glass, appears analogous to a category of behavior, lying. Both concepts, glass and lying, could be developed through observation and discussion of their qualities as unfolded through study of concrete examples. The 1871–1872 test followed similar lines: "6. What means would you employ in promoting justice and truthfulness in your pupils?... 8. What is the design of object lessons? How would you conduct an object lesson upon quicksilver?"[83] Both truthfulness and quicksilver, these questions suggest, have inherent meanings that may be expressed through careful questioning. The lessons in these cases were not simply lessons on objects, but as Pestalozzi, the Mayos, and Sheldon intended, explicitly linked to the development of moral reasoning and judgment.

Composing Narratives and Making History

Early historical works on Oswego graduates celebrate a pantheon of the school's teachers. These innovators moved from Oswego to nearly every state in the United States and several other nations, bringing with them variations of Sheldon's pedagogy.[84] The efforts of two of these educators—Mary Alling-Aber and Sheldon's daughter Mary Sheldon Barnes—suggest how object-lesson pedagogy shaped the production and the interpretation of texts. Both women extended the object lesson idea to create reading lessons and historical analysis that reflected the thinking skills developed through the systematic training of the senses. Their examples—developed for young children and college-age students—highlight the flexibility of the object lesson to structure intellectual work at a range of levels.

Mary Alling-Aber, who graduated from the Oswego Normal School in 1869, adapted a specific form of object-based composition for the children in her classroom.[85] Pauline Agassiz Shaw, daughter of Louis Agassiz, funded a primary school at 6 Marlborough Street for the children of Boston's elite. In the early 1880s, Alling-Aber began what came to be considered an experiment in education in Shaw's school.[86] Alling-Aber appreciated the goals of object lessons but feared that the object-lesson training she received at Oswego dictated classroom practice that was too formal and did not emphasize the natural acquisition of knowledge along with the development of observational skills. She critiqued Sheldon's object lessons on "thimbles, scissors, chairs" as a "farce" that did not take advantage of children's actual experiences, curiosity, or knowledge. She described a little boy who told her that "kindergarten was a place where people pretended to do stuff, instead of actually doing it."[87] She wanted to give children the chance to do things.

In the early 1880s, she developed a curriculum organized around real-world observations and called it an "Experiment in Education." The idea of the school was that students would learn literature, natural history, and history along with the normal primary school skills of reading and figuring. During class she wrote student descriptions of objects on the blackboard, taking down the exact words of the children and creating a text for the class. She had these responses printed and distributed to her students. The printed compositions became the children's first reading lessons. The student compositions were privately printed in two volumes that document the content of Alling-Aber's classroom exercises. Future Harvard historian Samuel Eliot Morrison was a pupil in the Marlborough Street School in the 1890s, which he remembered as a "really progressive school for those days." He noted that the teachers there "dramatized the most ordinary subjects for us."[88] Ordinary subjects, from Indian corn and magnets to sheepskin and geometry, were the basis of Aber-Alling's frequent lessons.

The lessons that Alling-Aber published as part of her book *The Children's Own Work* (1883) range from the simple answers to questions like "What do children do?" (answer: grow) to more complex discussions of class trips to historic sites, the properties of soil, and the functions of various plants and minerals.[89] A composition lesson on wool begins with a description of an actual piece of sheepskin, with the wool attached. The child narrating the composition, probably a boy in this case, is obviously handling this object. He moves from talking about the object to discussing how wool was made into thread via a wool-wheel and later into cloth on a weaving loom "in old times." A recollection and description of a picture showing a man washing a sheep in a river before shearing adds another kind of context to the piece of sheepskin. The child then described different colors of wool flannel he had handled, noting the threads in the samples as well as those in his own suit. Next, the child attempted to weave worsted wool with the help of classmates, a process that illustrated the relationship between the warp and weft. After recalling a time when sheepskins were used for clothing, the child explained how felt predated woven cloth and some of its qualities ("The wool is thick, soft, and oily. Each fiber of wool is made of little scales that overlap each other."). Finally the physical qualities of the sheep, along with its diet, digestive system, cloven feet, and horns, link the animal to other animals in its family.

This two and a half page "composition," narrated by a child and written by the teacher on the board prior to printing, addresses most of wool's natural, material, and social history. The child revealed an understanding of where wool came from, how it became cloth, the other uses it has been put to over time as well as the natural history of the sheep that produced the wool. Certainly this information was not drawn solely from observation of the sheepskin, the pictures, the pieces of flannel, or the colored worsted. Rather, these items became opportunities to talk about and in some ways hold this information. The composition, considered in light of the student's expanded knowledge of and experience with the topic, suggested how a child might craft a complex story around an object.[90]

Other examples reflect a more direct interest in the material qualities of the items considered and what they may instruct via comparison or analogy. For example, a student described as under the age of ten noted the relationship between different forms in "The Cube and the Pyramid":

> I have a cube. I have a pyramid. The cube has six plain, square faces. The cube has twelve straight edges. The cube has eight corners. Some of these crystals of rock salt are perfect cubes. This pyramid has five plain faces. This pyramid has eight plain faces. This pyramid has five corners. The face on which the pyramid stands is the base of the pyramid. The corner of the pyramid, which is opposite the base, is the apex of the pyramid. These crystals of quartz have pyramids at one end. They are six-sided.[91]

This short description revealed an understanding of two shapes and found analogies between these shapes and natural forms students observed in their classes. Furthermore, the observation led to lessons in counting and basic geometry. The technical terms children employed in this lesson like "apex" or "pyramid," Alling-Aber explained, were tools they were eager to use once acquired. In other cases a child traced a visual analogy between the shape of a strawberry and the dome of the Massachusetts statehouse; another thought apple blossoms looked like balls of popcorn. The goal was to teach children to create knowledge both from and through their observations, teaching them to observe and to think through their perceptions of the material world.

In these examples, what children actually perceived combined with, augmented, or correlated with what children believed. The lessons could never be based solely on physical perceptions of material things. Rather, these lessons served to teach patterns of thinking with and through objects. In describing the effects of her experiment on her students, Alling-Aber mentioned their strengthened perceptive abilities but also noted that her students learned to ask questions, discovered "that opinion without knowledge is folly," were better at remembering things, and were more patient when it came to developing new ideas.[92] Ella Flagg Young, teacher, school administrator, and professor of education in Chicago, wrote that Alling-Aber's goals put her more in line with her teachers at Oswego and with their methods than Alling-Aber herself might have admitted. Young pointed out in her 1903 study of Alling-Aber that the teacher's claim that at Oswego she had learned "to watch the pupil's mind more than the subject being taught" was key to understanding her pedagogy and the intellectual debt she owed to her own teachers.[93]

Sheldon's daughter, Mary Sheldon Barnes, took her training at Oswego in a different direction. She became a historian and produced several books of historical documents designed to teach students and teachers how to "make history," as she put it, and to understand and respond to current events. Her object-lesson approach to historical sources became a way to train students for citizenship.[94] In 1871, she left Oswego for the University of Michigan, where she entered the sophomore class as part of the second group of women admitted to the university.

Sheldon Barnes frequently wrote home about the impact her Oswego training had on her learning at Michigan. She was thrilled to note that a professor, who had actually voted against admitting women to the university, had praised her preparation and told her "that I had more 'method than matter' which I consider as the highest compliment of all."[95] He referred to her ability to critically approach the process of learning as opposed to simply remembering facts. For Sheldon Barnes, memorization was "barbarism." This emphasis on method, on thinking, was the goal of her father's object-lesson curriculum, which separated the ways of approaching an object—method—from the object itself—matter. Sheldon Barnes lamented the effect memorization had on her as a student, writing to her parents, "All this drill is good for me, I suppose, but I feel almost as though I were losing the power to think the way I used to." She continued, "I am more and more in love with Pestalozzianism every day of my life and would be so glad could it only touch the highest departments of education. Of course it will eventually, but as Miss. Perry remarks in regard to dying, it's long to wait." Poking fun at her melodramatic college roommate, Sheldon Barnes wondered if these methods of teaching would ever spread to the college and university classroom.[96] Her Michigan teachers told her to study books, just as artists should study fine art, to find perfection. But, trained in the Oswego method, Sheldon Barnes believed, "We must improve by comparison of our own efforts with perfection." Her historical source method for the study of history was one way to approach this problem.[97]

After graduating from Michigan, Sheldon Barnes returned to Oswego, where she taught a range of subjects before accepting a job teaching history at Wellesley College in 1876. There, she assembled packets of primary source documents for use in her seminars. Instead of offering college students narratives for passive consumption, as her teachers at Michigan had advocated, she gathered and edited collections of primary documents to help students think through historical problems. A few years after leaving Wellesley she began to publish these documents in a series of books, *Studies in General History* (first published in 1885), *Studies in Greek and Roman History* (1886), and *Studies in American History* (1893).[98] She included personal narratives, letters, laws, and maps as well as images of artifacts, such as wooden-soled shoes worn by a Confederate soldier and representations of places, such as a sketch of a mining camp in Denver.

The idea was that students would come to their own conclusions through the documents about the people and events represented. In the preface to *Studies in American History* Sheldon Barnes explained, "In using the sources the pupil must do his own feeling and thinking; no one tells him that Drake was a pirate or that the last days of Columbus were pathetic and bitter with ingratitude; he has the chance to see these things for himself, his opinions are formed his sympathies aroused by the nearest possible contact with the man and the deed." Like an object lesson that mandated the experience of a material thing, like glass or silk to understand its qualities, the idea was that document study led students to a deeper appreciation of history through their own experience of it. Students might read a Walt Whitman poem, a personal account of a slave trader, and a plea from a Native American to simply be left alone on his land. She instructed students to make timelines, to fill in blank maps, and to study pictures. For example, she included a view of a Native American boy wrapped in a blanket upon his arrival at the Hampton Institute intended to be compared with a picture of the same student upon graduation wearing a cadet uniform.[99] Through a series of questions, students were to think through the historical problems addressed in the sources and be guided to possible answers. For example, regarding the Indian Question, Sheldon Barnes asked, "Give two proofs that Indians can be civilized. What do the Indian children learn in the Hampton School? Why is it necessary to teach them these things? What good does it do to teach them these things?" These leading questions allow for only a few possible responses. As one Massachusetts teacher who worked with Sheldon Barnes's books noted, "The questions produce freedom in *thinking* and at the same time direct and keep the thought in right channels."[100] Her carefully edited sources suggested the expansiveness of historical study but limited her students' responses to those she considered correct.[101]

Just as Sheldon and Mayo suggested that object lessons could teach a student to reason morally, Sheldon Barnes believed that the process of studying historical documents could teach a student to make judgments as a citizen. She wrote in the preface to *Studies in American History,*

What is more to our purpose, it is only by dealing with the sources of past history that our pupils can be rightly trained to deal with the historic sources of his own time and to form independent and unprejudiced judgments concerning the mass of opinions, actions, institutions, and social products of all sorts in which he finds himself involved. In other words, whatever else our young people will become, citizens they must be and the citizen must constantly form judgments of the historical sort, which can only be based upon contemporary sources. To enable him to do this should perhaps be the primary aim of the study of history.[102]

Sheldon Barnes makes it clear that students will face a world filled with sources of information, not unlike the many different objects that concerned her father, and that students would need to make sense of them on their own. In *Studies in General History* she put an even finer point on this issue claiming, "In short, we Americans are all making history, an American history of a sort that no man has ever made before us and which lies entirely in our own hands to shape according to our best judgment of all that goes on about us from year to year."[103] For Sheldon Barnes the study of historical documents was the best way to develop this judgment. She challenged her students to try to answer the "questions of today," which she defined in her *Studies in American History* as about race, suffrage, economic disparity, the tariff, and political reform, by reading the newspaper and seeking documents that could offer different perspectives on these matters. Her books of historical documents would have offered practice in deriving ideas from a range of sources. Just as the study of objects could lead to the development of abstract thought, these documents could help students make personal and political decisions based on sound evidence and reasoning.

The Moral of the Story

E. A. Sheldon believed that there was a direct link between sensation and volition—understood as the power of willing—a theory that drew on his understanding of the HCS's teachings, particularly the writing of Elizabeth Mayo. Mayo's initial goals in creating object lessons were linked to a broader religious mission that would help children understand God's work through the material world. In her book on shells, she explicitly noted that empirical study could quickly devolve into atheism if children did not recognize the work of God's hand in all of their lessons.[104] In this basic way, their object lessons were moral lessons because they encouraged children to marvel at God's work. A school essay written in the Oswego Normal School in the 1860s, likely by the young Mary Sheldon Barnes, expresses this sentiment. After describing the role of senses in the appreciation of nature's teachings, she goes on to argue that "the Bible and nature go hand in hand," explaining how the observation of nature "begets a faith in truth, humanity and God."[105]

However, this was not the only moral lesson to be gathered from study through observation. Elizabeth Mayo stridently claimed in the introduction to her *Lessons on Objects*, "As the sphere of observation is enlarged, and the pages

of history, or the fields of science, are explored, the minds accustomed to accurate investigation, will not rest content with less than satisfactory evidence,
either in morals or science."[106] As children were learning to appreciate God's
work, the development of their reasoning powers would also heighten their
abilities to make moral decisions. For the Mayos, as for Sheldon, the process
of learning to look at objects was central to the development of one's ability to
reason. Carefully arranged encounters with specific objects were the key that
would open the door to this possibility. In this object-centered morality, material things understood and experienced within this ordered system acted on
students through their senses and were intended to shape them into moral, reasoning beings.

The connection between morality and perception is a key theme in nineteenth-century American culture. Hypocrisy was a threat to nineteenth-cen-
tury-American society. As Americans faced a reality shaped by increasing
social and geographic mobility, everyday encounters with new individuals
could lead to worries about hypocrisy and sincerity and a desire to be able to
judge the actions and identities of the people around them. These same perceptive abilities, whether the "suspicious eyes" required for consumers of spirit
photographs in the 1860s or the nagging anxieties engendered by famed huck-
ster P. T. Barnum's claim that all business transactions are a humbug or a deception, were necessary in navigating this world. On a daily basis, individuals had
to be able to judge for themselves whom they were meeting, whether a product
was authentic, or if they were making a risky decision.[107] Educator Warren
Burton explained in 1865 that only by learning to observe and compare could
children develop the ability to deal with "King Sham," who dominated all dry
goods stores, groceries, and other shops. Training in observation was a bulwark
against fraud.[108] Writing to Burton in 1863, Birdsey G. Northop, an agent of the
Boston Schools, lamented, "So far as relates to intellectual training, I heartily
concur in the sentiment of Ruskin, 'The more I think of it, I find this conclusion more impressed upon me, that the greatest thing a human soul ever does
in this world is to see something, and tell what it saw in a plain way. Hundreds
of people can talk, to one who thinks; but thousands can think, to one who can
see.' "[109] In this environment, discernment and decision-making had to be an
individual responsibility.

Furthermore, in the unstable world of the 1860s, with established forms of
reasoning shaken by the carnage and true horror of the Civil War, object lessons
offered an appealing possibility for moral education. This moral system did not
rely solely on precedents, laws, or faith.[110] Moral lessons had been an important
part of antebellum American education. Often told through illustrative tales,
these stories could be completely textual, like biblical or classical fables, or they
could be visual, with a picture standing in for the narrative. Instead, with object

lessons children were taught "not [to] rest content with less than satisfactory evidence" but to examine and consider all sides of a problem for themselves through individual sensory investigation. The hope was that children would understand why an action was moral or immoral through reason and evidence, just as they understood through observation that glass was transparent. Within the prescribed program of study, practitioners believed that children could develop the ability to think through their interactions with material things. Pictures had even broader instructional possibilities.

3

Picture Lessons

In January 1876, *Schermerhorn's Monthly* published an engraving by the illustrator Frank Beard to accompany a two-part article called "The Object Lesson."[1] Each detail of Beard's picture exemplifies the pedagogical trend. The picture makes it clear that a successful object lesson consisted of more than a single object. The classroom portrayed in the engraving is located inside a large school building; it is lit through big windows along the one exterior wall and contains orderly desks in orderly rows. Each desk seats a pair of boys or girls. There are no books in this classroom and only a single blank slate is visible on the desk of one boy. The walls are tiled with large charts, pictures, and maps. Four frames of mathematical shapes echo the double-hung windows; lithographs of various lizards and reptiles, easily exchanged for other pictures, are spread over the front wall of the classroom; a huge wall map of the world, a representation of the planets' orbits, a smaller map of the state of Florida, and a picture of two men poking an animal with long spears fill in the available wall space. An unused blackboard is tucked into the far corner. At the front of the room, on a raised platform, a well-dressed man and woman sit behind the teacher's desk silently observing. To their left, a boy gestures toward the map of Florida with a pointer. To their right, a small table supports what appear to be several varieties of turtle. A teacher stands in profile facing her students. All eyes are on her and the writhing turtle she dangles in front of her by the back of its tail. The minute hand on the clock ticks towards 9:45, the moment the fictional Miss Lee's object lesson is set to begin.[2]

According to the two-installment story that accompanied the illustration, Miss Lee's students had been waiting all weekend for their promised Monday morning object lesson on turtles and had been instructed to learn whatever they could about these fascinating animals. Located somewhere north of New York City, in a town that had plenty of fishing holes and backyard gardens, the fictional classroom was filled with a range of children, all able to contribute some personal experience with turtles to the classroom discussion. Every child in this fictional classroom benefited from object lessons particularly the troublesome children like "Idle Dick," and "Careless Mary." Idle Dick,

Figure 3.1. "The Object Lesson," *Schermerhorn's Monthly* (January 1876), frontispiece. This fictional teacher offered her students an object lesson that traced connections between the turtle in her hand and the pictures, maps, and specimens arrayed in her classroom.

a boy something like Huck Finn, would rather fish than attend school, but he had a great deal to share with his classmates about turtles. He recalled the time a snapping turtle clasped onto his dog Bowser's lip and clung there even after it was decapitated. He theorized that a box turtle had a shell just like the pattern on his mother's old hair comb that he had found in the attic. Careless Mary, known for her messy clothes and shiftless manner, revealed that she cared deeply about her flowers and described the geometric turtle she had seen eating her beloved begonias. Other children, like the son of the richest banker in town, had dined on green turtle soup in Delmonico's restaurant on a trip to New York City. A girl recently relocated from Georgia described how her father's coachman "Uncle Jim" had pointed out a large snapping turtle, which he called an "alligator cooter," and taught her about eating turtle eggs. Each child could bring to the conversation a small piece of information from his or her own experience tasting, seeing, or touching turtles. Miss Lee's job was to organize and develop those experiences into knowledge through the study of pictures, specimens, and maps.

Miss Lee was an ideal object teacher: she asked questions, led her students to observe closely and to differentiate and organize their observations. She linked what they knew to what they did not know and incorporated geometry, geography, and even commodity histories into their lesson. First she moved the students through an array of categories of turtles and tortoises, describing their habits and habitats and the different patterns found on the carapace and plastron. Next, she taught them how turtles were used: for food, in the production of goods for sale, and for their eggs. Children were shown the handles of some penknives, eyeglass frames, and jewelry that had been produced from turtles. They learned that turtle eggs contained "turtle butter" used for lamps, cooking, and oiling machines. The students discovered (to their horror) that in some places hot coals were used to loosen and then pry the turtle from his shell while it was still alive, a process Miss Lee explained was analogous to scalping. The children expressed sincere sympathy for these unfortunate animals and would therefore think twice before purchasing a shell-handled knife.

In other places, sailors harvested turtles for their meat and shells, turning huge animals onto their backs dragging them to their ships, likely the scene illustrated in the corner of the classroom. Finally, the different kinds of turtles offered an opening into the study of faraway places and different cultures. Miss Lee was quick to correct Idle Dick when he referred to the "rascally niggers" who removed turtles' shells to make things like his mother's comb. She explained that they were "closer to Malays than to negroes," correcting his coarse language as well as the meaning behind it. She challenged students to find the locations she discussed on the wall maps like the Tortugas or the Galapagos Islands, suggesting she had taught them about those places before. As the lesson closed Miss Lee reviewed what they had learned through questions and conversation. Unlike lessons organized around reading and memorizing, the children were forced to make connections between disparate topics and to remember and re-contextualize past experiences, performing the critical thinking often praised by twenty-first-century educators.

Object lessons like these emphasized the link between learning how to observe and learning how to think. As the author of this detailed two-installment lesson explained, "The great use of object teaching, properly understood, is to teach a child to observe and think, and the observation and thinking cannot be accomplished, till there are objects presented to the mind for it to observe and think about." Real three-dimensional objects—like the dangling snapping turtle that eventually bit a hole in poor Miss Lee's dress sleeve—could be presented as a start. Just as important, children needed to learn in an environment that supported their intellectual development, moving outward from the object to other contextual, visual materials. As the author explains, "The whole arrangement of the tables, desks, and maps, blackboards, drawings, and charts on the walls show that this is a school where minds are developed and thoughts elicited."[3] In addition to the central material things, in this case a snapping turtle and a range of casts, pictures completed the pedagogical environment and presented information one could not discern solely through the examination of a material thing.

Miss Lee's classroom is an idealization of the environment for which publishers and educators designed their teaching materials. Schermerhorn and Co., a New York City retailer of object teaching aids, published the magazine, which helped readers imagine how its products could be used. The detailed classroom illustration itself provided a clear lesson in how a classroom should look and how a teacher should address a complex topic. In this classroom, children were learning to look at pictures and maps as part of their object lessons and to organize the information found in those pictures as part of their learning. For educators who could not travel to an educational convention or visit modern schools, close study of Beard's illustration provided them the opportunity to abstract pedagogical concepts from the detailed picture. Pictures worked in just the same way in primary school classrooms.

Picture lessons, a variety of object lesson that gained popularity throughout the latter decades of the nineteenth century, were conveyed through the study of pictures as opposed to just the study of material things. The images did not simply stand in for objects but, like language, were another way to abstract and organize information about the material world. The prints under consideration were supposed to be treated as the material, concrete subject of an object lesson–based curriculum, a system that examined things for their qualities, sorted information into categories, and developed conceptions based on these perceptions. As with the study of a three-dimensional material thing, these picture lessons structured the ways children were taught to view pictures. Reinserting the pedagogical lithographs into the lesson plans created for them defines a viewing culture developed through object-lesson pedagogy. In it, children are taught to see lithographs both as material things and as tools for discerning elusive qualities or aspects of daily life, whether related to moral behavior, the natural world, or labor. This viewing method promoted an active engagement with visual sources as it produced pictures that directly linked to the world beyond what they depicted. When studying images, children were supposed to learn to sympathize, or perhaps even empathize, with the people and animals illustrated, gaining access not simply to what their senses might register but to a deeper conception of what was represented.[4] Object lessons centered on the study of pictures taught children how to organize and understand these observations. Inevitably, these lessons shaped the ways adults and children viewed pictures beyond the classroom and imbued images with new potential meanings.

Object Lessons and Visual Teaching Aids

By the time object-lesson methodology had spread through the United States in the 1860s, teachers had been using pictures for diverse pedagogical purposes for centuries. Locke advocated that children be exposed to images and objects because children learn through their senses and by responding to experience. By the late eighteenth century, primers and other forms of visual learning were a common part of the education of young children, ranging from emblem books to sets of Mrs. Trimmer's *Scripture and History Prints* for the walls of elite nurseries.[5] By the early nineteenth century, pictures were often used as illustrations for stories or as mnemonic devices to help children remember specific words, letters, or concepts.[6] Charts depicting letters and related pictures were in popular use in the antebellum American classroom. Most common schools in this period pursued a basic curriculum of reading, writing, mathematics, some grammar, perhaps geography, and most important, moral and religious training.[7] Visual teaching aids were adapted to all of these ends but not necessarily to provide the training in perception, comparison, and description that would be found in object lessons.

Similar to the New England primer in form and goals, early nineteenth-century American illustrated lesson cards like those produced by Munroe and Francis in Boston in the 1830s were frequently used in the classroom. These large cards linked pictures with letters of the alphabet, sometimes adding descriptive texts and reading lessons. Instructions for teachers, counting lessons, or moral directives like "Love God" were often printed on the reverse.[8] These pictures were not necessarily intended to convey information but instead served as illustration for the text or simply as a way to remember the name and sounds of the displayed letter: a picture of a wolf for the letter "W." Another example of these letter and picture cards included a classroom chart of a buffalo taken from a sketch by Titian Ramsey Peale from the 1830s. It simply stood in for the story of the buffalo on the printed chart.[9] In her 1838 school journal, which recounted her time as a student at the Greene Street School in Providence, Rhode Island, Hannah (Anna) Gale suggested how such pictures might have been used. She described a spelling lesson illustrated with a picture:

> One of the words which were given us today was "canibal [*sic*]." After giving us the definition, he [Mr. Fuller] told us he had the picture of a canibal by [?], that was found wild in the woods. He had a most beautiful face, very bright and expressive, but his form was very bad, his limbs being very long the gentleman to whom he belonged for a time was very sorry to part with him, he could not bear to think that this beautiful boy would return to [his] tribe and become a maneater.[10]

The picture was simply an illustration of a short narrative, the goal of which was to spell and define the word cannibal and suggest a moral lesson. Instead of training the eye, the picture helped Anna Gale learn her spelling lesson. The story was not designed to help her draw connections or observe patterns. She was moved to sympathize with the lovely young man, even though she misspelled the word.

German "concept picture" lessons offered similar visual lessons. Pestalozzi's term *Anschauungsunterricht* was understood by the Mayos and American adopters of Pestalozzi's theories to be "sense perception exercises." In Pestalozzi's Swiss schoolrooms pictures of ladders and windows were replaced with study of the actual objects—but the pictures remained.[11] In nineteenth-century German-language lessons this term also referred to sheets of pictures of everyday objects meant to illustrate concepts. This practice dates back to illustrated collections of every item or idea a child might encounter from Johann Amos Comenicus's seventeenth-century *Orbis Sensualism Pictus Quadrilingus* and Johann Siegmund Stoy's eighteenth-century *Bilder-Akademie für die Jugend*. These nineteenth-century wall charts or large-format books were intended to help children learn to name items included on the charts in a range of categories re-lated to different themes.[12] *Bilder zum ersten Anschauungs-Unterricht* included illustrations of classroom items. It shows a set of large-format concept picture cards displayed on a stand to be shown to schoolchildren, suggesting how the book may have been used. Starting with familiar objects from the schoolroom, the book goes on to present domestic scenes, weapons, animals, and industrial tools, moving from the familiar to the less familiar. The same images appear in different variations in other books characterized as part of this genre, often with text in both German and French naming the object or picture (Plates 5 and 6).[13]

English and French books based on this model also provide short essays and exercises to help parents and children look at pictures together. In some cases these texts are similar to the lessons intended in an object-lesson curriculum, in that they are supposed to help children learn to look at images. One pair of texts translated into both English and French from German, called in English *The Picture-Book of Elementary Ideas* (1865), offered specific lessons that helped chil-dren count items depicted and discuss the scenes presented in pictures, making observations and identifying the items shown.[14]

These picture sheets and books were not object lessons, though they came from a similar impulse: to help children understand the relationship between an external material world and words used to identify those concepts. In many cases, collections of picture cards or larger bound books of prints included images that depicted the ways pictures were to be used. An early example is William Darton's *The Rational Exhibition* (ca. 1800), which presented stories il-lustrated with detailed prints, grouped as a collage on the cover with a teacher pointing out details to a group of boys and girls.[15] The *Picture-Book of Elementary Ideas* presented an image of a mother or female teacher examining the pictures with small children, pointing out various elements. Pedagogical illustrations that depict the use of the pictures highlight the artifice and function of these teaching aids. Like the classroom object lesson from Oswego that challenged children to describe the difference between a leaf and the picture of a leaf, the images suggest engagement and observation as opposed to a simple representation of reality. Hybrid lessons that include both physical objects and two-dimensional pictures further emphasized the material qualities of images.

Object Pictures

A buttery baked good, an Encore Biscuit, could also offer a classroom object lesson. Instead of including a picture of the item, the actual cookie became a teaching aid. Arranged as part of the first lesson in "Oliver and Boyd's Object-Lesson Cards on the Vegetable Kingdom," the cookie helped instruct children in the mysterious process through which stalks of wheat stitched onto the center of the card could become a tasty treat. A length of tightly braided straw-plait, a coiled knot of macaroni, and a rectangular patch of paper served the same end (Plate 7). These things were all derived from and central to the meaning of wheat, which, along with the short composition printed below, the objects helped to define. In a schoolroom object lesson, such familiar items could lead to the study of human ingenuity, the complexity and curiosity of the natural world, or the wonder of God.[16]

"Wheat" is the first of twenty lesson cards on plants ranging from the oak tree to seaweed. Each of the lesson cards measures roughly fifty by thirty-three centimeters and includes actual specimens of "raw and manufactured materials" stitched onto cards along with a short essay detailing the chosen plant and its connections to the commodities displayed and sometimes a picture. A boll of cotton resides next to brightly colored calico; oak bark connects to squares of tanned and untanned leather; a cypress leaf is displayed beside a pencil. A paraffin candle, a lump of coal, and a hunk of jet flank a scene depicting a decaying, ancient forest, while a small terracotta pot and a clay pipe are sewn beneath images of Persian potters at work and a profile view of a vase. Rather than a cabinet of curiosities, this set of object-lesson cards includes extremely common items that were curious only in their connection to one another, their origin, or their qualities. By redefining actual cookies, straw, or macaroni as the subject of a classroom exercise, these pedagogical tools attempted to transform children's daily experiences into learning opportunities and narratives. The items themselves and not simply their representations had instructional value—even when the items were permanently affixed to cards and became analogous to images.

Ancient Forests of Coal Measures.

COAL.   SHALE.   JET.

Trades : Miners, Stokers, Coke Burners, Gas Manufacturers, Paraffin Manufacturers, Jet Carvers.   *Uses :* Fuel, Gas, Paraffin
Oil and Candles, Coal or Aniline Colours, Jet Ornaments.

Coal.   **Paraffin.**   **Aniline Colour.**   **Jet.**

Coal is one of the most important necessaries of everyday life. It is essential for warming buildings, cooking food, making GAS for lighting, and raising STEAM for propelling machinery for manufacturing and other purposes. It is needed for Locomotive Engines and Steam-Ships, for the conveyance of passengers, merchandise, and munitions of war.

Wood was the earliest form of fuel, and Coal is vegetable matter in a FOSSIL state. In remote ages the earth's surface was in many parts covered by dense forests of cone-bearing trees, gigantic ferns, club-mosses, and strange-looking plants, through which crawled huge reptiles, frogs, and other curious animals. Through GEOLOGICAL changes these great forests, having been covered up, lay buried for ages under other STRATA, and now constitute the COAL-FIELDS found in various quarters of the globe. There are several varieties of Coal, each having certain peculiarities. The Coal is got by MINING, often at a great depth, one PIT at Monkwearmouth, near Newcastle, being 1900 feet deep, and so extensive that the WORKINGS extend for two miles from the bottom of the SHAFT. The Miners are exposed to great and fatal dangers from fire-damp, choke-damp, and water.

GAS is produced by heating Coal—and for this purpose Cannel Coal is best—in air-tight vessels, called RETORTS. In the process of manufacture the Gas comes off as vapour, leaving the COKE, COAL-TAR, and AMMONIA-WATER behind. The Gas requires to be purified before passing into the GAS-HOLDER, and thence through the "Mains" and other pipes.

Coke, which is produced in the course of Gas-making, or by burning coal dross or CULM, in close furnaces or ovens, is largely used for smelting Metals, and for engine fires. From the Ammonia-water the useful chemical substances SAL-AMMONIAC, CARBONATE OF AMMONIA, and ALUM are prepared. From the nasty black Coal-Tar, with its disagreeable odour, CARBOLIC ACID, NAPHTHALINE, BENZOLE, and, more wonderful still, the brilliant ANILINE DYES, MAUVE, MAGENTA BLUE, etc., are all produced.

Paraffin, that beautiful semi-transparent substance rivalling the purest wax, is made by distilling BITUMINOUS SHALE in cast-iron retorts. It comes off as a thick black oil, and is afterwards refined. It is either used as Oil, or moulded into Candles.

Jet, of which so many beautiful ornaments are made, at WHITBY and elsewhere, is the FOSSIL GUM from the trees of long-buried forests, which is dug out of the earth and carved in various forms, for Brooches, Earrings, Bracelets, etc., etc.

OLIVER AND BOYD, TWEEDDALE COURT, EDINBURGH.
LONDON: SIMPKIN, MARSHALL, HAMILTON, KENT, AND CO., LIMITED.

Figure 3.2. "Coal, Shale, Jet," No. 11 from *Oliver and Boyd's Object-Lesson Cards on the Mineral Kingdom.* A hunk of coal, a candle made from paraffin, a brilliant purple created with aniline dye, and a piece of polished jet suggest the varied uses of coal, shale, and jet as featured on the Oliver and Boyd's Object-Lesson Card. *Cotsen Children's Library, Department of Rare Books and Special Collections, Princeton University Library, Princeton, NJ ([CTSN] Elephants 91569 no. 2).*

Oliver and Boyd of Edinburgh began publishing "Object-Lesson Cards on the Vegetable Kingdom" in the early 1860s. In the mid-1870s they developed the Animal and Mineral Kingdoms, completing the tripartite Aristotelian scheme with two additional sets of fourteen cards each. As with the cookie, substances derived from animals and minerals were affixed to these cards. Dried cochineal insects transformed into vivid reds, a tube of sand into glass, and an engraving of a calf into a patch of skin with hair and a dried, cracked square of gelatin were all affixed to the cards. Bancroft Bros. in San Francisco created an American version of the series in 1890. The selected animals, plants, and minerals remained fairly static over the years in which these cards were produced, as did the objects chosen to represent the topics, but the narratives that went along with the items changed considerably. That the same material objects and pictures could be considered for very different ends suggests the flexibility of this kind of object lesson. At the same time, the necessity of including both objects and pictures highlights the different qualities and information these forms could convey about the substances at the heart of each lesson.

On a basic level, object-lesson cards could form the foundation of classroom study designed to reintroduce children to the origins and meanings of the material things they encountered in their daily lives. Such a collection was well suited to classroom teaching. It fit neatly into a varnished wooden box; each numbered card could be easily displayed for the duration of the lesson. Organized in this way, objects and specimens were already grouped into sets around specific natural substances. Metal spoons, bone combs, many kinds of textiles in various states, dyes, food, even the type-metal that printed students' schoolbooks were assigned to naturally occurring or naturally derived categories of substances rather than understood as individual products or resources. Instead of focusing on the qualities of individual objects, these collections suggested that commodities and various states of commodities were qualities of naturally occurring substances. Each set of object-lesson cards functioned as a sort of "Industrial Museum," a concept that had been an important part of public education and display since the Crystal Palace Exhibition in London in 1851.[17] Industrial museums housed collections of industrial products, commodities, and natural materials employed in manufacturing and economic development.[18] In the classroom, smaller collections served similar purposes, forming the nucleus of and modeling a private classroom collection, which teachers and students were encouraged to augment with their own everyday discoveries. Quotidian items of foreign origin were viewed as particularly constructive, creating a material geography through the origins of the substances displayed.

Oliver and Boyd and Bancroft Bros. both packaged their object-lesson cards with specific instructions for their use in the classroom. As object lessons, both sets took up the study of the material aspects of wheat, tea, coffee, cotton, the whale, the honeybee, mercury, and other items, often through the same or similar objects, but they employed very different framing. Oliver and Boyd offered teachers the hope that the study of plants would "assist in awakening the minds of the young to a perception of the power, wisdom, and goodness of God" and give them "a desire to extend their acquaintance with the natural objects around them."[19] This explicitly evangelical goal sought to teach children about God's plan through the study of nature.[20] Linking commodities to different kinds of natural goods overtly included them as part of God's creation. In contrast, Bancroft Bros. offered a far more secular directive closely aligned with curricular standards in public schools. Casting the cards as useful for object teaching, language study, subjects for composition, geography lessons, and natural history surely helped sell these sets—"for every grade of scholars from the most primary to the most advanced."[21] Furthermore, they encouraged teachers and students to approach the objects with their own knowledge and experience.

The narratives printed on the individual lesson cards also reflect this distinction. The lesson on wheat published by Bancroft Bros. in 1890 appears materially similar to the Oliver and Boyd example. Though the items affixed to the Bancroft version have not survived, the items' ghosts and their labels document similar biscuit, plaited straw, macaroni, and paper specimens, with the addition of a tube of starch, still sewn in place. Their narratives are in stark contrast. Oliver and Boyd noted the many species of wheat, the common plant's amazing properties, and the "wonderful" way it reveals God's work. In addition, one species of the plant (darnel) is even identified by its biblical name (tares). Yet God has been erased entirely from the Bancroft lesson on wheat. Instead, specific varieties of flour, details of its production and uses, and the Egyptian history of its cultivation explain the six objects. Since the objects themselves were the center of the lesson, the absence of God in the Bancroft text did not stop the company from recommending and sending their quite secular cards to the Deseret Sunday School Union for the illustration of scripture lessons in 1897.[22]

The text printed on each card was simply one possible lesson on the subject displayed. The objects themselves held the most potential for meaning and could contain these printed narratives as well as the written compositions students might be instructed to create about them.[23] In one surviving collection of object-lesson cards, the teacher has cut the text away from the objects entirely. Perhaps saving the information for his or her private consumption and presentation, the dramatic cropping forced students to look, touch, or smell (in the case of cedar or cocoa) the lesson, relying solely on their senses. There is no established narrative, simply a group of related objects. This modified set suggests that the ways in which these cards may have been used does not necessarily align with the goals of their creators—indeed, this teacher had cut away Oliver and Boyd's religious message. Unlike a text, which may be read and copied again and again, object lessons challenged teachers and students to draw their own connections among objects. One person's individual experience necessarily varied from another's. Even when mediated by text or detailed lesson plans, the objects themselves offered some of the instruction.

The potential of a material thing to convey information was at the heart of object-lesson pedagogy. Sometimes, however, an object alone was not enough. As with Miss Lee's turtle lesson, maps and illustrations could provide necessary information that complemented and shaped the ways children viewed an object. In some cases, illustrations addressed a problem of scale or provided crucial narrative details about a given substance such as its mode of manufacture, point of origin, function, or history. In these cases, each image addressed a specific aspect of an item's meaning. For example, an image of a beached whale, with living cetaceans spouting in the background, is the only way to visually represent the entire whale and to explain the connection between the animal and the spermaceti and sliver of whalebone on the card. In the case of the oak tree, it was not possible to represent the annual growth rings, a fascinating aspect of the tree's natural history, through a material item; a small engraving was necessary. But no image could adequately explain the difference between tanned and untanned leather. Only samples could show how tannin derived from oak could transform the substance. The objects and images offered access to different qualities of each item.

Though the cards were primarily visual, with the objects permanently glued or sewn to the paper substrate, their physical qualities provided crucial information. The smell of cedar, the texture of raw silk, and the shine of gold leaf were all qualities considered essential to the substances and therefore necessary for students to experience. Seeing the actual leaves glued or sewn onto the cardstock would allow students to identify a maple tree or an oak tree in their own community, gathering their own leaves for comparison. In several cases, the cards addressed topics explicitly about representation and image or art making. Specimens of type, samples of paints and varnishes in glass tubes and actually painted on the surface of the card, and hunks of marble and granite introduced students to the materials commonly used for creating representations. These cards potentially turned a painting or even

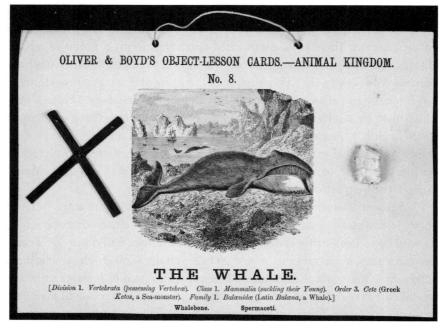

Figure 3.3. "The Whale," No. 8 from *Oliver and Boyd's Object-Lesson Cards on the Animal Kingdom*. The image of the whale helps explain the substances—whalebone and spermaceti—that Oliver and Boyd chose to include on the Object-Lesson Card. *Cotsen Children's Library, Department of Rare Books and Special Collections, Princeton University Library, Princeton, NJ ([CTSN] Elephants 91569 no. 1).*

any printed matter into the subject of a material lesson. With the emphasis on process as opposed to content, these lessons highlighted the artifice of representation. For example, the cards on type-metal, an alloy of lead, antimony, and tin, included a stereotype plate and an example of an impression made from that plate directly on the card. This impression is similar to all the other information-bearing text printed on that card and each card in the series. This emphasis on artifice recast all pictures and texts as potential object lessons.

The power of object lessons does not lie in their visual complexity. The combination of objects, images, and text implied that the layering of different kinds of information—mediated in different ways—could enhance a student's understanding of the topics to be examined. This layered abstraction was not about creating a visual source but an intellectually complex one. For example, in 1876 the Perkins School for the Blind in Massachusetts, the first school for the blind in the United States, founded in 1829, specifically requested a set of object-lesson cards like those Oliver and Boyd made for their students. Rather

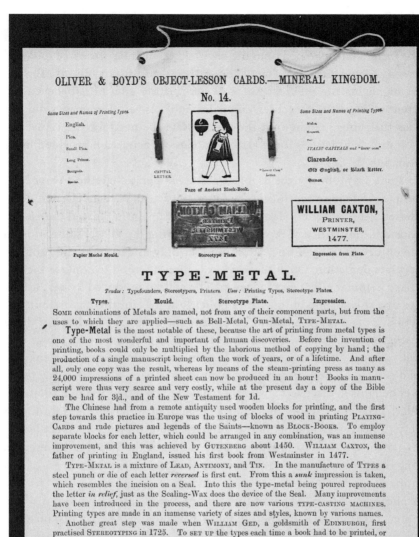

Figure 3.4. "Type-Metal," No. 14 from *Oliver and Boyd's Object-Lesson Cards on the Mineral Kingdom*. The card on Type-Metal transformed the printed card itself into the subject of the lesson by emphasizing the way it was created—in the process all printed texts became the subject of a possible material lesson. *Cotsen Children's Library, Department of Rare Books and Special Collections, Princeton University Library, Princeton, NJ ([CTSN] Elephants 91569 no. 2).*

than a visual collage of material things, images, and texts, which would be useless to their students, the school requested that the information conveyed by the images be embossed onto the page and the text be presented in raised letters, in conjunction with "tactile illustrations" of various objects. This request highlights the different kinds of information educators believed the different parts of the object-lesson cards could convey. The images did not replace the things; neither did the text obviate the need for the actual object or a related picture. These various modes of abstraction provided more information.[24]

In some ways these hybrid object-pictures operate like the *trompe l'oeil* paintings of late nineteenth-century American artists William Harnett, John Frederick Peto, and John Haberle. This genre of painting forced the viewer to consider the artifice of representation, drawing the viewer's attention to the legibility of the painting, attention that only underscores the problem of accurate depiction. Object-lesson cards do not intend to confuse the eye but have a similar effect on the viewer. The collage produced by pasting flat leaves or a silk cocoon onto a card implicitly argues for the impossibility of a picture, a mere representation, to capture the necessary qualities of those items. Haberle's *A Bachelor's Drawer* (1890–94) presents many things that actually appear on object-lesson cards or in classroom lessons—a penknife, a needle, a pipe, a bone comb, glass, a range of papers—in such a way that a viewer delights in discovering whether they are real or represented (Plate 8). Similarly, Haberle's ability to render a range of materials printed through a variety of processes highlights the different kind of printing object-lesson cards taught children to identify. Appreciation of the nuanced differences among these various printing techniques is necessary for the success of this painting.[25]

A photograph from a turn of the century New Jersey classroom displays the object-lesson cards pinned along a blackboard. At that distance are the items stitched onto the cards obvious as three dimensional, or is that a question, as it is in Haberle's painting? Is that part of the lesson? Instead of storing the cards in a wooden box until needed, they are displayed as decoration. From this photograph it is impossible to determine whether students were able to get close enough to feel the softness of rabbit fur or to test the magnetic powers of iron. But even in this setting the cards seem to make clear that images alone do not necessarily convey all that may be needed for successful lessons. Picture lessons take this notion further by assuming that images of daily life are not transparent windows onto a scene but may be visual tools for identifying the central qualities of moral values or abstract ideas.

Figure 3.5. Detail of classroom photograph, ca. 1900. Object-lessons cards were not always used in prescribed ways, as these cards would have been out of reach to the students in this turn-of-the-century Princeton, New Jersey, classroom. *Collection of the Historical Society of Princeton.*

Picture Lessons and Moral Impressions

Strict object teachers would have disapproved of the New Jersey school's choice to display teaching aids on the classroom walls. A promiscuous display of pedagogical images could be as hazardous as rote memorization to the intellectual development of children. Starting in the 1830s, English object-lesson innovator Elizabeth Mayo made it clear that pictures of objects were no substitute for actual physical objects of study. In her first book on the study of shells she noted, "The plates which illustrate this work, have been drawn from specimens actually presented to the class: They are intended as an assistant to the teacher, but not as a substitute for the shells themselves in the instruction of pupils."[26] In another instance, she instructed her student-teachers at the Home and Colonial School (HCS) in London that lessons with pictures for two- to seven-year-old children must first emphasize the distinctions between objects and their representations as part of the lesson before using images in any classroom exercise.[27] Pictures that were used for instruction were not simply pictures that stood in for objects, like the pictures presented in German concept picture cards or alphabet cards.

Instead, structured looking practices were employed in the study of carefully
selected images to develop children's thinking abilities. Students were taught to
identify the "moral impressions" or "conceptions" embedded in visual sources to
link singular images to other pictures, objects, and personal experiences.

These methods shaped picture lessons throughout the British colonies from
Canada to India to New Zealand and were the foundation for the picture lessons
advocated by Sheldon in Oswego. Analysis of lesson plans designed by both the
HCS in London and by Sheldon for two closely related series of lithographs
reveals an active, empathetic viewing culture shaped by object-lesson pedagogy.
The two series of lithographs, one produced by HCS in England sometime after
1847 and another produced by the American Sunday School Union (ASSU)
between 1847 and 1853, are roughly the same size, twenty-eight by thirty-eight
centimeters, though they are in different formats. The HCS example survives as
individual picture sheets, which could be easily displayed in the classroom. The
ASSU prints are bound in a book along with short essays describing their use,
though they were likely also available as individual sheets.[28] E. A. Sheldon used
the ASSU prints as the centerpiece of a series of object lessons. These lesson
plans taught children not only how to look at images but also how to understand
the ideas embedded in visual sources more broadly and to apply those ideas to
their daily lives.

Formal picture lessons were structured as object lessons. Students
were first instructed in developing "perception," observing the pictures
and describing what they were looking at and what the actors were doing.
Then, the students were to understand "conception," interpreting the
actions presented in the images. In decoding the concept embedded in the
represented story, they were to consider what came before and what came
after the scene they viewed, to see how the image might "excite interest,
and call out sympathy." Through this understanding of the ideas presented,
they were directed to apply the lessons observed to their own conduct and
circumstances, to draw certain qualities from the pictures that they might
apply to their own experiences.[29]

A lesson plan Sheldon published in 1862 highlights the distinction between
perception and conception as applied to a lithograph from the HCS and ASSU
series variously titled "Leading the Blind" and "The Kind Child" (ca. 1850s, Plate
9). The image shows a young girl leading a woman with closed eyes and a full
workbasket across a bridge that spans both a river and the width of the lithograph.
In the lesson that accompanied this picture, students were first instructed to describe the scene, to recognize that the woman was blind through closely looking
at the way in which she was represented. Next, they were told to close their own
eyes and walk around the classroom to develop the "conception," the concept,
the notion, of being blind. Blindness was a quality of this image. Children were

to sympathize, if not empathize, with this woman by isolating and adopting the central quality that defined her image.[30]

One of Mayo's disciples, Rebecca Sunter, who led the Infant Model School at the HCS, also wrote her own lessons on these pictures for children in her *Home and Colonial School Society's Manual, for Infant Schools and Nurseries*. Based on everyday scenes from domestic and child life, the lessons were to help children see the nuances of a typical situation in order to develop children's "moral impressions," which were like sense impressions or the term Sheldon used "conceptions." These could be developed through exercises. She offered three explicit steps:

1. Children examine the picture, and endeavor to make out the story, the teacher aiding them by questions, and exciting their interest and feelings.
2. The children [are] to determine the character of the actions delineated, and from what disposition those actions spring.
3. The lessons [are] to be applied to their own conduct.[31]

Sunter detailed a model lesson on the lithograph, "The Cruel Boys Robbing the Bird of Her Little Ones," which represented two boys stealing a bird's nest. This lithograph includes two unruly boys climbing a high tree to steal a bird's nest on one of the highest branches (Plate 10). The children were instructed to examine the picture and discuss each part, noting details that might not be obvious at first glance like the effort that went into the creation of the bird's nest and the motherly love of the bird, whose nest and babies were to be stolen. After helping the children understand the feelings of the personified bird and sympathize with her, the lesson shows ways the cruelty of the boys may be linked to the powerlessness of the little bird that can do nothing to stop them. Next the children were supposed to apply this lesson to their own actions and consider times when they had a choice about whether or not to be cruel.[32] The text that accompanied the ASSU's publication of this lithograph is similar and asks the "Young Robbers" how they would feel if someone were to seize their brothers and sisters and destroy their home? Lessons instructed children to view the picture in a specific and not particularly surprising way—stealing a bird's nest is a cruel act that kind children should avoid.[33]

Sheldon's lesson on this lithograph expands on this interpretation by casting the boys' actions as one aspect, one quality, of orderly or disorderly living. He applied to this image the basic principle of object lessons, moving from the familiar and accessible to the unfamiliar. This lesson was part of a multistep curriculum unit that included first helping students physically understand the foundation of a moral life: order. It starts with a lesson that instructed students to arrange material items, like a cup in a saucer, snuffers in a tray, and unfolded clothes, in a neat way. The children were to interact with these objects to emphasize order. Then they had a lesson on the bird's nest lithograph. To Sheldon, it was a structured place created by a loving mother bird that was destroyed by the boys. The next lesson was on proper behavior in different places and circumstances—children were asked to discuss behavior at home, at church, and in the streets.

The final lessons in the unit linked the "Young Robbers" to additional images. The lithograph variously published as "Saturday Night" or "The Industrious Man" presents a workingman returning to his neat home and family on Saturday night, to an empty chair waiting by the fire and a teacup on the table (Plate 11). The details of this scene were to be dissected by the children to teach them how the kind of order they experienced in placing a cup on a saucer or snuffers on a tray was a crucial aspect of a good life lived by good people. All the different components of this lithograph fed into this conception of daily life and prepared them for the next image, titled variably "The Light of the Week" or "The Happy Family," which depicts the same family on Sunday morning. In this series of lessons, the cruel boys robbing the mother bird and industrious man are in opposition to each other. Both are crucial agents in the destruction or creation of a happy home—whether for birds or people. The lesson learned from the boys stealing the bird's nest simply expressed one quality of a larger orderly system.[34]

Although no target age is indicated for these lessons, they were likely intended for younger children, from six to seven years old. For slightly older children, picture lessons were not simply supposed to give them moral impressions but to further categorize and apply those moral impressions to religious or historical topics. A model lesson on an unidentified print given at the Oswego Normal School makes this point clear. A lesson from 1870 was recorded as it was given to eight-year-old children on the concept of self-sacrifice. The lesson was organized around a picture of a boat sinking in a storm. A vignette of two white children and their father's slave, evocatively named Coffle, center the teacher's description of the lithograph. There is not enough room in the lifeboat to save everyone. The print records Coffle's last words, "Tell Massa Coffle did his duty," as he is depicted helping the children into the lifeboat and preparing to drown. After discussing the tragic scene the teacher and students characterize his actions as laudable and "self-sacrificing"—dying so that others may live. The children list other people and actions that might fall into this category, including Jesus and soldiers, presumably from the Civil War. The lesson of this life or death decision is then explicitly translated into children's daily lives. A child does not have to die to be "self-sacrificing." Helping one's mother, feeding the sick, or giving up one's seat, according to the teacher would make one more like Coffle and therefore pleasing to God. The concept of "self-sacrificing" defined in an extreme case was used as a concrete example to help organize and name a whole range of observable behaviors.[35]

It is not clear whether the print of Coffle's sacrifice was an image explicitly designed for classroom use, but it did not have to be. Sheldon noted in the seventh annual report of the Oswego Board of Education that though specific pictures were made for object teaching, any picture could be approached with this method.[36] Popular lithographs could easily be the basis of a picture lesson, in which a student was directed to observe, discuss, and organize information drawn from an image. For example, a Currier and Ives lithograph, "The Four Seasons of Life: Old Age 'The Season of Rest,'" depicts the happy old age of a married couple, sitting together in a well-appointed interior, by a fire with a child, likely their granddaughter. As the foundation for a picture lesson, it could suggest the rewards of hard work, loyalty, and fidelity in marriage, and the importance of family and faith, represented by the large Bible at the center of the picture. All of these values might be qualities of the peaceful domestic scene depicting happy old age. As part of a series of four images, the print may also encourage comparison of the relationship among the four linked scenes.[37] The same method could be applied to E. B. and E. C. Kellogg's "Increase in the Family," in which a girl's treatment of her kittens is analogous to the ways her mother and grandmother treat her (Plate 12).[38] Most mid-nineteenth-century American genre paintings could have served this purpose as well. This is not to suggest that object-lesson methods shaped the creation of genre paintings, a chronological impossibility. Rather, genre painting is suited to this kind of classroom study because of its reliance on cultural types and familiar narratives, key elements of lithographs employed for picture lessons.[39]

This application of picture lessons may be familiar to art historians and similar to the ways some contemporary scholars attempt to draw information from visual sources with an emphasis on description, narrative, and their broader implications. Yet in the nineteenth century, picture lessons offered surprisingly expansive interpretations of visual sources. As children were taught to move from perception (description) to conception (lessons and ideas embedded in the depicted scenes), they were instructed to link visual sources to their own experiences and choices. This final step forced children to empathize with figures and types presented in the scenes from mischievous boys to tragic slaves—transforming images into aspects of one's daily life and into tools for reasoning and making decisions.

In classroom object lessons, a candle and a pencil might be defined as cylindrical, or whalebone and India rubber might be elastic, constitutive qualities of these objects. In picture lessons, the idea of self-sacrifice, like the cruelty of the boys, are qualities drawn from images, analyzed, and applied to other situations. The explicit identification of these qualities helped develop children's "moral

Figure 3.6. "The Four Seasons of Life: Old Age 'The Season of Rest,'" New York: Currier and Ives, ca. 1868. Prints did not have to be created explicitly as teaching aids to serve a pedagogical purpose. This image, designed for display in a mid-nineteenth-century home, could be used for structured picture lessons. *Library of Congress, Prints & Photographs Division, LC-DIG-pga-00716.*

sense," similar to the way rough and smooth or pungent and sweet objects helped to sharpen students' senses of touch and smell. As an object teacher might use a cone of sugar or a swatch of silk to stand in for all sugar or all silk, and later all kinds of sweetness or silkiness, specific pictures could similarly stand in for broader sets of moral precepts, rooting moral and religious training in visual collections of specific everyday actions.

Visualizing Natural History and Social History

Just as Sheldon and Mayo had adapted object-lesson methods for moral instruction through images, school administrator Norman Allison Calkins and lithographer Louis Prang applied object-lesson methods to the study of natural history topics and to the investigation of skilled labor and trades. In the 1870s, the pair produced two sets of object lesson-based lithographs for the classroom accompanied by detailed teachers' manuals. Both sets of teaching aids were designed to train children's observation abilities, employing the lithographs as tools to help students identify patterns in their daily life. Like moral lessons drawn from narrative prints, these lessons required students to apply information drawn from the images they studied to their lived experiences. As Calkins explained in the manual he wrote to accompany *Prang's Aids for Object-Teaching*, "The passive recipient cannot be a real learner." Instead students had to learn how to "observe intelligently and with system," simultaneously treating classroom aids as material things and identifying patterns in and qualities of those images.[40]

Calkins was an experienced, practical educator committed to object-lesson pedagogy. From 1862 until his death in 1895 he served as assistant superintendent of the Schools of the City of New York and was the superintendent of the primary departments starting in 1862.[41] His experience in New York inspired his project to make natural history "specimens" accessible to urban children. Not all schools could provide the snapping turtles and casts Miss Lee brought in to engage her students, but all increasingly felt a responsibility to introduce students to nature. Calkins and Prang's *Natural History Series* met this goal through picture lessons.[42]

Calkins's many object-lesson books were built on the same sense training prescriptions put forth by Mayo and Sheldon. He emphasized observation through a variety of lessons: the study of shapes, color, counting lessons, and lessons on the human body, in addition to object lessons on everyday items. In the 1870s, he produced an extensive catalog of object teaching aids for home and school; these included a broad range of classroom teaching aids and books that suggested the variety of approaches that might fall under the rubric of "Object Teaching"—from blocks for very young children to collections of minerals for school students.[43] Included in his catalog were specialty items that could be purchased at educational stores and teachers' agencies like Schermerhorn's in New York City as well as simple items that could be acquired in one's own town. For example, suitable objects like "coarse sandpaper, window glass, India rubber, blotting paper, whalebone, a piece of leather, a steel spring, rattan, sponge" were easily obtainable and could help any teacher give "lessons on qualities." Emphasizing the need every teacher had for his own work, he noted that "the kind of object is of much less importance than the manner of giving the lessons," particularly the lessons included in his *New Primary Object Lessons*.[44] His writing emphasized that object lessons was a method, not simply a set of objects or pictures.

Calkins filled several pages of his catalog with one application for this method: *Natural History Series for Schools and Families: Animals and Plants Represented in Their Natural Colors and Arranged for Instruction with Object Lessons*, a new pedagogical project designed to use pictures to meet the goals of an object lesson–based curriculum, without the use of specimens. Calkins collaborated with Joel Asaph Allen, an assistant at Harvard's Museum of

Comparative Zoology, to produce detailed scientific information classifying all of the animals and plants presented in the series. Prang and his artists represented this information, along with colors and sketches taken from life, in vivid chromolithographs. Allen, probably best known as an ornithologist, had been a student of Louis Agassiz at Harvard and had learned via his teacher's famous "case study method." With such a foundation, it is not surprising that Allen would agree to collaborate on a project that taught children to observe, to order, and to find meaning in observations, as opposed to learning through texts.[45]

Calkins's specific directions as to the use of these teaching aids made it clear that it is not the accurate information contained within these cards that mattered most to him. Rather he aimed "to furnish necessary steps in observation and comparison for preparing children to examine, as opportunities present, the various animals and plants that come within their sphere of observation, and thus to introduce them to the true study of nature."[46] In order to serve this end the picture lessons replicated the actual study of nature in a creative way. The lessons comprised cards of two sizes organized according to different modes of classification: first, by birds, quadrupeds, and plants; then within those categories into subgroups or orders—for birds, for example, swimming birds, wading birds, birds of prey, and scratching birds. Within these categories, a central bird was selected that was most familiar to children, the Mallard Duck, the Great Blue Heron, the Golden Eagle, and the Wild Turkey, and this was used to make a large lithograph (roughly thirty-five by twenty-five centimeters, Plate 13). As Calkins noted in his advertisement for the series, "Each larger one contains a single animal as a representative of a family, and also the distinguishing parts enlarged."[47] The "distinguishing parts" could also be described as the central qualities of the category of animal or plant.

The object teaching that Calkins described intended to teach children what they did not know through information they already had, applying a basic principle of object lessons to looking at and organizing pictures based on central, easily observable qualities.[48] The dozen small, playing card–size lithographs that accompanied each of these larger cards presented the different members of the families that fell under the same order. For example, the card on Wading Birds presented a large picture of a Great Blue Heron, which would be displayed along with smaller cards depicting a Flamingo, an Ibis, and an Avocet, birds similar to the Heron in significant, observable ways. Children were not supposed to memorize relationships among these animals. They were to discern them through observation. The large card of the familiar Mallard Duck could be related to a dozen smaller cards that depict other swimming birds that have similar features like webbed feet and a beak adapted to eating fish. Cards of quadrupeds and plants followed similar rules. The familiar Domestic Cat could introduce children to the exotic Ocelot, Royal Tiger, or Jaguar (Plate 14). The Gray Squirrel, whose teeth were different from those of the cat, could inform children about Woodchucks and Gophers. The cud-chewing Cow opened a door onto the study of Chamois and Sheep. Plants were examined in the same way.[49]

Calkins then instructed the children to relate the smaller pictures to the larger pictures or to other sets of cards. Calkins elaborated,

> Although beautiful as pictures, these natural history chromos are not designed to be suspended on the walls of the school-room as ornaments. To be most useful and to effectively accomplish the objects for which they were designed, the smaller pictures must be put into the hands of the pupils while the larger illustrations are suspended before the class, thus enabling the children to make separate comparisons with a view to training them individually to observe the prominent characteristic belonging to different kinds of animals and plants.[50]

Putting the smaller chromolithographs into the hands of the children encouraged them to look closely and also enabled them to have the sense that they were examining something physically and materially different from the other cards in the series. This material form also allowed for simultaneous comparisons across images that highlighted the related qualities that might be found in each of the cards in the series. For example, the fact that all swimming birds had webbed feet could be emphasized by comparing the duck to other cards from the same family or to the clawed feet of scratching birds. The study of function led to a discussion of climate and geography.

Calkins spelled out the reason for this project in his *A Plan of Instruction Embodied in Prang's Natural History Series*. Children, whether they lived in cities or in the countryside, he explained, did not know how to observe; they looked around "in a promiscuous manner" with no particular intellectual goals in mind. They could not identify the unique categories of the things they encountered every day. He argued that training in observation, while they were under the age of ten, would help them develop "habits of self-acquisition in knowledge" and become better students generally. The study of nature's beautiful forms would refine their sensibilities and develop their taste. In some instances, children were asked to examine a cat at home or to bring in leaves and roots that matched the different shapes they studied in school. These lessons brought the observation taught in the classroom into their homes and helped them see and apply the patterns beyond the large and small cards.

Calkins also produced a manual for teachers to provide them with specific scientific information about each of the items studied.[51] He emphatically instructed teachers in the proper use of these visual aids, which required knowledge of this technical information. "There is no danger from 'cramming' children," he

comforted his teacher-audience, "when they [the students] learn from observation."[52] Plus, he described an added benefit of the new knowledge: children
would be encouraged to be kinder to animals because they would know more
about them and better understand their lives.[53]

The series of lessons Calkins recommended included different ways of
training children to observe, to organize, and to compare visual information
geared to different age groups, from the youngest primary school students to
older students who might supplement their study with advanced reading in
natural history—as well as for parents who wanted to instruct their children
at home. The goal for all students was the same: to be able to distinguish char-
acteristics that were defining features of the different groups of animals and
plants through observation and comparison. The entire series was intended
to make a visual argument through shared qualities, that groups are naturally created, ordered, and understood through observable similarities.[54] The
pictures were not "ornaments" as Calkins explained; they were abstractions of
key ideas.

The observation and categorization facilitated by teaching aids like those of
Calkins had been intended to happen in the classroom with groups of related
material things. A tray of varied minerals could be used for this purpose, or a
group of prepared specimens. A classroom scene from the Perkins School for
the Blind from the 1890s captures a group of visually impaired girls touching
a range of taxidermy quadrupeds, from a platypus to a monkey. They were
likely instructed to use this experience to develop and then organize their sense
perceptions, through touch, about these animals. In the process they were to develop the abstract concepts shared by this whole family of creatures.[55]

After completing their *Natural History Series*, Prang and Calkins worked together on another object-lesson project motivated by the same basic goals. Just
like the Natural History Series, *Prang's Pictures of Trades and Occupations* were
"to be used as materials for training children in habits of systematic examination
of real objects." This time the objects of their gaze were items and places related
to different occupations.[56] The urban schoolchildren Calkins knew in New York
City likely had less exposure to work, apprenticeship, and professional training
than previous generations of children. These lessons were intended to teach
them about the origin of the material things around them, whether garments or
apple pies, and to introduce them to potential trades, for both men and women.
In the process, children were to see the tools and techniques of various trades
as linked. The baker is dependent on the farmer for produce, while the house
carpenter needs the blacksmith to make his tools. The series was based on the
premise that if children were simply to go and observe different occupations,
they would not understand the most important aspects—or qualities—of
each trade. They would miss patterns and not appreciate the work that went

Figure 3.7. Zoology; Subject of Lesson: Mammalia, Perkins Institution, ca. 1893. A class of girls from the Perkins School for the Blind studies and sorts a collection of mammal specimens. *Perkins School for the Blind Archives, Watertown, MA, AG13_05_0031c.*

into the creation of everyday things. Calkins described the goals of the twelve-lithograph series.

> These representations are intended to be used as a means of awakening a desire to know more about trades and occupations in which people are daily engaged, and of furnishing a ready means of pointing out the various kinds of materials, tools, and acts of labor, required in carrying them on, and leading pupils to understand the relations of these operations to the common welfare of all.[57]

The "representations" were training materials designed to develop the child's ability and desire to observe the tradesmen at work and convey information that would help the child intelligently approach the sites of labor he or she was studying. The lithographs served to stabilize the tasks students would observe into discrete steps, making a complex production process visible, legible, and even noble. Students were supposed to gain an understanding of what it would be like to work in these environments and, just as important, to understand the material history of the things around them. Focusing on imparting the method of observing and comparing material things, the series of lessons encouraged children to use the prints as tools to begin their exploration of various trades, their implements, and products.

The twelve vividly colored cards present a range of trades and occupations, including those of carpenter, shoemaker, tailor, blacksmith, lithographer, gardener, farmer, baker, tinsmith, and printer, as well as two spaces of domestic labor: the kitchen and the farmyard. Each card is roughly thirty-one by fifty centimeters. In most instances the trades are shown in various stages, as in the tailor's shop, where both the production and retail aspects of the trade are shown or in the lithographer's studio where different steps in the printing process are detailed. Instead of simply introducing children to possible occupations, the different trades were studied and defined by different qualities. Each trade has central defining features that may be dissected and understood by discerning students. In some cases the trades depicted like the *Shoemaker* may have appeared foreign or old-fashioned to students familiar with ready-made goods produced in factories (Plate 15).[58] But the lessons allowed children to focus on the individual worker, to imagine how each employed specific tools, and to consider the items produced.

Part of the process of learning to look at both these pictures and the items depicted in them was seeing that the labor was a quality of the objects students studied, from the clothing they wore to the food they ate. This process echoed Karl Marx's analysis of commodities in *Das Kapital*. The labor depicted in the images becomes simply another quality of a pair of pants, a tapioca pudding, or a house. In the same way, material details like shape, color, weight, or texture accessed through sensory engagement are qualities of those things. Calkins and Prang did not discuss the value of the goods they study in specie directly; rather the picture lessons emphasized the social value of skilled workers, who produced to serve the common good.[59]

To meet these pedagogical goals, Calkins devised a four-tiered lesson. First, students were led by their teacher to examine the pictures carefully, to determine the trade depicted, the function of necessary tools, and the items produced. Next, the children were instructed to actually visit a shop in which this trade was practiced and to return to the picture with new information and questions about the trade. For example, after such an experience their teacher might instruct, "Point out in the picture before you, some tool which you have seen a blacksmith use, and tell us what he does with it."[60] Looking at the picture the children might then point to the tongs on the floor or the anvil being used to fashion horseshoes. Examining the kitchen scene, they might consider the ways the clock above the sink might be an important instrument (Plate 16). Third, the students and teacher return to the pictures to learn "what the persons represented in the picture work upon; what they work with; why they do the given work; what

articles are made; what is being done with that which is made" through conversation. This facet of the lesson was to correct "mistaken notions" about how
and why people work and to help students see that manual labor is "a means by
which the necessaries and comforts of life are supplied."[61] These more abstract
observations—which encompass personal motivation and consideration of why
workers might "strive to become skillful in their work"—suggest the conceptions
Mayo or Sheldon may have drawn from these images had they applied their own
lessons.[62] Finally, depending on their age, students presented an oral or written
sketch of the studied trade encompassing everything they had learned.

Trades and Occupations instructed students to see the items around them as
lessons on that labor. This is particularly true of the lessons on printing and lithography, which taught children to treat printed texts and lithographs as manufactured objects. The lesson on lithography begins with a categorization of all
printed material into three categories: printing from raised lines, printing from
lines sunk below the surface, and printing from flat surfaces.[63] Instructors were
encouraged to offer the lithographs of the "Trades and Occupations" series as
an example of the "flat" method, challenging students to study the teaching
aids as documents of a mechanical process with certain physical qualities. *The
Lithographer* represents each stage in the process of producing a lithograph, from
grinding the stones, to the artist's reverse copy of an original in lithographic
crayon, to the eventual printing, and back again in a circle (Plate 17). Old, worn
plates rest beside the stone-grinder to be repurposed for a new picture. Each
of the four workers is shown in action, with arms bent, emphasizing that their
active labor created and in some way still animates the physical classroom lesson.
If students chose to follow up with a visit to an actual lithographic studio as part
of their assignment, not only would they be able to identify an etching-trough
or a hand press, but they would also understand how their teacher's tools were
created.[64]

Object-lesson pedagogy, whether applied to the study of pictures or other
things, deemphasized the acquisition of knowledge from books in favor of observation and personal experience. Calkins and Prang's lesson on lithography
reinforces this theme. Similarly, their chapter in the teachers' manual on printers
includes samples of the impression created by a range of type, from "Great
Primer" to "Old English," highlighting the object nature of that book and any
printed text.[65] Other object lessons reinforce this point. A set of object-lesson
cards on type-metal, an alloy of lead, antimony, and tin, includes a stereotype
plate and an example of an impression made from that plate directly on the
card (Figure 3.4). Samples of type dangle from thread between two columns of
different varieties of printed lettering, like that in the teachers' manual for *Trades
and Occupations*. The impressions created by the type and the stereotype plate
are similar to all the other information-bearing text printed on that card and each

card in the series. Printed images and texts become like any other object: created from naturally occurring substances and produced through several individuals' skilled labor.[66]

In both the *Natural History Series* and *Trades and Occupations*, Calkins and Prang followed the cardinal rule of object lessons: use the familiar to get at unfamiliar concepts. Their lithographs and detailed lessons gave students tools to discern patterns that structured the natural world and to discover the work embedded in material things. In the process, picture lessons complicated the familiar and gave children access to new information and new ways of finding information.[67]

Picture lessons did not teach children to accept images as a window onto reality. Object teachers were often explicit in making this point, noting that while a picture may be a less "arbitrary" symbol than a word and "bears some resemblance to a real thing"—it appeals to "only a single sense" and cannot be fully trusted.[68] Rather, images became ways of ordering and conveying information. Pedagogical lithographs, when viewed through the step-by-step unfolding process of object lessons, taught children how to know and to understand their material world as opposed to simply accepting common knowledge about it. Picture lessons directed children to consider: What is the central quality of this image? Why is it morally right or wrong to act in a certain way? Why is this a squirrel or that a tinsmith? What can I know from my own experience and not from a picture of that experience? The insistence on personal experience and empathy reflected an anxiety about a perceived disconnect between what children said they knew and what they actually learned, a gap that had implications for a person's ability to reason. Object lessons offered through and on pictures could help a young citizen learn to understand real from representation, to develop the power to make good decisions, and to understand that the order of nature and the value of work may be encapsulated in familiar things. As Elizabeth Mayo explained, "Minds accustomed to accurate investigation, will not rest content with less than satisfactory evidence, either in morals or science."[69] Picture lessons were supposed to give children additional tools to investigate the origin and meanings of things they encountered every day—as one writer put it, "This *thinging* forms the only true basis for *thinking*."[70]

4

Object Lessons in Race and Citizenship

Around Thanksgiving 1899, Hampton Normal and Agricultural Institute student Louis Firetail posed for a photograph. Firetail, a Crow Creek Sioux, mounted a small platform in the front of fourteen of his fellow Native and African American classmates and their teacher. Photographer Frances Benjamin Johnston snapped the picture, which has been described as a scene from an American history class. Yet Firetail's portrait comprised a very specific kind of classroom study. Like the taxidermy eagle perched on the table behind him and the geological specimens in the case against the wall, this young Sioux man, who had recently returned from a summer on a New England farm and studied carpentry at Hampton, was an object lesson.[1]

Frances Benjamin Johnston's photograph of Louis Firetail is one image in a series of beautiful, haunting, and compelling publicity photographs taken at Hampton.[2] Like the photographs Johnston would later take of the Tuskegee Institute, the Carlisle Indian School, and the Washington, DC, public schools, these photographs depict the students at Hampton in class, engaged in work, and at rest, as well as the campus buildings, the surrounding area, and the homes of Hampton graduates. These well-known images have had a long afterlife and have an even longer bibliography.[3] Scholars and critics have interpreted Johnston's photographs in a variety of ways, often holding onto the presumed transparency of the images and their interpretation of racial uplift linked to manual labor.

Commentators have analyzed Johnston's emphasis on the tractable, quiet, hard-working bodies of African Americans and Native Americans and at the same time noted the ways the photographs attempted to document the positive, observable effect Hampton had on the lives of its students and their communities. However, these analyses do not consider the full range of Johnston's photographs of Hampton, now held at the Library of Congress, preferring to focus on her more famous images of Hampton, as selected for publication in the *Hampton Album* and a 1966 exhibition at the Museum of Modern Art in New York City.[4]

Figure 4.1. Frances Benjamin Johnston, "Louis Firetail (Sioux, Crow Creek), wearing tribal clothing, in American history class, Hampton Institute, Hampton, Virginia," 1899. Louis Firetail is presented to his class as an object lesson in this iconic photographic by Frances Benjamin Johnston. *Library of Congress, Prints & Photographs Division, LC-DIG-ppmsca-12031.*

There is something else going on in these images. Taken as a group, they reflect a central but understudied aspect of Hampton's educational philosophy. Image after image emphasizes active student engagement with material things as the primary source of knowledge and pedagogical development. These object lessons are the intellectual framework of Hampton's curriculum.

Object lessons were employed at the Hampton Normal and Agricultural Institute and its associated primary school, the Butler School (later the Whittier School), from 1868 to roughly 1900. Johnston's photographs mark the end of that period and provide an avenue to visualize the different ways the practice and rhetoric of object-lesson pedagogy infiltrated the Hampton curriculum—from history class to Kitchen Gardens. This mode of pedagogy was at the core of Samuel Chapman Armstrong's "education for life" philosophy when he founded Hampton after the Civil War. The school's curriculum focused on drawing information out of material things through the study of objects and on learning from experience through labor and later manual training. Hampton's curriculum reflects the object-lesson pedagogy that was extremely popular when the school was founded. Armstrong's arguments for a "scientific rather than classic" course at Hampton were racist, complicated, and problematic, but they were also in line with developments in progressive education.

At the same time, visitors to the school, federal officials, and members of the community were instructed to view the school's students and graduates as material evidence—as living "object lessons"—of what African American and Native American students could become after an education at Hampton. Hampton transformed this classroom practice into the explicit observation of people as well as objects and pictures, a process that served to define certain types and tropes as exemplars even as the pedagogy was intended to expand students' critical thinking ability by teaching them to observe and reason for themselves. By transforming students into lessons, Hampton brought the idea of the object lesson out of the classroom and into the broader community, changing the cultural meaning of this practice.

Object Lessons for Hampton Students

In 1868, when Armstrong founded Hampton, the school's initial mission all but mandated the inclusion of object lessons. Hampton's stated purpose was "to prepare youth of the South, without distinction of color, for the work of organizing and instructing schools in the southern states."[5] Best practices for primary school education in progressive common schools in the 1860s and 1870s included object lessons. A close look at Hampton's publications, including the college catalogs, annual reports, and the *Southern Workman* newspaper, reveals that these lessons were everywhere. Even when the phrase "object lesson" is not explicitly mentioned, the emphasis throughout the curriculum is on the development of observation and experience-based learning. Sensory education, proponents believed, would lead to right feeling and critical thinking.[6] Several graduates of the Oswego Normal School spent time at Hampton and deemed the school's curriculum in line with their training.[7]

Armstrong's decision to found Hampton likely had roots in his childhood in the Pacific. He grew up in Hawaii, where his father, Richard Armstrong, was a missionary and the minister of public instruction. Although object lessons did not attain wide popularity until the 1860s, educators and missionaries long knew about the methodology through the work of the Home and Colonial Teaching Society in England and through Henry Barnard's *American Journal of Education* in the United States. For example, a Hawaiian teacher from Maine named Ingraham described employing a form of object teaching in his 1856 classroom at the Hawaii Free School, noting that he cut a watermelon into sections to teach his students fractions.[8] Richard Armstrong believed that his children should develop practical, hands-on skills as well as book knowledge and had young Sam apprenticed to a carpenter, even as he prepared for entrance to Williams College.[9] This same philosophy drove Richard Armstrong's missionary schools, which included "character-building" manual labor, as central to the intellectual and moral development of native Hawaiians. The value Samuel Armstrong would later place on both primary education and manual labor reflected his hope in their potential to help freed slaves, just as he believed they had helped native Hawaiians. He would point to the Hilo Boarding and Manual Labor School for boys as a potential model for Hampton. At the same time, Samuel Armstrong's rhetoric about manual labor as character building also dovetailed tightly with the primary pedagogical sweep of his modern curriculum.[10]

There is likely another reason that object lessons in particular came to be such a big part of the school's curriculum: racist notions about the aptitude and nature of Hampton's students led to the use of this mode of pedagogy. The 1874 book *Hampton and Its Students by Two of Its Teachers* portrayed the capacity of African American students in a way that a period educator would understand as perfectly suited to an object lesson–based curriculum. In describing the Hampton student body (which in 1874 did not yet include Native Americans), the authors said:

> Our students learn with average readiness, and show more than average perseverance, but find their chief obstacle in an inability to assimilate the ideas which they receive. . . . [A]s children [they] formed no fixed habits of thought. The formulation of ideas and their expression in words are invariably difficult for them, and at times it is fairly pitiful to watch their efforts to catch and crystallize into language a thought which they feel to be slipping from them back into the realms of mystery whence it came.[11]

The idea that African American students were not able to "crystallize" thoughts is something object lessons, which were intended to concretize abstract concepts into language, promised to address. A. P. Harris, an early chronicler of the Oswego method, concurred: "The Pestalozzian methods were peculiarly adapted to the awakening mind of a race, which had been forced for centuries to derive its ideas from the concrete, a race from whom books and most forms of abstract thinking had been rigorously removed."[12] A school report from 1869 included the following subjects, "object-teaching, reading, music, geography, grammar, English composition, mathematics, natural philosophy, history, and civil government."[13] White southerners believed that race was not simply a visual category but one that involved all of the senses. Some white southerners may have assumed that African Americans sensed differently and relied more on "lower" senses— touch, smell, and hearing, rather than sight—which were heightened through use.[14] Their supposed ability to sense more acutely than whites could make them appear to be particularly susceptible to the study of material things.

When Captain Richard Henry Pratt brought native prisoners to Hampton from Fort Marion in 1878, cultural stereotypes about Indians further reinforced the use of object lessons for their education. Many Americans were familiar with the pictograms of the Plains Indians through examples produced by or sent to the prisoners at Fort Marion and believed that Native Americans communicated through images of objects.[15] When describing Indian fitness for "school room work," Helen Ludlow, an instructor at Hampton, contrasted their supposed ability to *observe* with their inability "to get hold of new ideas." Such a combination of traits would have rendered object lessons the ideal pedagogy for this situation, leveraging this presumed ability to observe as a way to improve intellectual development.[16] In fact, while object study permeated the curriculum, the phrase "object lesson" was most often applied to the education of Native American students.[17] Instead of simply conveying information or teaching children skills, like reading, writing, and basic math, Hampton educators tried to show students how to acquire knowledge and to address perceived shortcomings in their ability and early development.

The racist language found in educators' descriptions of Hampton students suggests that lessons that might have been considered better fitted to younger white children in the North were considered appropriate at Hampton for older students (who were typically over the age of fourteen).[18] The perceived differences in the perceptual abilities of Native American and African American students at Hampton is one aspect of the ways these groups were viewed: both were considered potentially deficient by Hampton staff, but their deficiencies were manifested in explicitly racial ways. Armstrong believed blacks were poor workers because they had historically been "worked" while Indians had never learned to work.[19]

Hampton employed object teaching in a number of ways: in the museum, in the classroom, at the practice school, in training students to be teachers, and through the pedagogically (and financially) prescribed physical labor of the students. First, in order to conduct object lessons, Armstrong worked quickly to develop teaching collections that could be employed to instruct the students about other cultures, geography, history, and general studies. In 1868, he asked his mother, who was still living in Hawaii, to send "specimens of coral, lava and curiosities of all kinds" for use in classroom instruction.[20] School catalogs noted a "Cabinet of curiosities" to which missionaries abroad were encouraged to donate cultural objects.[21] The Hampton University Museum was founded along with the school and featured teaching collections from around the world, with particular focus on African and Native American collections. In 1881, Armstrong appropriated $300 to collect Indian materials from the Crow Creek reservation, and other collections, notably the Blake Indian collection, augmented these items.[22] In the early twentieth century a curator's report noted that the museum would be an aid to all geography and history classes and would provide objects, pictures, and lantern slides for the directed or independent study of foreign cultures, geography, history, and commodities.[23]

By the 1870s, the school had a substantial collection of philosophical apparatus, allowing students to take part in scientific object lessons, or what the school's catalog would later describe as "Object lessons in Physics and Chemistry."[24] Johnston captured such a lesson in the photograph that has been captioned, "A class in mathematical geography studying earth's rotation around the sun, Hampton Institute, Hampton, Virginia." It depicts a class of twelve men and women studying astronomy and the seasons of the earth through the examination of individual globes. Courses in natural history (later called nature study) were also taught through conversation and with objects.[25]

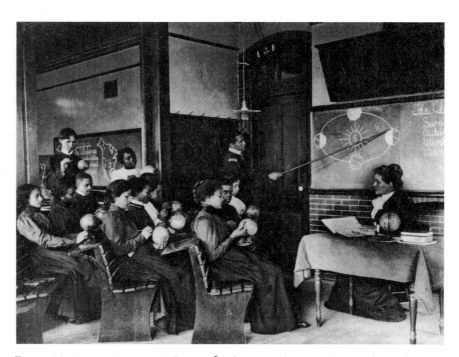

Figure 4.2. Frances Benjamin Johnston, [A class in mathematical geography studying earth's rotation around the sun, Hampton Institute, Hampton, Virginia], 1899. Photographed by Frances Benjamin Johnston, a dozen male and female students study the earth's rotation around the sun. *Library of Congress, Prints & Photographs Division, LC-USZ62-62376.*

Plate 1. Educational specimen box, for the education of children, assembled in England, mahogany, ca. 1850. Collections of everyday objects and substances were arranged and sold to aid teachers in classroom instruction. The materials in this box were likely designed for use with Elizabeth Mayo's *Lessons on Objects. Victoria and Albert Museum, B.5:1 to 5-2009.* © *Victoria and Albert Museum, London.*

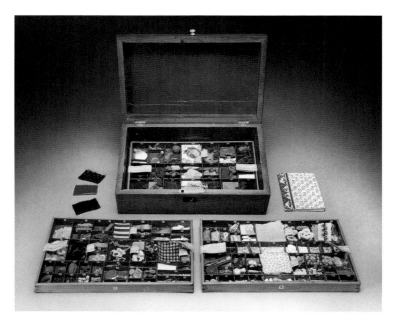

Plate 2. Specimens of Articles in Common Use, Great Britain, ca. 1830, wooden box containing 141 specimens of material, predominantly natural, with booklet. This box was likely created as a teaching aid in the early nineteenth century. *Yale Center for British Art, Paul Mellon Fund.*

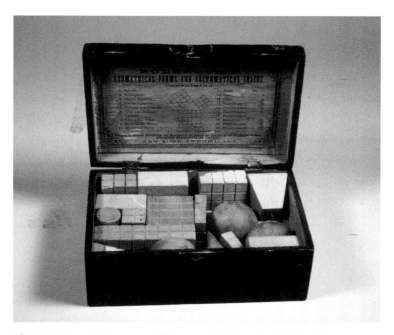

Plate 3. Holbrook's Geometrical Forms and Arithmetical Solids, 1859, paper and wood, 3 9/16 x 8 11/16 x 5 11/16 in. Wooden teaching aids like "Holbrook's Geometrical Forms and Arithmetical Solids" invited children to compare objects of different shapes and sizes. *Behring Center, Division of Medicine & Science, National Museum of American History, Smithsonian Institution, 1986.1025.*

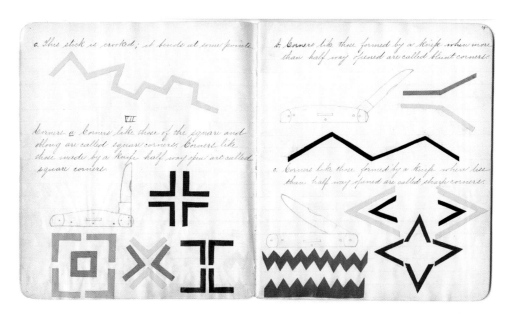

Plate 4. Fanny Rothkopf, "Class III" notebook, 1877–1881. The notebooks of pupil-teachers trained in object-lesson methods suggest how ideal lessons could be translated for classroom use. *Archives of the Alumni Association of Hunter College, 1872–2005, Box 124, Folder 3, Archives & Special Collections, Hunter College Libraries, Hunter College of the City University of New York.*

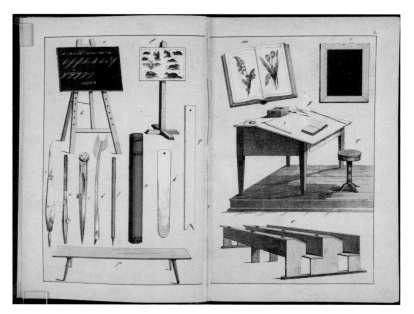

Plate 5. *Anschauungsunterricht* card from *Bilder zum ersten Anschauungsunterricht,* ca. 1850s. Object-lesson cards like this one depict how such teaching aids might be displayed in the classroom, in this case a card featuring small mammals presented on a stand. *Cotsen Children's Library, Department of Rare Books and Special Collections, Princeton University Library, Princeton, NJ ((CTSN) Euro 19Q 44901).*

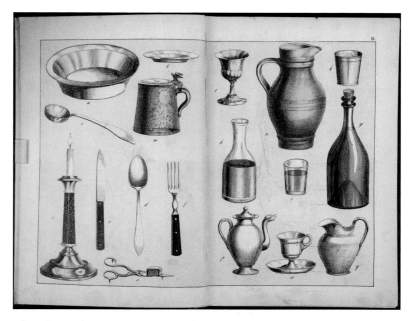

Plate 6. *Anschauungsunterricht* card from *Bilder zum ersten Anschauungs-Unterricht,* ca. 1850s. *Anschauungsunterricht* cards could present common objects, like candle snuffers and wine bottles, for study in the classroom. *Cotsen Children's Library, Department of Rare Books and Special Collections, Princeton University Library, Princeton, NJ ([CTSN] Euro 19Q 44901).*

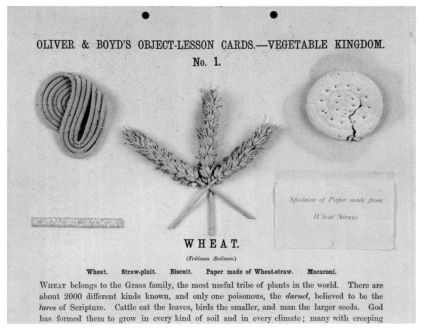

OLIVER & BOYD'S OBJECT-LESSON CARDS.—VEGETABLE KINGDOM.
No. 1.

Specimen of Paper made from
Wheat Straw.

WHEAT.
(Triticum Sativum.)

Wheat.   Straw-plait.   Biscuit.   Paper made of Wheat-straw.   Macaroni.

WHEAT belongs to the Grass family, the most useful tribe of plants in the world. There are about 2000 different kinds known, and only one poisonous, the *darnel*, believed to be the *tares* of Scripture. Cattle eat the leaves, birds the smaller, and man the larger seeds. God has formed them to grow in every kind of soil and in every climate; many with creeping

Plate 7. Detail of "Wheat," No. 1 from *Oliver and Boyd's Object-Lesson Cards on the Vegetable Kingdom.* Oliver and Boyd's object-lesson card on wheat featured an actual biscuit and macaroni in addition to wheat-based paper and plaited straw affixed to the card for use in the classroom. *Cotsen Children's Library, Department of Rare Books and Special Collections, Princeton University Library, Princeton, NJ, ([CTSN] Elephants 91569 no. 1).*

Plate 8. John Haberle, *A Bachelor's Drawer*, 1890–94, oil on canvas, 20 x 36 in. Like object-lesson cards, late nineteenth-century American trompe l'oeil paintings challenged visitors to assess the relationships among objects, printed materials, and painted surfaces. *Metropolitan Museum of Art, purchase, Henry R. Luce gift, 1970, 1970.193.*

Plate 9. "The Kind Child" from *Cautionary Tales*, after 1847. "Leading the Blind" or "The Kind Child" offers a picture lesson on the qualities required to complete a good work. *Cotsen Children's Library, Department of Rare Books and Special Collections, Princeton University Library, Princeton, NJ, ([HSVC] 22831).*

Plate 10. "The Cruel Boys Robbing the Bird of Her Little Ones" from *Picture Lessons Illustrating Moral Truth*, ca. 1850s. This children's story suggests the connections between the boys' cruelty and the overall disorder suggested by the scene. *Courtesy Winterthur Library, Printed Book and Periodical Collection.*

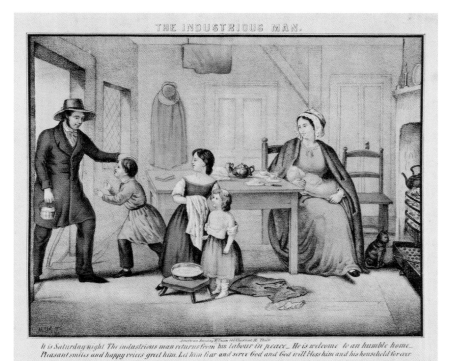

Plate 11. "Saturday Night" or "The Industrious Man" from *Picture Lessons Illustrating Moral Truth*, ca. 1850s. In this illustration, children could identify details that presented an orderly interior as part of a happy, industrious life. *Courtesy Winterthur Library, Printed Book and Periodical Collection.*

Plate 12. "Increase in the Family," Hartford: E. B. and E. C. Kellogg, 1860. Genre scenes not explicitly designed for instruction could become the subject of structured pictures lessons. *Harry T. Peters Lithography Collection, National Museum of American History, 228146.*

Plate 13. "Mallard Duck" and related cards, *Natural History Series,* ca. 1872–73. Caulkins presumed that children would be most familiar with the mallard duck featured as the largest image in this group, a familiarity children could leverage to understand the other animals. *American Antiquarian Society, Worcester, MA.*

Plate 14. "Domestic Cat" and related cards, *Natural History Series*, ca. 1872–1873. By studying the common domestic cat, children could learn about the less familiar ocelot, tiger, and jaguar, which shared similar features. *American Antiquarian Society, Worcester, MA.*

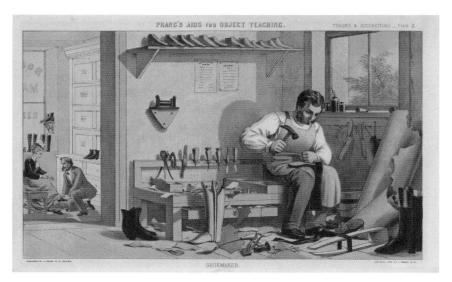

Plate 15. "Shoemaker, Trades and Occupations" from *Prang's Aids for Object Teaching*, ca. 1877. *Prang's Aids for Object Teaching* helped students understand various kinds of labor and tools as qualities of the trades depicted, like shoemaking, and the objects produced by those trades. *Library of Congress, Prints & Photographs Division, LC-DIG-pga-07880.*

Plate 16. "Kitchen, Trades and Occupations" from *Prang's Aids for Object Teaching*, ca. 1877. The twelve different cards suggested a variety of possibilities for work, including the work that may have taken place in a domestic environment like the kitchen. *Library of Congress, Prints & Photographs Division, LC-DIG-pga-04045.*

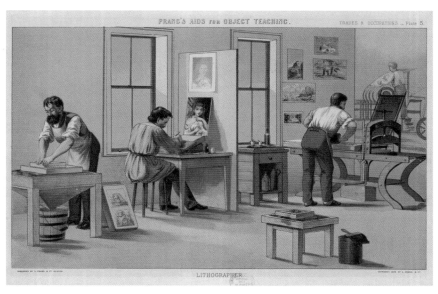

Plate 17. "Lithographer, Trades and Occupations" from *Prang's Aids for Object Teaching*, ca. 1877. The lesson on the lithographer taught children to recognize all of the pedagogical prints they were studying as the product of a specific kind of labor. *Library of Congress, Prints & Photographs Division, LC-DIG-pga-07879.*

FOR PRESIDENT,
GROVER CLEVELAND.

FOR VICE-PRESIDENT,
ADLAI E. STEVENSON.

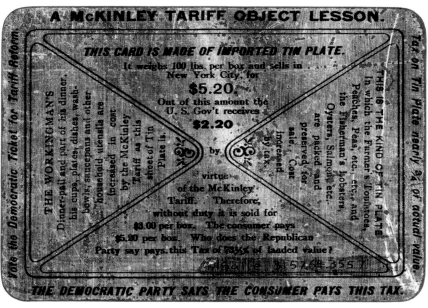

A McKINLEY TARIFF OBJECT LESSON.

THIS CARD IS MADE OF IMPORTED TIN PLATE.

It weighs 100 lbs. per box and sells in
New York City, for

$5.20.

Out of this amount the
U. S. Gov't receives

$2.20

by

virtue
of the McKinley
Tariff. Therefore,
without duty it is sold for
$3.00 per box. The consumer pays
$5.20 per box. Who does the Republican
Party say pays this Tax of 73½% of landed value?

THE WORKINGMAN'S
Dinner-pail and part of his dinner.
his cups, plates, dishes, wash-
bowls, saucepans and other
household utensils are
increased in cost
by the McKinley
Tariff as this
sheet of Tin
Plate is.

THIS IS THE KIND OF TIN PLATE
In which the Farmer's Tomatoes,
Peaches, Peas, etc. etc. and
the Fisherman's Lobsters,
Oyster, Salmon etc.
are packed and
preserved for
sale. Cost
increased
by tax.

Vote the Democratic Ticket for Tariff Reform

Tax on Tin Plate nearly ¾ of actual value

THE DEMOCRATIC PARTY SAYS THE CONSUMER PAYS THIS TAX.

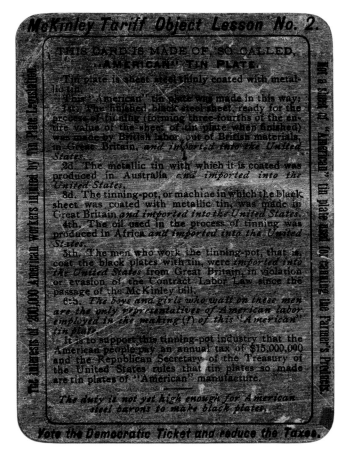

Plates 18 and 19. Presidential candidate Grover Cleveland's campaign created a pair of object lessons in 1892 that were both about the production and use of tin and actually printed on cards made out of tinned sheet iron.

Plate 18 (opposite): "A McKinley Tariff Object Lesson," DiSalle 315264.3557, *Division of Political History, National Museum of American History, Smithsonian Institution*; Plate 19 (this page): "A McKinley Tariff Object Lesson, No. 2," Tin-Cleveland/Stevenson RSN 81698X05, Reverse. *Division of Political History, National Museum of American History, Smithsonian Institution.*

Plate 20. "Decker Bros. Grand, Upright, and Square Pianos," Decker Bros., New York, n.d. The patterned interior and the cadence evoked by the dancing girl suggest the sounds produced by the upright piano advertised in this trade card. *Advertising Ephemera Collection, Baker Library, Harvard Business School (olvwork88844).*

Plate 21. "Le Page's Liquid Glue," Russia Cement Company, Gloucester, MA, n.d.
A trade card for "Le Page's Liquid Glue" makes the tactile quality of the glue—perfect for
glass or broken hearts—visible. *Advertising Ephemera Collection, Baker Library, Harvard
Business School (olvwork80274).*

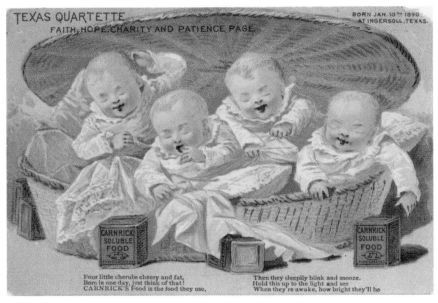

Plate 22. "Carnrick's Soluble Food," Reed & Carnrick, United States, n.d. The quadruplets displayed on this metaphoric card—a card that shows the babies both sleeping and wide awake when held up to light—are presented as material evidence of the health of "Carnrick's Soluble Food." *Advertising Ephemera Collection, Baker Library, Harvard Business School (olvwork80329).*

When Pratt first brought the group of Plains Indian prisoners of war to Hampton in 1878, the school responded with "object lessons."[26] Ludlow described the curriculum intended for students in the Indian Department as initially centered around the study of things, "The methods of teaching are those in modern use for their grades, with adaptations to the conditions: Language and number lessons with objects, geography with molding sand and map drawing; reading." Later they were to move on to "arithmetic, history and drawing." Only then did they enter the normal school's junior year, usually spending five years in all at the school.[27] For younger native students, objects and object lessons, lessons on pictures, and basic drill usually replaced books for the first three years of classroom study. Because of their perceived abilities to observe, these Native American students were believed to have a "native keenness of perception" that fitted them to the study of natural history, which they pursued through Prang's lithographs.[28]

Hampton was, as its name indicated, also a normal school. Teachers were trained in pedagogical methods and permitted to teach and observe instruction in the school's practice school in preparation for their own mandatory teaching experiences. In 1878, Armstrong invited Colonel Francis Parker and his students from Quincy, Massachusetts, known for the "Quincy method" of object teaching, to give a teacher's institute. Parker's hands-on methods emphasized students' real-world knowledge and skills. For example, Quincy was known for its granite quarries. Parker used a specimen of granite from their quarries and another from a New Hampshire quarry as the foundation of a conversation lesson in comparison for his students. The children of granite men could tell the difference between the two samples, and in looking closely at the materials with this in mind, were able to understand the nature of physical evidence.[29]

Through the work of Parker's teachers, the students in the normal school were explicitly instructed in how to teach with objects. Of course, this mode of teaching was not exactly what some parents were expecting, even though it was employed in various forms in northern schools. In 1879, the *Southern Workman*, Hampton's newspaper, reported on the new pedagogy: "The object lessons given to the little children of the Butler School this winter by a trained teacher from Col. Parker's famous schools in Quincy, Mass. have proved quite trying to the faith and patience of some of the parents, who thought that because the little ones did not bring home books to study they could not be learning anything."[30] Directing the focus away from literacy was clearly troubling to parents who viewed it as the central goal of primary education and a tool they had been denied under slavery.

Parker's methods could be applied in schools where books might not be readily available. W. E. B. Du Bois described the rural Tennessee schoolroom in which he spent his summers off from Fiske in the 1880s as little more than a log hut, an experience that suggests how basic some of the Hampton students' classrooms would be.[31] Even when teachers could obtain books (and Du Bois taught with Webster's spelling book), object-lessons, object-lesson charts, or reading charts for their students, they did not always last. Caroline F. Putnam, who helped establish and run the Holley School near Lottsburg, Virginia, reported to *Harper's Weekly* in 1874 that her object-lesson charts, along with books and maps, were "torn down from the walls and thrown away" by "rebel hate," presumably to prevent the African American students from learning.[32] Parker's methods addressed a reality that would affect many Hampton graduates who would go on to become teachers. But parents, who wanted their children to learn to read as quickly as possible, did not find these methods acceptable. In Johnston's photograph of a schoolroom scene organized around a lesson on Thanksgiving, the children are constructing a model of a log home and may read writing on the board, but there are no books in the classroom. The lesson likely focused on discussion and observation.[33] Another view of a similar classroom reveals a lesson on cotton, as students learn to twist thread between two fingers. Some desks appear to have books and paper on them, but the emphasis is on the students studying the material properties of raw cotton together. What might such an activity have meant to their families? There was another form of imported object lesson at the Butler School that parents found disconcerting: the Kitchen Garden, a program that had its origins far from Hampton.

Figure 4.3. Frances Benjamin Johnston, [Thanksgiving Day Lesson at Whittier], 1899.
A group of primary students in the Whittier School build a model of a log cabin to study the first Thanksgiving. *Library of Congress, Prints & Photographs Division, LC-USZ62-123937.*

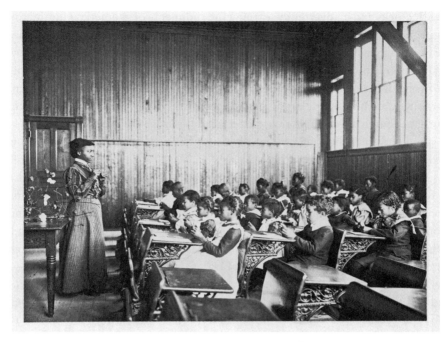

Figure 4.4. Frances Benjamin Johnston, [Lesson on Cotton], 1899. Students twist bolls of cotton between their fingers to understand their material properties. *Library of Congress, Prints & Photographs Division, lot 11051-4.*

Hampton's Kitchen Garden

Domestic education pioneer Emily Huntington described what she viewed as the problem of finding well-trained household help in the introduction to her 1877 book *The Kitchen Garden*. The poor children she taught at the Wilson Industrial School for Girls on the corner of Eighth and Tompkins Square in New York City were not lazy good-for-nothings trying to shirk their lessons in household work. They were not willful Irish "Bridgets" who would tyrannize newly married wives and long for the freewheeling life of a shop girl, often lampooned in the newspapers. Rather, her girls were gloomy. They were anxious and puzzled. Their little faces were "prematurely old." They did not complain, but longed to play. To Huntington, their suffering was obvious. They were not resistant to their lessons but were not able to absorb what she was trying to teach them.

All this changed in 1876 when Huntington visited her first kindergarten class. She went to a class in Henrietta Haines's private school for girls, where Maria Kraus Boelte, a German immigrant, had first established a kindergarten class in 1872.[34] Gazing at a long table full of happy, wealthy children playing with blocks and inadvertently learning the rudiments of geometry, Huntington imagined the same table full of happy potential servants arranging tiny dishes or sweeping with toy brooms tied up with a bright bow. They would learn how to respond to the demands of service without anxiety and would learn how to control their bodies and faces so that no one would know if they were not having fun. Huntington hypothesized that kindergarten methods, designed to teach children about their environments and to train their senses so that they would grow into thinking, feeling adults, could be used to teach poor girls how to feel like servants.[35]

Using the same methods as kindergarten teachers, Huntington devised a "Kitchen Garden" intended to transform the urban children she saw as unhappy working girls into well-trained domestics. The object lessons, songs, dances, and other activities of the Kitchen Garden did not intellectualize this labor. Instead, these activities naturalized service as an innate part of any girl's body through proper training. In the Butler School at Hampton, which served the children—aged six through thirteen—of the local African American community, the program linked somatic training for service to both race and gender, as the Kitchen Garden classes contained an equal number of African American boys and girls.[36] Furthermore, this course fit perfectly with the manual training devised for male and female students of all ages. Just as the Kitchen Garden methods cultivated and defined the sensory qualities that defined domestic workers in the last quarter of the nineteenth century—from responding to a bell and properly salting soup to managing one's emotions—the labor at Hampton trained students' bodies and minds.

The first kindergartens in the United States date to the 1850s and the movement began to take off in the 1870s. Friedrich Froebel, who had studied with Pestalozzi and was the inventor of kindergarten, created the pedagogy as a way of linking children's inner state with their external activities through play.[37] As adapted for the American context by Elizabeth Peabody and others, the pedagogy contained several components designed to teach children about the unity of this inner and outer world. There was music, for singing and dancing, active games that involved various forms of moving in a circle, and the manipulation of "gifts," specific objects designed for play. These gifts included soft balls of primary and secondary colors, wooden balls, boxes of cubes and wooden forms, sticks for stick laying, and peas for pea work; there were also perforated boards for sewing, paper for weaving and folding, patterns for pricking with pins, and clay or wax for molding. Examples of material created in these classes survive to document the nature of these activities. These materials allowed children to create forms of increasing complexity, from solid forms to be arranged in patterns to clay that could be worked and formed into any desired shape. Along with these activities, moral instruction and sometimes gardening completed the children's experience.[38]

Huntington gained more than a clever name for her school when she appropriated the kindergarten concept. She adapted every major component of this system of education for her students and added some aspects of contemporary primary school pedagogy, such as questions and answers and object lessons geared toward older children.[39] Stick-laying, paper folding, arranging objects (similar to building with blocks), paper pricking, and clay molding were all directly adapted for the acquisition of domestic skills. Kindergarten songs such as "Brotherly Love" or "The Cuckoo" were transformed into songs on how to iron or properly sweep a room, as were active games and dances. The curriculum begins with stick-laying and paper folding, easily applied to setting the table and folding napkins, activities that require a sense of order. Rather than follow a diagram, as Miss Huntington had instructed her students before she discovered the kindergarten method, students learned through specifically controlled movements, often keyed to a chord on a piano. As chords were struck they arranged different items. As they practiced, they learned not how to position these items but more important, concepts of straightness and order. This skill is described in a song that went along with these exercises:

> This to straightness trains our eyes
> And we quickly grow so wise
> 'Twill only take a moment's look
> To see the slightest turn or crook.[40]

The pupils were learning how to identify order—whether a crease was straight or cutlery parallel—just as other kindergarten pupils might learn to distinguish primary and secondary colors, or a sphere from a cube. Similarly they came to appreciate the smoothness of properly ironed cloth and the sound of squeaky clean dishes. Not only did they train to respond to music, but they also learned to sing songs, and the songs they learned were intended to help them remember how to properly complete their work, turning the lesson into both an aural and oral experience.

Kitchen Garden students also received "gifts," purchased from Schermerhorn's Educational Bureau on East Fourteenth Street, the same New York City educational supply company that sold traditional kindergarten materials. Like the boxes of blocks given to each child as "gifts" in a kindergarten, in the Kitchen Garden each child had two individual boxes—one containing small dishes and another containing tablecloths, knives, forks, and napkins. They were taught to set the table by chord, a process that linked each activity with a specific chord on the piano. Moving slowly and in unison, the children learned how to neatly remove items from the boxes and properly arrange them on the table. Instead of ordering the blocks in fanciful forms, they positioned the items according to specific rules and knew how to remove them, glassware first, after their pretend meal was complete. Sweeping, washing, ironing, and other skills were taught in similar ways.

Specific kindergarten gifts, like the eleventh gift, were also modified. Instead of pricking lessons that taught children how to prick out pretty pictures, transferring an image from a card to a piece of paper with a needle-like punch—a skill that could be used to transfer patterns—they were taught to prick out butcher's diagrams. A bucolic image of a cow from a kindergarten manual easily became a diagram of beef, with the brisket, the sirloins, and the hind shaft keyed to a numbered list. A happy sheep became mutton, comprised of the shoulder, the neck or rack, the loin, the leg, and the breast; a pig became pork. All were to be carefully copied.[41] Similarly, for the twentieth gift, modeling clay; instead of molding clay into shapes that could teach unity, the notion that a cube could become a sphere of the same mass, they were taught to knead lumps of clay into loaves of bread.[42]

Girls learned how to interact with their potential mistresses through active games that taught them how to react to the bell indicating a caller or how to properly listen to a message—standing to listen intently. "Waiting on Door," a song and active game, had the children gather in a circle; each girl took a turn ringing a bell, a pretend doorbell. Different girls practiced responding to "the door" in an appropriate way, showing the guest into the circle or politely telling her that Mrs. Brown "wishes to be excused." One newspaper account suggests that "mistress" may leave rather long messages to test the memory of the serving girls.

Another song, "Good Manners for Girls," which went along with the molding lessons, a kind of personal molding analogous to the molding of clay, described how girls were to move through the world. As they sang the song, they were to emulate the actions described: The girls were to move with a light step, to speak gently, to bow as they leave, to rise when addressed, to stand quietly with folded hands when spoken to, to conceal their emotions ("Strange those people can't conceal all they know and all they feel/one can read in every look like an open book"), to cross their legs at the ankles, to always hold the door and never let it slam. Another song specifically taught girls when food needed salt. It begins with the seemingly plaintive verse "Oh dear, what can the matter be? Dear! Dear! What can the matter be? Oh dear! What can the matter be," describing a savorless scene in which someone forgot the salt; and it explains what to salt and how the salt should be pounded and sifted.[43]

"A GAME MEANT TO TEACH US TO WAIT ON THE DOOR,
AND SHOW YOU THE WAY IF YOU'VE NOT BEEN BEFORE."

Figure 4.5. "Waiting on the Door" in Emily Huntington, *How to Teach Kitchen Garden; or, Object Lessons in Household Work* (New York: Doubleday, Page & Co., 1903). Kitchen Garden classes taught children how to feel like servants through hands-on activities, games, and songs. *Schlesinger Library, Radcliffe Institute, Harvard University.*

Huntington's Kitchen Garden lessons were devised to help servants feel a certain way, suggesting that specific ways of tasting, touching, hearing, moving, and speaking were considered central qualities of the bodies of servant girls. These lessons emphasized the bodily skills girls needed to identify order and disorder: how to listen to directions and to manipulate materials, how to set a perfect table or shape a round loaf. The students did not simply acquire facts but gradually developed the bodily conceptions of the labor necessary for service.

Perhaps because of its positive associations with the kindergarten—often referred to as the "Paradise of Childhood"—the Kitchen Garden concept spread quickly. More likely, potential employers trusted the rhetoric of kindergarten as a successful and "natural" form of pedagogy that could cultivate unruly children into trained domestics. From the 1870s through the 1910s, press accounts emphasized that girls in these programs were playing with "toys," that learning was fun and natural, and that the program was a success. The positive press accounts of Kitchen Gardens as games obscured the differences between these courses and kindergarten. Instead of children under the age of six, most

Kitchen Gardeners were around ten. Many of these courses could be offered after regular school hours, but for some children there was the suggestion that this was their primary education. An extended treatment of the practice in *St. Nicholas Magazine* in 1881 gets around this sticky issue by creating a main character from a wealthy family who suffers from poor eyesight. Since she could not learn by reading, the Kitchen Garden engaged her other senses, allowing her to learn in spite of her infirmity. Some newspaper commentators claimed that Kitchen Garden graduates did not always go to service but instead married well and were excellent wives and mothers. Hinting that those claims may have been fabricated, Miss Huntington promised to place any girl over the age of twelve in a respectable position upon completion of the course.[44]

The New York Kitchen Garden Association exported the concept to other US cities as a way to deal with what was framed as an increasingly serious servant problem. Before long it appeared in urban areas across the United States, in Canada, and even in Belfast—where it attempted to intercept Irish servants before they immigrated to the United States.[45] In Boston, a Kitchen Garden was opened for the children of the wealthy so that they could learn how to run their households and manage their servants.[46] In 1880, the *New York Times* reported that the Kitchen Garden was on its way down to Hampton Agriculture and Normal Institute. From Hampton, the leaders postulated, the method could be transmitted through its trained teachers throughout the South.

Hampton was an ideal place to begin a Kitchen Garden course. Its "learning by doing" curriculum was heavily inflected with manual training and object-lesson pedagogy. When the program began in its practice school in 1881, Hampton parents railed against this mode of instruction. In the words of Elizabeth Hyde, the principal of the primary school, "Many of the [parents] object to having their children in the 'Kitchen Garden Class' because they think they are being made servants of." These parents, who had higher ambitions for their educated children, were absolutely right. Hyde continued her report, boasting of the Kitchen Garden's success,

> One small boy of twelve who was seen waiting on the door and table so won the heart of one of the lady visitors that he was taken up north to do this work in a beautiful house just outside of Philadelphia. This answers the question sometimes asked: Is it practical to teach boys the Kitchen Garden?[47]

This student's experience, plucked from a classic Kitchen Garden game of "waiting on door," may have been atypical, but it certainly highlights the goals of the program. Not all children would necessarily become servants through this course, but the course intended to teach children how it felt to perform this role.

In spite of early parental protest, the program was very popular with visitors to Hampton. Hyde noted in 1883 that the twice-weekly Kitchen Garden class had received visitors, such as the lady visitor from Philadelphia who employed a Kitchen-Gardener, in every recitation for months, to the point of impeding students' progress.[48] Furthermore, the class could lead to more advanced opportunities for older girls to learn sewing and boys to learn carpentry in the workrooms of the Normal School.[49] Photographs taken nearly two decades later captured this class as a regular part of the school's curriculum. Frances Benjamin Johnston's 1899 photograph captioned "Eight African American children, in kindergarten, learning washing and ironing at Whittier Primary School, Hampton, Virginia" does not mention the industrial nature of the course. It presents small children learning to iron and wash, as if it were a game—their posture and tiny sad irons no different from images published in Kitchen Garden materials.[50] The dollhouse behind the children does not suggest an introduction to an imagined future but is yet another way for them to learn how to put things in their proper place and or how to run a house through play—a form of sense training.[51]

Figure 4.6. Frances Benjamin Johnston, "Eight African American children, in kindergarten, learning washing and ironing at Whittier Primary School, Hampton, Virginia," 1899. The washing and ironing these small children are learning in the Whittier Primary School is closely related to Kitchen Garden lessons designed to train the senses of domestic workers. *Library of Congress, Prints & Photographs Division, LC-USZ62-120667.*

Learning by Laboring

In *Up from Slavery*, Booker T. Washington described his Hampton "entrance examination" as a form of manual labor. When he arrived at Hampton after an arduous journey, he looked like a "worthless loafer or tramp" and had to prove himself through work before he could be admitted to the school. Asked to sweep a room upon arrival, he knew that the task was not simply about cleaning but about knowing how his teacher understood cleanliness. He had to show that he had the ability to understand the requirements of a simple manual task and the ability to clean a space even to the standard of a "'Yankee' woman who knew just where to look for dirt." He had to prove his ability to observe. He dusted the room four times, moved every piece of furniture, and checked each corner and closet. The fact that he framed this task as his entrance exam suggests how physical and mental labor were integrated at Hampton.[52] In the Kitchen Garden, educators tried to naturalize service as part of children's bodies. The work component of the Hampton curriculum pushed these notions further, conflating physical and mental work. Just as object lessons linked sensing and thinking, Hampton linked laboring and learning, the head, heart and hand.

In the early years of the school, Hampton students could expect to conduct farm or mechanical labor for up to five hours a day in addition to taking academic classes.[53] Formal industrial training did not begin at Hampton until later in the school's history, but hard manual work was there from the start to prepare students for the life of labor Armstrong expected its African American graduates to face.[54] Armstrong frequently described the moral goal of this work as developing "industry" and "industrious habits."[55] Ludlow, writing for the school, summarized the object of industrial training in three points. It was to give students a means of earning a living and help them support themselves through school. But, first and foremost, its goal was "to build character: stimulate the mind, form habits of industry, promptitude, accuracy and self help." At Hampton, African American students for whom the work typically funded part or all of their tuition primarily performed this labor. For the most part, native students were funded through government treaties. Ludlow argued that this was a great disadvantage for those native students because it denied them "a valuable means of true education and progress."[56] This linking of physical training with mental growth, not merely the acquisition of skills, links the labor to intellectual and personal development. While different in many ways, at Oswego, E. A. Sheldon also advocated manual training as pedagogically relevant. He lectured on the "mental effect of manual training," not to train children for trades, but as another way of developing children's ability to understand their world and their place in it through the senses.[57]

Representations of labor, in this model, could also be representations of thinking and problem solving. Johnston's well-known, beautifully composed photograph, "Students at work on a house built largely by them," depicts carpenters at work on a staircase. It emphasizes the students' active engagement with all parts of the process, a job that required understanding of materials and a self-awareness that permitted six people to work in tight quarters, even if only for one perfectly staged photograph. Similarly, her related photograph of the exterior of what is possibly the same house under construction depicts the students as if part of a larger working machine.[58]

Images of Hampton students engaged in manual labor, much of which would have been viewed as outmoded by 1899, may suggest a way of representing reasoning that is not obvious to modern viewers. While manual labor was not necessarily an appropriate interpretation or application of this pedagogy at Hampton, intellectual reasoning may still be linked to labor in this context. As depicted in Prang's lithographs of trades and occupations, each aspect of these jobs required specialized tools and skills. While actual manual training is not equivalent to classroom exercises organized around lithographs of trades, there is a shared, underlying interest in the sense-based, experience-based processes of production and a celebration of the inherent value of the labor in both scenarios.

Figure 4.7. Frances Benjamin Johnston, "Students at work on a house built largely by them," 1899. Frances Benjamin Johnston presents Hampton students working collaboratively on a building project, as if each is part of large complex machine. *Library of Congress, Prints & Photographs Division, LC-USZC4-8176.*

Hampton Students as Object Lessons

In addition to learning by a variety of object lessons, Hampton students were transformed into living object lessons during their time at the school. Armstrong said it quite clearly in a report to the American Missionary Society in 1882: "At Hampton there are ninety and at Carlisle there are nearly three hundred Indians—boys and girls—who are learning civilization as an object lesson, and are themselves an object lesson."[59] A *New York Times* article from 1900 put an even finer point on it:

> It is a normal school in the sense that it is intended to teach teachers, but the teachers it turns out are not necessarily engaged in schools; the instruction they receive goes far beyond the usual scope of teachers' work, and the instruction they impart after they go out is of a nature, influence, and variety such as do not exist in the schooling with which we are most of us familiar . . . instruction in honorable and productive labor.

The article continues, "Wherever they are living they are as a rule giving object lessons in honest industry and thrift and in the self-respect that goes with these."[60] The students were supposed to be teachers, but they were to offer instruction both actively in the classroom and passively by example. Hard work learned at Hampton was intended to train graduates to be better able to spread the Hampton idea throughout the South.[61]

Booker T. Washington, Hampton's most famous graduate, often employed the metaphor of the object lesson in his speaking and writing.[62] He was a trained teacher and certainly understood the import and purpose of an object lesson. Washington frequently described graduates of Hampton and similar schools as "object lessons." He relied heavily on this metaphor to argue for the efficacy of normal schools, institutions that could bring the entire South into the classroom. For example, in 1891 he wrote, "Hampton, Tuskegee and other institutions have been able year after year to present to Southern white people object lessons showing the value of an educated colored man, letting them see that an Educated man was a help rather than a hindrance to the progress of the South." Later, when stating the need for "strong Christian leaders who will live among the masses as object lessons" or "a class of leaders who go out among the people as object lessons, as centers of light," he returned again and again to the simple classroom metaphor.[63] Washington and Armstrong frequently applied this metaphor not only to individuals but also to their homes, businesses, and farms. Even Hampton itself would later be described as an object lesson in what an industrial school could become.[64] The pedagogical strategy of object lessons was intended to teach students how to observe and to think, in the process transforming the student into a moral person and thinker. By extension, all members of a community could benefit from this kind of lesson.[65]

The metaphor of the object lesson came into increasingly frequent use by the end of the century, but applying it to the bodies and efforts of teachers conveyed a specific meaning. In some ways it became a material way to argue for respect, equality, and citizenship or recognition of the rights of citizenship. Instead of claiming these rights based on civil rights of inherent equality, the bodies and actions of African American and Native American graduates provided material evidence. They had to offer affirmative evidence of their worth. Object lessons were intended to teach students to observe, leading from the close study of material things to the development of abstract concepts. The material thing was necessary because it captured or crystallized the abstract idea to be developed. To call a Hampton graduate an object lesson was not merely to apply a metaphor but to argue that he or she was the embodiment of the concept of industry or morality. As in any object lesson close study of these individuals could help to develop the theoretical concepts as well as the ability to recognize them through observation. This ideal is discomforting and problematic, then and now, but considered as an idea to be developed, like the idea of pungent through pepper or of elastic through whalebone, the Hampton graduate, as object lesson, embodied a way of thinking as well as a way of being. Armstrong and Washington could employ these trained teachers and industrious workers to spread their message and their mission.[66]

Hampton tried several ways of documenting the material success and abilities of its students. When some of the first Native American boys and girls arrived at Hampton in 1879, Pratt invited the prominent sculptor J. Clark Mills to take casts of the students' heads for the National Museum, just as he had done of the prisoners at Fort Marion.[67] One way Hampton measured and shared the success of its pedagogical methods was through the before and after photographs of students. These photographs depict children dressed in the native clothing they wore upon arrival at Hampton, and later, after training at Hampton, portraits reveal them transformed into "civilized" students who dressed and carried themselves like any city-born, refined, white students. The success of this propaganda relied on a viewer's ability to recognize the visual and material rhetoric of posture, clothing, and facial expression to determine the status of the students on display. Mary Sheldon Barnes's use of before and after pictures of a Hampton student in her popular history schoolbook of primary sources, *Studies in American History* (1891), suggests the ubiquity of this visual rhetoric.[68] The photograph of Louis Firetail, standing in front of his classmates in "tribal" dress, complicates this comparative practice.[69]

INDIAN BOY ON ARRIVAL
AT HAMPTON.

(After a Photograph.)

INDIAN BOY AFTER WORK-
ING AND STUDYING AT
HAMPTON.

(After a Photograph.)

Figure 4.8. "Indian Boy on Arrival at Hampton" and "Indian Boy after Working and Studying at Hampton," in Mary Sheldon Barnes and Earl Barnes, *Studies in American History* (Boston: D. C. Heath, 1893), 384–385. Before and after pictures of Hampton students often emphasized the transformative power of the school by replacing their traditional "Indian" clothing with the Hampton cadet uniform.

An Object Lesson

Frances Benjamin Johnston's photograph of Louis Firetail depicts a class in the midst of an object lesson. Every student gazes intently at Firetail. His teacher holds what appears to be a Sioux rattle like a conductor's baton and leads her class through the exercise. The photograph documents an object lesson in progress; Firetail stares straight ahead, like the eagle behind him, while his fellow students stare at him. This photograph was captioned at some point as a scene from an "American history class" and may depict an exercise similar to pageants and tableaux that took place at Hampton to commemorate historical events.[70] For example, in 1892, as reported in *The Southern Workman*, students celebrated Indian Citizenship Day, which commemorated the passage of the General Allotment Act, or Dawes Act.[71] It included "historical characters of special interest to the Indians well represented both by suitable costumes and speeches." The same article described tableaux performed for Longfellow's birthday from "Evangeline," "Hiawatha," and "The Courtship of Miles Standish," which likely included native characters. Finally George Washington's birthday was celebrated with "old-time costumes." The article continued, "An object lesson of this kind often makes a more vivid and lasting impression than a recitation of history in the class room."[72] Did Firetail perhaps offer a similar kind of "vivid" lesson?

Indian students from Hampton also served as another kind of object lesson. Like the African American students described by Booker T. Washington and the students captured in before and after photographs of students, they served to physically document the power of the Hampton idea. In May 1882, General Armstrong and two of his native students visited members of Congress in Washington, DC, to petition the government to honor treaties made with tribes, to fund schools, to grant individual Indians land, and to recognize Indian legal rights under US law. Prior to *Elk v. Wilkins* (1884), in which the Supreme Court ruled that John Elk could not vote in Nebraska because he was an Indian and therefore not a citizen, the potential of Native Americans to become citizens was in question. As part of this presentation, a Pawnee student and a Shawnee student, dressed in the cadet uniform of Hampton, made a presentation. Described as the "object lesson of the evening," the young men told their own stories before leaving the platform. They returned dressed in "full Indian toggery," speaking to each other in sign language, but their graceful gestures and picturesque appearance was not quite right. A commentator noted, "Their clothing was too clean, their manners too refined. Their first impression was the strongest, and the audience instinctively knew that Hampton had eradicated the savage."[73] By dressing as Indians, they convinced the audience of their civility.[74]

Perhaps Firetail, posing for Johnston's camera as well as for his teacher, served as such an object lesson. On first glance, his costume appears to be generally appropriate to his broadest tribal affiliation. But the different parts of his assemblage are not quite right. The shirt is belted, which is not typical, and may even be worn backward, as the fringe is not falling properly. Neither his shirt nor his leggings fit correctly. His bonnet is made of eagle feathers, but not the typical wing feathers one would expect. His pipe looks as though it could be Lakota, his necklace or breastplate appears to be Blackfoot Crow, and the designs on his pipe bag are likely eastern woodlands. Even his teacher, who leads the class with a rattle in her hand, holds the item upside down.[75] Firetail probably knew these things as he posed for the camera.

Firetail had been at Hampton since September 1897, roughly two years prior to this photograph. He had spent the previous summer in western Massachusetts learning to be a farmer.[76] His hair is likely a wig, as it would have been cut on arrival, and he probably knew his classmates far more intimately than his rigid stance may suggest. It is likely, however, that he had a no more personal relationship with the objects he wore than with the natural history specimens on the table behind him. In fact, Frances Benjamin Johnston's photography collection includes a photograph of another young man wearing the very same shirt.[77]

There is another image of Louis Firetail in the Hampton archives, taken three years later by an anonymous photographer. In the 1902 photograph taken on the Crow Creek reservation in South Dakota after he left Hampton, his face is hidden by his hat, but his dress could not be more different from the Johnston image. His thick striped tie, wide brimmed hat, and watch fob suggest an assimilated and quite fashionable man. This photograph was possibly taken to document his wedding to Minnie Finley, a Caddo Indian from Oklahoma who graduated from the Carlisle Indian School in 1899 and worked as a seamstress.[78] Their September 1902 wedding was reported in the *New York Times* because a white schoolteacher on their reservation married a native man at the same time. The photograph in his Hampton student file shows a similarly dressed young man. In his file he is described simply as "farming, nice wife and children." In correspondence with Hampton, Firetail described his work as a carpenter in South Dakota and his plan to build a house using the skills he honed at school. He wrote to Hampton in 1902 that an increase in his salary gave him "renewed energy and determination to uphold the Hampton idea."[79]

Figure 4.9. "Mr. and Mrs. Louis Firetail, Crow Creek Reservation, South Dakota 1902," glass slide. This shadowy image of a glass lanternslide provides a glimpse of Louis Firetail (later Fire) and his new wife, Minnie Finley, at Crow Creek, South Dakota, on the occasion of their wedding. *Hampton University Archives.*

Figure 4.10. Louis Firetail student record photograph. Louis Firetail's photograph from his student file at Hampton presents a fashionable young man wearing his choice of clothing—not his cadet uniform or the costume Frances Benjamin Johnston photographed him wearing. *Hampton University Archives.*

Louis and Minnie Firetail are photographed leaning against a fence. In this scene there is nothing obviously "Indian" about this young couple. Several years earlier a missionary described the role of educated young Native Americans at the Crow Creek reservation. She described educated young couples like the Firetail (sometimes Fire Tail and later simply Fire) family:

> I could show you home after home, occupied by Hampton students, built by themselves and beautifully kept. The young men and women in them are models—anybody might be proud of them. They are object lessons to their own people and show to others what can be made of Indians.[80]

These competing images of Louis Firetail could act as two different kinds of object lessons, Crow Creek at Hampton, Hampton at Crow Creek. Louis, it seems, was able to negotiate both worlds.

Johnston's publicity photographs suggest that various iterations of object lessons continued to be central to Hampton's curriculum and self-image at the end of the century. At the Paris Exposition of 1900 her photographs won a grand prize as part of the American Negro Exhibition. Along with photographs of prominent and successful African Americans and information about their accomplishments, incomes, and professions, her photographs helped document the school's success.[81] At Hampton, the phrase "object lesson" was shorthand for a series of pedagogical goals that encompassed more than empirical evidence. Johnston's images appear to depict students laboring or, in Louis Firetail's case, as objects. An understanding of object lesson pedagogy suggests a more dynamic, if ambiguous, view of these images: manual labor could be a mode of thinking; Firetail's costume a document of his civility. Object teaching instructed students in how to interpret bodies and labor as well as material and visual culture, both inside and outside the classroom.

In March 1894, Booker T. Washington, then president of the Tuskegee Normal School, shared the stage at Carnegie Hall with US president Grover Cleveland. The men were there to support the Home Missions of the Presbyterian Church by asking for financial support for schools and churches throughout the South. In particular they requested funds to supply impoverished communities with living object lessons. Washington offered his audience a success story that they could help replicate throughout the Black Belt:

> Go with me into their Church and their Sunday-School, through the model farm and house of this teacher, and I will show you a community that has been redeemed, revolutionized in industry, education, and religion by reason of the fact that they had this leader, this guide, this object lesson to show them how to direct their own efforts.[82]

The educated graduate proved the ability of African Americans to be full moral and economic citizens. Simultaneously, this object lesson or community leader both taught and embodied the skills inherent in citizenship. The idea of the object lesson adeptly conveyed these interrelated goals. Both presidents understood the utility of the term.

5

Objects and Ideas

In 1892, presidential candidate Grover Cleveland produced a pair of object lessons to protest the McKinley tariff, a law designed to protect American products with high duties on many competing foreign imports. Like the classroom lessons with which the American electorate had grown up in the preceding decades, Cleveland's lessons relied on the close study of a material thing: two rectangles of tin, one of the commodities most heavily taxed by the tariff (Plates 18 and 19). Roughly the size of a trade card, the tins featured Cleveland's and Adlai Stevenson's pictures on one side, printed on a rectangle of paper affixed to the tin. On the reverse of the tin cards, two different, detailed object lessons are printed on the cards in black lettering. The different texts offered competing stories about the tin on which they were printed. Like the classroom object lessons that aimed to teach children about the origin of the everyday items that surrounded them, these lessons explained in clear, easy-to-understand terms the meaning of tin and the inequity of the tariff. The cards offered an understanding of what tin actually was, where it came from, how it was produced, how it compared to similar substances, and how it was used. This information, particularly the foreign and domestic aspects of its production and use, aligns closely with the kind of object lesson a child might receive on this substance in school. Qualities like "foreign" or "domestic" may not be sensibly observed in material things, but they were still qualities of objects, taught along with details of an object's material or social history. Instead of explaining the swelling national surplus, the unfairness of protectionism, or the uneven interests of American manufacturers, Cleveland employed an object lesson to show how this law affected Americans through the social life of a single commodity.[1]

The development of the American tin industry was one of the central goals of Ohio congressman William McKinley's Tariff Bill of 1890. Prior to the passage of the bill, there were no tinplate mills in the United States and most tinplate was imported from Cornwall, England. The high duties the tariff placed on foreign tin created an incentive to develop an American industry. It might drive up prices in the short term, advocates argued, but in the long term it would lower the cost. Tin was partially to blame for McKinley's loss of his Ohio congressional seat in 1890. The bill was passed only four weeks before the election and could not have dramatically affected the cost of tin by that time on its own. McKinley's local Democratic opponent preyed on anxieties and supposedly bribed peddlers to inflate the cost of tin wares to five times their pretariff cost before the election.[2] Since any potential benefits of the tariff were not yet apparent by Cleveland's 1892 campaign, tin remained a common political target.

The two object lessons are printed on identical tin cards, but lesson one is identified as made from "imported tin plate" while the other is identified as from "'American' tin plate," the former costing consumers an added duty of 73⅓ percent, the latter a commodity protected by this extensive tariff. Directed by the title "A McKinley Tariff Object Lesson," an observer would know to examine and compare the physical nature of the cards. The printed text mandates a close physical examination. The text on the back of the first object lesson is printed in four triangles that lock together to form a rectangle. To read the lesson one must read from top to bottom, then from the left to the center and the right to the center. Additional details are printed in a border that wraps around the edge of the central text. To read the text, a reader is forced to rotate the card. The second object lesson is printed vertically in a list of six steps. Again, the border wraps around the inner text, forcing the reader to rotate the card, emphasizing its shape and form. Their identical material qualities highlight the irony behind their competing identification as foreign versus domestic.

Card one explained the broad function of tin in the daily lives of everyday Americans. It is shaped into the cans and boxes that hold farmers' tomatoes, peaches, and peas and that preserve the lobsters, oysters, and salmon caught by industrious fisherman. It is the main material in the workingman's lunch pail, which he carries to his daily job, and the metal that is shaped into the saucepans and cooking utensils used by his wife as she prepares her family's meals. The tax on this simple imported material, when seen through the lens of its consumption, hurts average Americans. Farmers, fisherman, and workingmen and their wives eventually pay the 73⅓ percent hike in price.

Card two emphasized the production of tin as opposed to its use. In its focus on so-called American tin plate, this story highlights the many foreign steps in its production as it walks the reader through the story of this simple commodity's manufacture. Like the geographical histories of objects, this lesson offered a global history of a common everyday item including stops in Great Britain, Africa, and Australia. Many Americans, even then, may not have realized that the substance commonly called "tin" was short for tinned sheet iron. The printed object lesson went through six steps in the transformation of these sheets of metal into the tin used for cans and lunch buckets. First the great sheets of steel, the substructure for the tin, were made in Great Britain and imported into the United States. The tin that was to cover these sheets was produced in and imported from Australia. The "Tinning-pot," the machine used to cover the steel sheets with tin, itself was imported from Great Britain. The oil used to grease this machine came from Africa. Even the men working this machine, Cleveland claims, were imports, in violation of the Contract Labor Law. The sixth and final point made about its production, "The boys and girls who wait on these men are the only representatives of American labor employed in the making (?) of this 'American' tin plate," emphasizes the foreignness of its production. Only American children, who should be in school benefiting from such a complex object lesson, earn a pittance from this protected "American" commodity.

Cleveland's two sheets of tin were not the only object lessons employed to protest the tariff. The metaphor became one of critics' most common ways to levy commodity-based protests against the legislation. By the 1890s, most Americans were familiar with this basic way of reasoning from things through their own education or that of their children. The physical object lessons may not always survive, as in the case of Cleveland's tin cards, but descriptions of protests against the tariff highlight the utility of the object-lesson metaphor. In 1891, the *New York Times* reported that large sheets of "American tin" were displayed as an "object lesson" in the success of the tariff behind a large, plate glass window of the *New York Press*. Both the glass and the tin were protected by high duties on their foreign counterparts. Playing with the object-lesson metaphor, the tongue-in-cheek reporter described how the American tin, "hard to get hold of and slippery to hang on to," was dropped and shattered the window. Passersby joked that they never knew American tin, still a nascent industry, was "so substantial."[3]

Jewelers and others who worked in silver claimed their own "object lesson" on the McKinley tariff when they discovered the high duty placed on the specific kind of silver tissue paper used to prevent their products from tarnishing. Lime and other elements had to be extracted from this pure white paper for it to be a useful substance with which to wrap their shipped goods. After twenty-five years of effort, American manufacturers had yet to master this process, leading to widespread frustration. Silversmiths described the result of their attempts: their wares would arrive at their destination with "spots" because of the inferior paper. The American silversmiths and jewelers who created American products for American consumers had no choice but to pay high duties on paper imported from England.[4]

In addition to tin, glass, and paper, the dry goods industry provided a further "impressive object lesson" on the real cost of the tariff. One of these lessons consisted of an exhibition in which bolts of cloth, lengths of carpet, and examples of hosiery and blankets were displayed with specific labels as to their increased cost under the tariff. The black alpaca, transformed into dresses by the wives of laborers and mechanics, increased in cost by 115 percent. A sample of woolen suiting, a wardrobe staple described to the *Times* as "just what a working man would like to have for his best Sunday suit," went up in price from $0.45 a yard to $1.45, for the same fabric. The textiles on display served as a concrete example of who was paying the high tariff. The satin purchased by the rich man's wife had a duty of 50 percent; the mechanic's wife, less able to afford the high price, paid a duty of more than 93 percent for simple black cashmere.[5] American carpet manufacturers relied on imported wool to make their carpets. Though made and sold in America, these carpets were woven out of British wool, a textile tradition centuries old, and wool in the necessary quantity was not readily available in the United States. Fire sales of overstock carpets too expensive to be sold in secondary markets in South America or even to most consumers, provided object lessons on the state of the crippled industry.[6]

At the same time, proponents of the tariff also employed their own object lessons to argue for the power of protection. In March 1892, William Bowers, a Republican member of Congress from California, delivered "a Tariff Object Lesson" to the floor of the House in the form of a fifty-pound block of tin made in California. As a *Los Angeles Times* writer described, "It is getting to be quite the thing to furnish illustrations . . . by ocular demonstrations" to support a pro-protection argument. This material argument was intended to uphold the position that the United States could supply its own tinware.[7]

Writers frequently drew on the trope of the object lesson to make their point about how the division between foreign and domestic goods was not as easily or as thickly drawn as the McKinley tariff presumed. Goods defined as foreign were not necessarily bad for domestic industry, and the articles produced domestically were not necessarily protected or aided by the high tariffs. These lessons relied on a nuanced understanding of the history of commodities and trade networks. The notion of foreign versus domestic, like natural versus artificial or even animal versus vegetable, was a central point of pedagogy in object lessons. Teachers believed these ideas should be part of the close study of objects, even if the details were difficult or impossible to discover simply from classroom observation. Objects helped to create a material geography for children that went beyond the simplistic notions that pungent ginger root grew far away and fresh, brown eggs came from the farm just out of town. The actual material qualities, functions, and production history of material things, when examined via object lessons, gave students the opportunity to create original compositions based around material things. These essays were based on an individual's own observations or opinions and required children to identify and then explain in their own words the complex stories embedded in or swirling around material things. These object-based stories were an ideal way to address the problems of the McKinley tariff. More broadly, they taught several generations of children to look to objects for answers, or at least questions, about the meaning of daily life.

The stories children were taught to spin around objects help explain the highly symbolic world of the late nineteenth-century home. Objects in this environment often signified themselves and something more: discernment, wealth, taste, family, and history.[8] Museums and world's fairs in this period also relied on object-based epistemology to create material stories about commerce, history, and natural history.[9] This museum context is one of the few places scholars have located what they thought of as object lessons, limiting the definition of this historical practice to places—museum galleries or the World's Columbian Exhibition—where most academics believe objects were intended to instruct. However, this presumption overlooks the ways generations of children were taught to draw information from material things found in everyday settings. Furthermore, advertisers and manufacturers depended on these lessons to create the desire for and to sell products.

In an object lesson—which moved from observation to the identification of the qualities of objects, to the discussion of qualities not perceived through the senses, to the categorization and comparison of objects, and finally to composition—children were supposed to learn specific ways of approaching the material world, particularly commodities, and how to move from making observations to finding meaning in objects. It was not simply that children were taught new ways to draw information out of material things but that they were given a language through which they could consider the potential meanings of things, a language and a mode of looking that shaped larger cultural patterns and concerns.

This kind of learning may be unfamiliar to twenty-first-century academics, increasingly dependent on keyword and full-text searches to conduct research. But an understanding of and comfort with the non-lexical, the value of pausing before a thing as well as a text, is at the center of the intellectual, social, and cultural history of late nineteenth-century America. Examination of early psychological theories, fiction, and marketing suggests that object lessons document a historical way of thinking—or "thinging"—grounded on the material world. This approach to the concrete gave children and adults a way to make sense of the diverse things at the center of late-nineteenth-century capitalism.

Commodity Training

The list of items covered by the 1890 tariff bill reads like the opening pages of an early object-lesson manual. In its attempt to enumerate every important imported commodity, it includes a long list of obscure and ordinary things, from cochineal and cocoons to porcelain and magnets.[10] The detailed listing of items is a key to a material description of each import and notation on how it would be taxed under the tariff, just as the table of contents in many object manuals linked items like tortoise shell and starch to lessons on those topics. Perhaps this visual similarity added to the desire to read each commodity listed as a sort of object lesson. More important, it highlights the commodity status of most of the substances included in lessons on objects in the manuals of Mayo, Sheldon, Calkins, and others.

Though object lessons rarely emphasized the precise exchange value of the items studied, the focus on production, country of origin, and use value suggested various commodity situations in which these objects might be placed. The labor that went into producing them, the distance they had to travel, and the function they served in various contexts was all part of their biographies and the compositions children were instructed to write about them in the classroom. In some ways, object lessons as education on commodities may be understood as a way to allay fears about the control of an increasingly abstract and distant market. This facet of object lessons makes the practice directly applicable to understanding and interpreting the material world outside the classroom.[11]

The eventual goal of most object lessons was the creation of compositions about material things. At the Oswego Normal School, Sheldon trained teachers to talk children through the observation of objects so they would learn to describe the qualities of the object they were examining and to contextualize and organize that information. Teachers were to place objects in front of children and to lead them, using careful questions, through a study of the object including its "natural history, manufacture, or composition [the material composition of the object]." Material things in various states were supposed to be displayed for the course of the lesson. For example, if the composition lesson was to be on flax, Sheldon directed that "the plant itself, the fibers when separated from the stem, the thread when spun, and the various articles into which it is manufactured, may be brought before the class and likewise a picture of the machinery employed in the manufacture."[12]

After working through a conversation and questions and answers on each of these topics, teachers instructed their pupils to write compositions about flax, testing students' comprehension and ability to organize the information. These lessons were geared toward older children, over the age of ten. The goal of the lesson would be to help them develop their ability to make sense of a material thing and simultaneously to see the raw substance—flax—transformed into useful products they might encounter on a daily basis. While the goal was sense training, the process offered its own material lessons. This lesson might not directly prepare students for understanding the difference between a hemp carpet and a burlap bag, which would be taxed differently under the tariff, but it would provide an introduction to the commodity's history and possible functions.[13]

The items at the center of most object lessons on qualities could be easily purchased by teachers in their own communities, leading to lessons on the items students and their parents would likely purchase and use. For example, N. A. Calkins declined to sell a set of objects for teachers in his *Object Teaching Catalog* because he wanted teachers to purchase the items locally. He recommended they collect "sand paper, window glass, India rubber, blotting paper, whalebone, leather, a steel spring, rattan, sponge, wool, sugar, a stick of candy, gum arabic, mustard, pepper, cloves, alum, salt, coffee and lead" from their communities.[14] Furthermore, his lessons on pictures, particularly the exercises he composed for the "Trades and Occupations" project he completed with Louis Prang, encouraged children to study laborers in their own communities while learning the process through which labor could become a product, whether through the creation of clothing in a tailor's shop or pies in a kitchen.[15] The labor becomes crystallized as part of the object's meaning and value. In this way, classroom lessons provide the stories explaining common commodities even as they developed children's sensory and reasoning abilities.

An example from the Bancroft Bros. Object-Lesson Cards further develops the notion that object-study may be linked to understanding the biography of objects in children's lives. A lesson on the rubber tree links an engraving of the unfamiliar tree to a common comb, a rubber band, a piece of gutta percha, a rubber stamp, and rubberized cloth. The objects are arrayed around a scene in which men gather sap from the huge rubber trees that is then exported to make inexpensive, disposable articles. The scene is generic, the shirtless men could be gathering sap anywhere hot, where (as noted in the text) the average temperature falls between 73 and 94 degrees. Different rubbers (which grow in different places) are appropriate for different applications and have been put to different uses through thousands of patents. The lesson may describe the innovations of Mr. Mackintosh in Glasgow and Charles Goodyear in Massachusetts, but these changes in consumption are not described as affecting the men from South America and some parts of Asia and Africa who were responsible for extracting the sap. The story is about the transformation of sap into common commodities. The information in this lesson cannot be determined through observation, but the objects themselves are linked to this story of production. Students learned to ask specific questions about the origins and history of the items around them that they might use to comb their hair or organize a bundle of papers.[16]

A lesson on tin produced for the Oliver and Boyd Object-Lesson Cards offered a similar biography of the substance. A hunk of tin ore, a toy tin dish, and a pewter child's gravy boat suggest possible states for the metal. Oliver

BANCROFT BROS. & CO'S OBJECT-LESSON CARDS.

VEGETABLE KINGDOM, No. 7.

RUBBER TREE.

Rubber Comb.
Rubber Cloth.
Elastic Cloth.

Gutta Percha.
Rubber Band.
Impression from Rubber Stamp.

India rubber, or Caoutchouc, is a product of the milky sap of certain kinds of trees and shrubs. It was first brought to the notice of the Europeans by the voyages of Columbus, who found the native Indians using it for various purposes, such as making bottles and shoes and smearing cloth with it to make the cloth water-proof. It is obtained from various trees growing in tropical parts of Asia, Africa and America. The best varieties, possessing great elasticity and durability, are the Para, Ceara and the Madagascar rubbers. The Para rubber is the best. It is obtained from a tree that grows in the thick, tropical forests of the Amazon valley. The tree is found in districts the temperature of which averages from 89° to 94° at noon and is never lower than 73° at night, and where it seldom happens that a period of more than ten days passes without rain. It grows to the height of 60 feet or more. The sap is collected in the dry season, between August and February. It is allowed to run from cuts made in the tree into cups placed to receive it. A clay mold is coated with the sap by being dipped into it and is then exposed to fire. The milk evaporates, leaving the rubber sticking to the mold. This operation is repeated until a sufficient amount of rubber is obtained and the mold is then broken.

Caoutchouc was first used by Europeans for erasing lead pencil marks. Hence its name "Rubber." Its use was confined almost exclusively to this purpose until the invention of water-proof **cloth**, called "mackintosh," by Mr. Mackintosh, at Glasgow, in 1823. To make this, one side of each of two pieces of cloth is smeared with rubber and the coated sides are then placed together and made to cohere by being pressed between rollers. The use of rubber was further increased by the discovery of the process of vulcanizing it. In this process the rubber is combined with a certain amount of sulphur, under the influence of great heat. The process was discovered by Charles Goodyear of Massachusetts, in 1843. Unvulcanized rubber becomes stiff and loses its elasticity under the influence of cold and becomes soft when exposed to warm weather and is very adhesive. Vulcanizing the rubber removes these difficulties and also increases its elasticity. Since the discovery of this process the uses of rubber have become innumerable. There are some two or three thousand patented applications of it. It is used for water-proof clothing and boots, for machinery belts and **rubber bands**, for **combs** and ornaments, for water hose and in many other ways. Its use for making **stamps** is a new and important one.

Gutta Percha is very much like rubber and is the product of the sap of a tree found in the Malay Peninsula. It is, however, not elastic. One of its most important uses has been for insulating telegraph wires, but in this use it is gradually being superseded by rubber.

BANCROFT BROS. & CO., PUBLISHERS, 120 SUTTER ST., SAN FRANCISCO.

Copyright, 1889, by Bancroft Bros. & Co.

Figure 5.1. "Rubber Tree," No. 7 from *Bancroft Bros. & Co.'s Object-Lesson Cards on the Vegetable, Animal, and Mineral Kingdoms, etc.* Lessons on substances like rubber linked raw materials to the creation of familiar commodities, like combs and rubber bands. *Cotsen Children's Library, Department of Rare Books and Special Collections, Princeton University Library, Princeton, NJ ([CTSN] E-000024).*

and Boyd's printed lesson on tin started with its historical uses, on the shields and breastplates of Homeric heroes, and traced its story through the production process of tin and tinplate goods, as well as that of related metals like pewter, Britannia, and bell metal. The printed composition, like the lessons on the back of the Cleveland object lessons, encompassed geography, production, and function.

The Philadelphia Commercial Museum, founded to permanently house the collections brought together for the World's Columbian Exposition of 1893 in Chicago, offered its own range of object lessons on commercially important substances. In addition to displaying and sorting objects from all over the world in the museum, in 1900, the staff created traveling museum boxes to be sent to hundreds of schools throughout Pennsylvania. The cabinets were designed for the documentation of a full world of commodities and the relationships among people, processes, and nations those items may suggest. The boxes were intended to support a clear pedagogical goal, "Commercial Education is a very large subject and can be divided into a great many branches. It is well however to begin in earlier years to learn something of those articles upon which commerce is based." The large cases consisted of a series of glass-covered drawers filled with varied substances; some contained an open cabinet for mounted photographs. The materials in the drawers were arranged in the following categories: "cereals, vegetable fibers, such as cotton; animal fibers, such as wool; food adjuncts, such as coffee and pepper; woods, minerals, and pictures illustrating the production and transportation of articles which enter into commerce."[17] The accompanying photographs included images of agricultural and manufacturing processes from around the world. As with other kinds of visual object lessons, the pictures provided supplementary information about the substances in the boxes, animating them in ways impossible for the raw materials to do alone. Unlike the cabinets designed to support Mayo's lessons from the 1850s, these collections were about conveying information about and the relationships among various substances.[18]

In each of these cases the study of objects led children to think about the origins and biographies of the material things they encountered every day. This material study led them to see things around them not merely as opaque substances but as things transformed into the subject of sustained analysis and consideration. The lessons tethered everyday commodities to concrete material stories. This analysis transformed their materiality and history into a biography, defining the relation between a person and thing as sets of stories and potential values. This relationship suggests the broad utility of object lessons as a way to think about and to talk about the material world more generally.[19]

Figure 5.2. Workers pack cabinets with drawers of natural history specimens. The Philadelphia Commercial Museum shipped collections of objects to schools throughout Pennsylvania. *Commercial Museum scrapbook, Courtesy of the Commercial Museum Collection, J. Welles Henderson Archives and Library, Independence Seaport Museum.*

A Pot of Green Feathers

An object lesson was an attempt to lead a child to a correct understanding of the meaning and history of a material thing. But, just as politicians and teachers worried about whether a consumer or a child might fully understand the real implications of the tariff or the meaning and origin of rubber through a material lesson, early experimental psychologists worried over the limits and possibilities of a person's perceptive abilities. In September 1882, G. Stanley Hall conducted an ambitious inquiry which he titled "Survey of the Contents of Children's Minds" in the Boston primary schools. He tried to discover how children actually perceived and understood their material and visual world prior to entering primary school. Inspired by a similar German study, he wanted to determine what children, particularly urban children, actually believed and how "concepts arising from their immediate environment" shaped their beliefs. The study was intended to serve the practical purpose of helping teachers know what their students actually knew upon arriving in school. This research, considered the first empirical, scientific study of children, is often described as the origin of the child study movement in the United States.[20] It also provided a new "scientific" foundation for object lessons and other forms of object-based study.[21]

Hall's researchers asked students 134 questions ranging from queries about their familiarity with animals, counting, color, and geology to the function of body parts or common religious conceptions. The study, which, like many of Hall's later studies, would not be considered scientific by today's standards, judged children as "ignorant" or "not ignorant" about these topics; respondents were grouped by gender, whether they were Irish or American, and whether they had previously attended kindergarten. Hall discovered that children had limited understanding and many misperceptions of a wide range of knowledge and experiences. Students were asked whether they had seen a watchmaker at work, knew where cotton goods came from, or could describe worms or rainbows. Some of their central confusions concerned the relationship between representation and reality, a problem particularly acute when applied to the study of the country or the natural world. For example, when asked to describe a cow, some children knew what it was, but believed it was merely the size of a fingernail, the size it might appear in children's books.

Other confusions stemmed from an ignorance of country life. The belief that skeins of wool grew on the backs of sheep and potatoes on trees or that butter came from buttercups hinted to Hall that urban children were benighted without instructive trips to the countryside. Still other questions suggested a misunderstanding of broader concepts, like the relationship between night and day or the notion that God took people to heaven in a balloon. The children were not completely incorrect to believe a worm swam through the earth; they merely applied their understanding of swimming fish to burrowing annelids. Hall hinted that Don Quixote's insistence that a windmill was a giant or a flock of sheep an army was not an issue of faulty perception but an indication of his particular experiences and worldview.[22] Shaping children's experiences by offering them object lessons or the chance to watch a tradesman at work and to travel to the countryside helped them develop a new knowledge base, stocking their minds with perceptions.

Hall aligned children's confused notions about the world with ideas about apperception, noting that children had these misimpressions because of their own limited but unique lives. Hall identified these "half-assimilated impressions, half right, half wrong" as problems that could be addressed through modern pedagogical methods. Unlike earlier advocates of object teaching, Hall did not necessarily accept that one could get the correct, true idea of an object through simply observing it. Instead, he believed one's own experiences and perhaps even those of one's race provided a context.[23] He recognized that the training of one's senses was crucial, if subjective, complicated, and unpredictable—just as they had been for Pestalozzi as he attempted to educate his son.[24]

The idea of apperception rested on this complexity. Drawing on German philosophy, it was initially employed to explain how individuals responded to and synthesized external stimuli in the context of their unique collection of experiences, as opposed to passively accepting an overly simplistic version of Lockean sense perception, which held that things could simply be imprinted on the mind. Thinkers like German philosopher and pedagogue J. F. Herbart emphasized that perception was a "process" as opposed to a discrete act.[25] The theory of apperception emphasized the role of the mind in making sense of the external material world. For example, early experimental psychologists such as Wilhelm Wundt and his students attempted to understand the connection between stimulus and response by timing subjects' reactions and attention to stimuli under different conditions. Psychologists and later educators believed variations of his theory could help explain how children learned new ideas, and in the case of Hall, how they acquired "half-assimilated impressions."[26]

In 1891, the British educator T. G. Rooper characterized the problem of observation-based conclusions in his pamphlet *Apperception*, subtitled "A Pot of Green Feathers." Republished in *School and Home Life* (1896), it was one of the first popular English-language treatments of Herbart's theories of apperception.[27] Rooper's essay was inspired by an object lesson he had witnessed several years earlier in which a student-teacher presented a class of young children with a fern. A young girl raised her hand and told the teacher it was "a pot of green feathers." Rooper argued that the girl's impression was not false, as it was based on her earlier experiences. She knew feathers, but not feathery ferns. Her experiences led her to wrongly identify the item. Rooper challenged parents and object teachers to offer children patterns of objects, showing them a variety of ferns or several different kinds of fish, to help children organize their sense perceptions.[28] Instead of suggesting object lessons as a simple answer to the problem, he revealed how sense training could help create patterns of thinking about the material world.

In a subsequent essay, "Object Teaching, or Words and Things," Rooper further addressed this challenge by examining how object teaching worked in the world beyond the classroom. He addressed the problem he introduced in *Apperception*: children and adults do not necessarily learn from what they observe or agree on the content of their observations. Rather, each individual matches his or her observations to previous experiences and knowledge. The object only "mediates" those experiences. He noted, "Something is supplied by the object and something else is supplied by the mind."[29] The actual object helped the viewer synthesize and understand old and new information by reminding the viewer of things seen before and potentially introducing a new concept. Unlike the arguments of educators earlier in the century that object lessons would counteract rote memorization or replace misperceptions with actual perceptions, Rooper viewed this process as teaching students "to come to a keen many-sided, and accurate observation of a familiar thing."[30]

Rooper's text opens with a real-world example to illustrate this split between an actual object and an observation of it. He described the visit of the German empress to London. During her visit four newspapers reported different descriptions of her dress. The *Times* noted that she wore gold brocade; the *Daily News* praised her "sumptuous white silk dress." The *Standard* described her "light mauve" dress, while the *Daily Chronicle* puzzled, "To us it seemed almost a sea-green, and yet there was now a cream and now an ivory sheen to it."[31] While one might dismiss the varied descriptions as plays of light on an iridescent, luxurious fabric, Rooper used this example to emphasize the point that the state of the eyewitness observer is as important as the object of his or her gaze. Though this may seem to be a potential threat to the efficacy of object lessons as classroom practice, Rooper advocated object lessons as a way to understand how one might relate sense perceptions to the information one may already have. To put it more broadly, object lessons helped explain how one could use previous experiences and sense perceptions to interpret the wider material world, whether fabric or feathers, beyond the walls of the classroom. For authors and advertisers, this broad applicability could shape the impressions of readers and potential customers.

Metaphors and Marketing

Object lessons appeared out of a classroom context as a useful metaphor before and long after Hampton students traveled the South as living lessons or Grover Cleveland employed them in his 1892 presidential campaign. The common classroom practice became a way to talk about learning from observation and from experience more broadly, offering a synthesis of information derived from direct observation coupled with the viewer's own memories and ideas. Authors, who may have first learned to write through object lessons in primary schools, adopted the concept as a literary trope and frequently employed it in short stories and essays starting in the 1860s. Sometimes the "object lesson" referred to a discrete material thing that taught the characters in a story a lesson, like the shrunken head of a murdered Peruvian paramour or a large shop bill translated into piles of silver coins to teach a wastrel wife the value of money.[32] It was often employed most effectively as a framing device, through which authors could describe their characters and narratives and teach their readers how to perceive and judge their subjects. For people who had grown up with the concept that it was better to be gently led to your own conclusion based on observation than to simply be force-fed new ideas, the object lesson became a useful way to teach the buying public what it wanted. Advertisers employed the concept to train potential customers in how to look at and desire their products.

An 1864 essay in the *Prairie Farmer*, published just a few years after Sheldon began to popularize object lessons in the United States, establishes how the idea of the object lesson may be useful to the storyteller. In "An Object Lesson," a young woman "rehearse[s] an 'object lesson' on the brick block opposite." Looking out her window onto her neighbors, she drew specific visual evidence from observing the dentist, piano teacher, and engraver who lived across from her on the second floor. She learned about their trades as well as their goals and character.[33] She reasoned like a detective, carefully noting the dress of the individuals, their age, station, and demeanor. As if anticipating the classic Alfred Hitchcock film *Rear Window*, she created stories based on what she saw: the shabby calico of a shop girl's dress could not be replaced until after she paid to have her tooth filled; a diamond-clad matron paid a thousand dollars for a new piano; an engraver tried to get as much work out of the limited daylight as possible. In each case the idea of the object lesson—precise observation, noting the qualities of certain individuals, finding patterns and drawing conclusions— allowed the observer to describe a scene that also told a story.

In "Object Lessons," another fictional story, published in *Godey's Lady's Book* in 1874, writer Tetia Moss described the havoc and unhappiness a group of fashionable, riotous, unchaperoned city women brought to their country carriage driver and themselves on a summer jaunt. The tools of the object lesson, she explained, were not simply good for the classroom. Rather, they were always useful because "those things that are seen and clearly understood are more readily laid away in that memory of ours." Not unlike the classroom picture lessons drawn out of religious or moral scenes published as lithographs by the ASSU, this verbal sketch offered a clear lesson, pieced together from its many descriptive details.[34] Moss's story, outlined on a metaphorical blackboard "from which no hand can ever erase the marks," linked the behavior of the rowdy women to the fate of one of their party, who ends up in a hasty marriage. In this tale, like the above example from *Prairie Farmer*, women were encouraged to use the object lesson to learn more about their communities, to assess what was happening around them, and to make judgments based on their own conclusions. The learning was not happening in the schoolroom, but they took its lessons and applied them to their daily lives. The ability to apply the lessons in observation acquired through the careful study of things in the schoolroom to daily life was one of the highest ambitions for object teachers.[35]

Just as powerfully, object lessons shaped how businesses marketed their products to consumers. A *Washington Post* article from the 1880s explored this aspect of applied object-lesson pedagogy. The essay analyzed images used in advertising as object lessons, noting that in "this pictorial age . . . the object lesson is not confined to the Kindergarten." The article went on to describe the object-lesson cards that came in tobacco products that helped instruct innocent youth about buxom, toothy beauties.[36] These object lessons, typically in the form of images of provocatively dressed women, clearly relied on another kind of sensory education: the physical, material, and sensual appeal that drove a consumer to desire a product. In fact, the idea of the object lesson itself was broadly incorporated into advertisements starting in the 1880s, in trade cards, magazines, and newspapers.

Bright, chromolithographed trade cards embraced the instructive possibilities of object lessons. Trade cards were the most popular form of advertising in the United States in the 1880s, as chromolithography became increasingly available and inexpensive.[37] Both in content and form, trade cards attempted to teach consumers specific lessons, both visual and sense-based, about the products being advertised. At the same time, the trade cards themselves had the potential to act as a kind of object lesson. They were easily handled and passed around; ordered in scrapbooks by color, content, or shape; and preserved. They were sometimes used for explicitly instructive purposes in the home or classroom. Advertisers employed many different techniques to create interest for the depicted products, like humor (often in the form of racist and sexist imagery) or collectible series of cards. Cards grounded in observation and the senses are simply one variety of trade card, but they are a type that helps explain the effect of object lessons on this form of visual culture.

Some trade cards emphasized this object-lesson aspect of their content more than others. A particularly clear example, "Mrs. Potts' Cold Handle Sad Irons," offers a classroom scene in which six children appear to be reciting a somewhat lampooned object lesson. Standing in a classroom, with a backboard, desks, and wall charts representing a map, the human body, and geometric forms, a seated male teacher dryly reads a question from a book. "What can we consider the most useful article in our households today?" he asks. His three female students quickly reply with the brand name of the advertised iron and are duly sent to the head of the class. The scene on the card does not feature an iron or students observing someone ironing. With a disengaged teacher simply reading questions and no explicit sensory engagement, it is exactly what is *not* supposed to happen in an object lesson. However, the printed black and white advertisement on the back of the card explains the meaning behind the teacher's question. The material qualities of the item, particularly its walnut handle that may be detached from the hot metal iron and affixed with non-conducting cement, allows it to heat more quickly and protects the user from burns. These physical properties would only be understood through experience

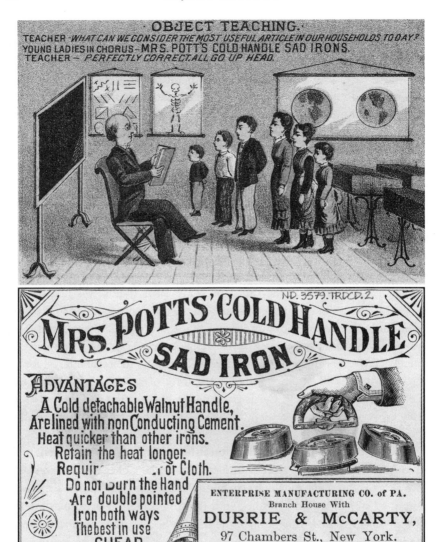

Figure 5.3. "Mrs. Potts' Cold Handle Sad Irons," ca. 1880s. The trade card for "Mrs. Potts' Cold Handle Sad Irons" played into the idea of object teaching, though there is no iron in the classroom for the students to study. *Grossman Collection (Col 838), Cabinet 8, Drawer 4, Box 8, courtesy Winterthur Library, Joseph Downs Manuscript Collection.*

and observation: the disembodied hand touching the cold handle with ease. The object lesson is imaginative, but like many other trade cards it relied on an understanding of the specific material properties of commodities as well as on viewers' imagined sense engagement.[38]

Trade cards that did not explicitly draw on classroom imagery also leveraged viewers' imagined sense engagement, whether sound, touch, or taste, to heighten the appeal of their products. An advertisement for a Decker Bros. piano, for example, depicts a woman playing the piano while a girl dances, another woman sews, and a boy gazes wistfully at the musician. All surfaces of the lithographed parlor interior are decorated with patterns and repetitive shapes and forms, a fully textured interior that does not preclude synesthetic, aural imagining (Plate 20). While the viewer of the card cannot hear the tone or action of the piano, the blithely dancing girl and the repetitive sewing of the women both rhythmically suggest the upright's music, echoing the piano's sound in their movements.[39] Touch is suggested through a series of cards advertising glue that illustrate the product's extreme stickiness, a tactile quality that could not be replicated on the actual cards.

A humorous card for Le Page's Liquid Glue, offers a scene in which a shoemaker has glued himself to his workbench to help him keep his New Year's resolution of temperance. Even his drunken, red-nosed cronies cannot drag him to the bar (Plate 21).[40] Another card for Le Page's Liquid Glue features a young woman, glued to a park bench while a man walks away, with the captions "The girl left behind me" and "A lady who keeps her place."[41] Similarly, Carter's Mucilage, "The Great Stickist," depicts a man whose overcoat is glued to his seat and cannot be pulled away.[42] The tactile quality of the glue is made visual. Taste could similarly be suggested through the healthful effect an advertised food had on those who consumed it. A metaphoric card designed for Carnrick's Soluble Food pictures healthy quadruplets born in Texas in 1890 and fed on this nutritious product (Plate 22). When the card is held up to the light, the babies' closed, sleepy eyelids seem to open, revealing bright, blue-eyed, active children; their hands are depicted as grasping objects, showing that these babies are fully engaged with their environment. Their round, fat faces and red lips suggest the physical value of this nourishing staple.[43]

Over time, magazine advertisements replaced trade cards in popularity. Some advertisements explicitly adopted the trope of the object lesson as a way to sell their goods. For example, a Copco Soap advertisement from *Munsey's Magazine* in the late 1890s employs the heading "An Object Lesson" to catch viewers' attention. A well-dressed, young woman, who could easily be a teacher presenting a lesson to a class, holds a bar of soap in her left hand and extends her right hand to the viewer. The text reads, "The woman who uses Copco Soap is an educator of womankind—she furnishes a lesson in comfort and economy, which, once learned, is never forgotten. Copco is the Perfect Soap, for the baby, the bath, and fine laundry—5 cents a cake. Sold everywhere."[44]

It invites potential customers to examine the product and to learn from their experience of it how the soap performs under various circumstances. The soap's material qualities, its utility for bathing or washing delicate clothing, can be readily discovered through thoughtful use. Other advertisements for the soap from the same periodical highlight these qualities, challenging the potential customer to learn why the soap is valuable and to look at how it might clean delicate glassware to assist a hostess in planning a perfect tea. These descriptions point to the specific, observable qualities of the product.[45]

Businesses also employed gimmicks they defined as object lessons as part of their advertising programs. For example, in 1895, Hornby's Oatmeal hired an extremely tall man and a very short man to walk about Boston wearing signs that read, "I eat H-O" and "I don't." The caption for images of this mismatched couple used in advertising described the comparative scene as "an object lesson in the powers of oatmeal to build up the system."[46] Advertisers capitalized on the notion that consumers wanted to come to an independent conclusion based on their ability to discern and weigh the apparent strengths of a given item. Object lessons both shaped and responded to this cultural dialogue.

Figure 5.4. Copco Soap advertisement from *Munsey's Magazine,* ca. late 1890s. This advertisement uses the object lesson idea to suggest that comfort and economy are qualities of Copco Soap. *Box 2, Folder 17, Series: Soap, Warshaw Collection of Business Americana, 1838–1953. Archives Center, National Museum of American History, Smithsonian Institution.*

An Object Lesson.

The woman who uses COPCO Soap is an educator of womankind—she furnishes a lesson in comfort and economy which, once learned, is never forgotten. COPCO is the perfect Soap, for the baby, the bath, and fine laundry—5 cents a cake. Sold everywhere.

The N. K. Fairbank Company, Chicago, New York, St. Louis.

Figure 5.5. "Two men who attract attention," ca. 1895. *Boston Sunday Journal*, March 31, 1895. The two men featured in this advertising campaign provided an object lesson in the power of Hornby's Oatmeal. *N. W. Ayer Advertising Agency Records, "Hornby's Oatmeal: Book 156," Series 02, Box 40, Folder 1. Archives Center, National Museum of American History, Smithsonian Institution.*

A Pause

In the final years of the nineteenth century, the classroom practice of object lessons gradually gave way to nature study, kindergarten, woodworking classes (like Sloyd, a Scandavian, craft-focused pedagogy), and the experience-based learning of John Dewey. Dewey's dislike and oversimplification of object lessons as rote learning prevented scholars in the history of education from taking the pedagogy seriously for decades or seeing how closely many aspects of it aligned to his own philosophy.[47] Politicians, advertisers, and authors continued to employ the idea of the "object lesson" as a metaphor or as a way to reason from objects. The power of this metaphor further erased its history. In 1903, Rebecca Harding Davis published a short essay entitled "A Great Object-Lesson" in the New York periodical the *Independent*. The author, best known for her novella "Life in the Iron-Mills," published in the *Atlantic* in 1861, mused on the recent death of Pope Leo XIII. She critiqued the Catholic Church for missing an opportunity to force individuals, regardless of their faith or politics, to pause and reflect upon his passing. Davis explained that "we all should be helped by object-lessons and pauses in our incessant work." The Liberty Bell, the American flag, an erupting volcano, the death of the pope or President McKinley, and even the sight of a drunken woman staggering in the street, baby in arms, all had the potential to serve as powerful "object-lessons." For the typical American whose knowledge of the world was "packed daily into his brain, done up in separate packages, labeled and ready for instant use," Davis hoped that such lessons, whether material or situational, would force an individual to think and make connections. She suggested that people should be drawn to observe and reflect on the world around them, not to be led to one particular lesson but to understand and appreciate "the electric fire that propels the world." This argument is in line with the early goals of object lessons, which considered the study of objects or learning through experience as both a means and an end. Consideration of Pope Leo's death would not be intended to honor the pope but to reflect on his importance and the meaning of his passing and why the idea of it mattered.[48]

Davis's definition of an object lesson as a pause is a helpful way to consider her novella *Life in the Iron Mills*. The story, often interpreted as an early example of realist fiction, focuses on the desperate life of an impoverished iron millworker named Hugh Wolfe and his deformed cousin Deborah. In addition to Hugh's physically draining manual work as a puddler, he is an artist who fashioned dramatic forms out of "korl," "scorl," or slag, the waste left over from the iron smelting process. The plot follows the hunchback Deborah who brings Hugh a late-night supper after her own work in a mill is done for the day. She lies to rest on an ash heap while he finishes his shift. That night a group of wealthy male visitors, including the mill owner and local doctor, inspect the mill and discover Hugh and one of his sculptures: a nude, muscular working woman carved from the korl. As the men praise and mock Hugh and his talent, Deborah manages to rob one of the men. Hugh is convicted of the crime and commits suicide. After serving three years in prison, Deborah goes on to live out her life with a kind Quaker. The story begins and ends in the narrator's home, in her library where she keeps Hugh's statue of the korl woman behind a curtain. The desperate look of the sculpture demands her attention.

Davis suggests the sculpture of the mill-woman carved from industrial garbage—all that remains of Hugh—can contain the entire tragic story. Davis did not use the phrase "object lesson" to describe the korl woman, but her notion of an object lesson as a pause is exactly what the korl woman demanded. For Davis, stopping to consider this object would allow one to see the hidden aspects of manufacturing that lie behind this crude form. Unlike the industrial products that were the subject of classroom object lessons, Davis's story focuses on the waste, both material and human, of the industrial process. While classroom lessons on iron, like the one produced by Bancroft Bros. in 1890, may have included a description of the "puddling furnace," the human cost of the product's labor is overlooked. Davis's "pause," like Hugh's transformation of refuse into an aesthetic object, disrupts and questions the fast-moving circulation of things. Her provocative call to pause and interrupt the flow of business and commerce suggests that an object lesson may offer a political or social critique as its pedagogical content.[49]

The idea of the object lesson as a pause that serves to focus one's attention on something solid and seemingly unassailable may be traced throughout the history of the practice, from the primary school classroom to the political sphere. The material thing, when understood as an object lesson, demanded close looking and sustained attention. When ideally presented in the classroom, this process forced children to question assumptions, to develop knowledge and understanding as opposed to memorizing the empty ideas represented in words. As Elizabeth Mayo hoped, "The minds accustomed to accurate investigation, will not rest content with less than satisfactory evidence, either in morals or science."[50] The goal was that the study of material evidence would force one to think more deeply and more clearly, learning how to reason even as one acquired new knowledge. Grover Cleveland, advertisers, and authors exploited this concept to lead their "students"—whether voters, consumers, or readers—to look closely and come to prescribed conclusions through their examination of selected materials.

To consider an object lesson as a pause is more than rhetoric. It gives a material thing a way to affect and to act on a thoughtful individual. That nineteenth-century children in the United States—and around the world—learned to pause in front of material things, to see objects as potentially holding knowledge and stories, opens up new interpretive possibilities for nineteenth-century material and visual culture. By understanding objects, pictures, and even people as embodying qualities that could be defined and organized, children and adults learned to draw abstract conclusions from their concrete perceptions. In a way, this practice helps explain the central role many scholars have given to the object-laden atmosphere of the late nineteenth century. More important, the study of object lessons suggests a central but forgotten way individuals reasoned from and through material and visual culture. That some nineteenth-century Americans learned or believed that things and pictures could stabilize or even crystallize ideas, however simple, should be part of the history of ideas in the United States.

Epilogue: Method over Matter in the Twenty-First-Century Classroom

A scholar of material culture does not need to be directed to pause in front of an object. The interdisciplinary study of material things is based on the concept that a material thing or its traces may contain information or meaning, whether valued for aesthetic, historical, biographical, technological, or other cultural reasons. These diverse goals have created a variety of approaches to the study of objects, all of which fall under the general rubric of "material culture." Some scholars profitably place things at the center of a nexus of historical documents, literary sources, biography, and local and cultural history; others apply the tools of the anthropologist and archaeologist to trace patterns connecting many objects; still others look for models within performance studies and consumer studies to understand how objects may have been animated by or even scripted various social and cultural behaviors; some have viewed objects as evidence of ways of thinking or worldviews.[1] To pursue any of these approaches, scholars are challenged to verbally express the information they find in material things. Numerous methods of object study have attempted to answer this call by providing a way of moving from object to language. For many scholars this desire comes from a research goal of giving voice to individual and collective experiences often overlooked in textual sources. It is in the potential of a regimented approach to find meaning in things that the practice of object lessons seems to align most closely to material culture.

The differences between the object-lesson method and contemporary material culture studies are obvious. In the first, the principal actors are schoolchildren as opposed to academics. In an object lesson, teachers hoped to show children how to perceive the world through the study of objects, to organize and to name their perceptions, and to write or tell stories about the things they studied. A material culture practitioner typically endeavors to answer or to frame an academic question about a larger community, cultural practice or pattern, a certain individual, or an unusual thing.

However, the common idea that one may derive information or determine value from the material world through systematic observation and a personally reflective way of engaging with objects is similar. Beyond that, teachers of material culture know that when presented with objects in the classroom—whether textual documents, works of art, or the stuff of everyday life—students make unexpected connections, think creatively, and have to defend their claims based on concrete evidence. Just as historic object teachers divided their work into "matter and method"—the subject of the lesson and the skills developed—such lessons both offer information about the past and open up new possibilities for thoughtful investigation and critical thinking.

Analysis of prescribed methods of object study—key to the training of material culturists—makes these goals clearer. Although there are many methods to consider, three classic texts stand out as most similar to formal object-lesson pedagogy. Charles Montgomery's "Fourteen Points of Connoisseurship," E. McClung Fleming's "Artifact Study," and the approaches of Jules Prown, worked out in numerous articles and books but most clearly detailed in "Mind in Matter," offer regimented ways to assess material things.[2] In each case, the method would lead a material culture practitioner to translate the details of a material object into ideas that may be expressed lexically. In the case of Montgomery, this process resulted in a rational evaluation of an object, oscillating between consciously subjective and objective observations to end in a connoisseur's appraisal. Students following Fleming's method would start with the identification of an item, beginning with its classification, comparison to other objects, and a consideration of cultural significance, and leading to an interpretation in line with their own interests and questions. Prown's method followed a somewhat different tack. Starting with a description of an object's physical qualities, the "internal evidence" of the object, he instructed students to deduce what they could about it through sensory, emotional, and intellectual engagement with the material thing, and finally to speculate about the object's meaning before moving to place it in a broader context.[3]

It is Prown's work, particularly "Mind in Matter," that resonates most deeply with object lessons. His method of starting with the physical object and spiraling outward through different modes of approach closely parallels the five-step object-lesson process that led a student through description, internal evidence, external evidence, and categorization to eventually arrive at composition. His call for bracketing or at least acknowledging the individual assumptions and cultural context of the investigator suggests the interpretive challenge of Rooper's green feathers or the empress's many dresses. Prown attributes the value he found in a systematic approach to cultural artifacts to his early training in both English and art history—first as an English major schooled in New Criticism at Lafayette College and later as an art history student at Harvard learning from German formalists. As he explained in a 2016 essay, the two approaches—whether to literary texts or art objects—are quite similar. Both rely on close analysis of a single key source.[4] Prown blurred the lines between literary text and material thing in his essay "The Truth of Material Culture? History or Fiction?" where he explored some of the ways objects could become metaphors or productive fictions, tools to access unexpressed cultural beliefs.[5] Elsewhere, he explained that a rococo Philadelphia side chair from the 1760s had "formal elements that reflect what was believed in Philadelphia at that time," and that the style manifested in the chair may "act as a kind of cultural daydream expressing unspoken beliefs."[6] This recognition and identification of material metaphor was rooted in careful observation, moving from concrete observation to abstract thinking through his method.

Two variations on an object lesson on similar chairs illustrate this methodological point. A 1901 cyanotype taken from a photograph by Frances Benjamin Johnston at the Carlisle Indian School presents an object lesson, sometimes called a conversation lesson when used for language instruction, in progress. Six Native American young men stand around their teacher's desk to study a common side chair, placed at eye level on the desk. The teacher stares at them intently. One could imagine a Prownian analysis of this chair, with students or a lone scholar considering its airy form, the way it required one to sit, evidence of a maker's hand or machine production in turning, or whether the curves of the seat indicate the kind of person for whom it was intended. In both a Prownian analysis and an object lesson, students could be led to find evidence of labor, material, trade, style, function, and meaning revolving around the object. As a historic classroom object lesson, the students may have initially discussed its geometry, developing the concepts and the associated vocabulary of perpendicular and parallel to describe the spindles and seat of the chair or its orderly form.[7] But there would be more. In the specific context of Carlisle Indian School, the chair could also be about craft practice and the students' potential to work, as native-made objects were explicitly considered "object lessons" in the promise of native citizenship through labor.[8] A chair could also consciously represent civility; the interior of a well-appointed, single-family home; or eating dinner at a table.[9] In some cases, the students themselves were called object lessons, suggesting the potential of these young men to be both the object and subject of such a lesson.[10]

A chair might be a lesson in civility, but a broken chair could be an object lesson in government critique, as viewed through a photograph of three broken chairs similar to the one at the center of the Carlisle classroom lesson. Between 1889 and 1893, E. Jane Gay, a reformer and photographer, traveled to Idaho with her companion, ethnologist Alice Fletcher, to live with the Nez Percés. In one photograph, Gay arranged three broken chairs: one with a missing

Figure 6.1. Frances Benjamin Johnston, "Conversation lesson, subject—the chair," March 15, 1901. Students at the Carlisle Indian School study a chair in a classroom lesson. *Library of Congress, Prints & Photographs Division, LC-DIG-ppmsca-18486.*

back, another with only one vertical support still tennoned into the seat, and another with just the curved arch of the bentwood frame. These "reservation chairs" were intended as a commentary on the agency that ran and supplied the reservation, then in the midst of implementing the Dawes Severalty Act. Gay explained that one could not recline comfortably in these chairs because "her chair had an Agency back and she knew that anything which depended on that would fall through."[11] Explicitly photographed and identified by Gay as an "object lesson," these chairs could offer a material critique of government policy. The broken chairs became an object lesson for broken promises, mismanagement, and disorder.[12]

These deductions and speculations, as Prown might call them, are informed not by an empathetic engagement with the object by a modern scholar, but through engagement with the history and the idea of the object lesson. The material details of the chair, read through this classroom lesson at Carlisle or Gay's photograph, keyed to a certain vision of material life with implications for the place of Native Americans within the United States. Of course, few material things arrive on a scholar's desk with explicit textual directions to be understood

Figure 6.2. E. Jane Gay, "Three broken chairs outdoors" from the album *Choup-nit-ki, With the Nez Percés,* 1889–1892. E. Jane Gay, the photographer for a government anthropological expedition, described these "reservation chairs" as an object lesson and used their variously broken forms to offer a political critique of US government policy toward Native Americans. *Jane Gay Dodge Papers, Schlesinger Library, Radcliffe Institute, Harvard University.*

as an object lesson, but the method itself may be applied to nearly any cultural artifact, whether made or collected. Many sources, like lesson plans, newspaper accounts, photographs, and teaching aids, invite such an interpretation.

The idea that one could see ideas in things was not a happy accident. Neither is it an ahistorical cultural notion or fiction molded through twentieth- and twenty-first-century material culture scholarship suggesting individual emotive, intellectual, and sensory responses to an object. Instead, nineteenth-century Americans may have found ideas in things because they were taught to do so. The history and practice of object lessons offer access to a historic mode of thinking with and through things and presents a new way to consider the practice of material culture.

These approaches—both past and present—have the potential to transform students into more dynamic and nimble thinkers. In the modern classroom an object-based lesson is successful when students are empowered to make their own observations and to develop the confidence to move from perceptions to conceptions, from what they perceive to the development of broader questions, problems, or theories about the subject of their examination and the worlds it reflects. Object-based classes or student research projects focused on things model a way of reasoning, from object to idea, from the concrete to the abstract, the familiar to the unfamiliar, that requires students to make connections across traditional disciplines. In these ways the study of material things is necessarily an interdisciplinary endeavor. The skills developed are broadly applicable well beyond the classroom to choices students make every day about the objects included in their lives.[13]

NOTES

Introduction

1. For example, Nobel Prize–winning economist Paul Krugman has used the metaphor more than a dozen times in his *New York Times* columns; Susan Stewart, "Promise Me, Elmo, You'll Stand Tall and Be Proud of Your Dad," review of *When Parents Are Deployed*, produced by Sesame Workshop, Cuba Gooding Jr., host, *New York Times* (1923–Current file), December 27, 2006; Jessica Benko, "He Survived Ebola. Now He's Fighting to Keep It from Spreading," *New York Times*, May 26, 2016; Somini Sengupta, "United Nations Chief Exposes Limits to His Authority by Citing Saudi Threat," *New York Times*, June 9, 2016; Jennifer Steinhauer and Laura M. Holson, "As Text Messages Fly, Danger Lurks," *New York Times*, September 20, 2008, p. A1. Furthermore, the phrase has been used to discuss race relations in contemporary America, as a way to acknowledge but not describe the lessons one may abstract from a racially charged situation. The July 2009 arrest of African American Harvard professor Henry Louis Gates Jr. at his home by a white Cambridge police officer, the allegations of racism against USDA worker Shirley Sherrod in July 2010, and the July 2013 George Zimmerman acquittal for the murder of Treyvon Martin are all key examples. All events have been described in various media outlets as "object lessons" and "teachable moments" for race relations.
2. For example, there is a book series published by *The Atlantic* and Bloomsbury, and regular "object lesson" columns that focus on material things in the online history magazine *Common-Place*, as well as in the *Journal of the History of Childhood and Youth*. Books that range from the history of science, to design studies, to theory all use the term. Lorraine Daston, *Things That Talk: Object Lessons from Art and Science* (New York: Zone Books, 2004); E. L. McCallum, *Object Lessons: How to Do Things with Fetishism* (Albany: State University of New York Press, ca. 1999); Sue Mitchell, *Object Lessons: The Role of Museums in Education* (Edinburgh: Her Majesty's Stationery Office, 1996); Ralph Caplan, *By Design: Why There Are no Locks on the Bathroom Doors in the Hotel Louis XIV, and Other Object Lessons* (New York: McGraw-Hill, 1984).
3. *Twelfth Annual Report of the Board of Education of the City of Oswego for the Year Ending March 31, 1865* (Oswego: S. H. Parker, 1865), 44–51; Elizabeth Mayo and E. A. Sheldon, *Lessons on Objects, Graduated Series: Designed for Children between the Ages of Six and Fourteen Years* (New York: Charles Scribner, 1863), 25, 382–385.
4. "Object Lessons," *Connecticut Common School Journal and Annals of Education* 5, no. 12 (December 1858): 365.

Chapter 1

1. *The Quarterly Education Magazine and Record of the Home and Colonial School Society* (London: Sampson Low, 169 Fleet Street, 1848), 1:58–74.

2. *Model Lessons for Infant School Teachers and Nursery Governesses Prepared for the Home and Colonial Infant School Society* (London: R. B. Seeley, 1838), v–vi.

3. *Quarterly Education Magazine and Record of the Home and Colonial School Society* (London: Sampson Low, 169 Fleet Street, 1849), 1:iv–v. Pestalozzi made the same claim regarding the revolutions immediately preceding the initial publication of *How Gertrude Teaches Her Children* in 1801. Johann Heinrich Pestalozzi, *How Gertrude Teaches Her Children*, ed. Ebenezer Cooke, trans. Lucy E. Holland and Frances C. Turner (Syracuse, NY: C. W. Bardeen, 1898), 226–227.

4. My understanding of the Enlightenment here is informed by Mark M. Smith's study of the senses in history and the historiography of senses that reveals the multisensory encounters central to empiricism. Mark M. Smith, *Sensing the Past: Seeing, Hearing, Smelling, Tasting, and Touching in History* (Berkeley: University of California Press, 2007), 31–32. Jessica Riskin's book *Science in the Age of Sensibility: The Sentimental Empiricists of the French Enlightenment* (Chicago: University of Chicago Press, 2002) provides a helpful context for understanding this aspect of the Enlightenment from a Continental perspective.

5. John Locke, *An Essay Concerning Human Understanding* (1689) in *The Philosophical Works and Selected Correspondence of John Locke* [electronic resource] (Charlottesville, VA: InteLex Corporation, 1995), bk. 2, ch. 1, sec. 2.

6. John Locke, *Some Thoughts Concerning Education*, 3rd ed., in *The Philosophical Works and Selected Correspondence of John Locke* [electronic resource] (Charlottesville, VA: InteLex Corporation, 1995), sec. 32.

7. John Locke, *An Essay Concerning Human Understanding* (1689) in *The Philosophical Works and Selected Correspondence of John Locke* [electronic resource] (Charlottesville, VA: InteLex Corporation, 1995), bk 3, ch. 4, sec. 11.

8. For example, Rousseau explains that Emile will learn to read when it suits his interest. Jean-Jacques Rousseau, *Emile or on Education*, trans. Allan Bloom (New York: Basic Books, 1979), 116–117.

9. Pestalozzi is long overdue for a new English biography. Kate Silber's biography first published in 1960 is still the most comprehensive English-language biography of the thinker. To most modern readers he is simply a name associated with Rousseau, Romanticism, or education, but he was a fascinating individual who linked his writing projects about family and community with his hopes for political reform and his pedagogical goals in a way that truly embodied the concept of "unity" often associated with his work. Much of the biographical writing about him seems to be colored by the legacy of his pedagogy as well as his own desire to rewrite his experiences.

10. Johannes Buss, personal narrative in *Pestalozzi and Pestalozzianism. Life, Educational Principles, and Methods of John Henry Pestalozzi; with Sketches of Several of his Assistants and Disciples*, reprinted from the *American Journal of Education*, in two parts, ed. Henry Barnard (New York: F. C. Brownell, 1862), 199; this anecdote is also in Pestalozzi, *How Gertrude Teaches Her Children*, 114.

11. This chalk drawing by F. M. Diogg, ca. 1804, is published in Kate Silber, *Pestalozzi: The Man and His Work* (London: Rutledge, 1960), 160.

12. This terracotta mask, ca. 1808, is published in Silber, *Pestalozzi*, 177.

13. A prime example of these classroom scenes may be seen in the engraving "Pestalozzi in His School," published in *Howitt's Journal* 77, no. 3 (June 18, 1848): 383. The image is after a drawing by the artist H. Bendel. Several artists recreated images like this one of Pestalozzi throughout the nineteenth century.

14. One key way Pestalozzi expressed his pedagogical views was through letters, which were edited and published, notably in his 1801 book *How Gertrude Teaches Her Children*. This excerpt comes from a letter Pestalozzi dated January 1, 1801. Pestalozzi republished these edited letters in 1820. The later version reflects changes to some of his theories, sensitively noted by the translators Lucy E. Holland and Frances C. Turner. Pestalozzi, *How Gertrude Teaches Her Children*, 43–44.

15. Roger De Guimps, *Pestalozzi: His Life and Works*, translated from the second French edition by J. Russell (New York: D. Appleton, 1892), 42.

16. Silber, *Pestalozzi*, 27. Pestalozzi's journal of his son's early years was published by one of his students and may have been edited to reflect some of the teacher's later thinking (after the 1774 date of the journal), though that is not clear. This interpretation is drawn on analysis of excerpts published in De Guimps, *Pestalozzi*, 36–51.
17. Silber, *Pestalozzi*, 18–30; Daniel Tröhler, *Johan Heinrich Pestalozzi* (Bern: Haupt Verlag, 2008), 32–33.
18. Barbara Beatty, *Preschool Education in America: The Culture of Young Children from the Colonial Era to the Present* (New Haven, CT: Yale University Press, 1995), 9–13.
19. Johan Heinrich Pestalozzi, *Leonard and Gertrude*, trans. Eva Channing (Boston: D. C. Heath, 1906), 134–135.
20. In his introduction to the 1906 edition of *Leonard and Gertrude*, psychologist G. Stanley Hall compared Pestalozzi's writing style to the colored wall charts, or *Anschauungunterrichts*, the pedagogue had helped to create, "The art [of the book], in a word reminds one of that of the large, colored charts for combined language and object teaching on the walls of so many German schoolrooms,—masses of strong colors, a crowd of things and persons, without attempted art or unity, but far truer to and richer in life for a child's eye than anything in the art galleries." Pestalozzi, *Leonard*, viii.
21. Silber, *Pestalozzi*, 37–46, 107–110; "Helvetic Republic," *Encyclopædia Britannica Online*, May 14, 2010, http://www.search.eb.com/eb/article-9039941.
22. The details about Pestalozzi's students come from a report that he submitted to the directory describing the initial twenty-nine boys and sixteen girls who arrived at his school, as transcribed by his biographer Roger De Guimps. De Guimps, *Pestalozzi*, 135–136.
23. This is drawn from Pestalozzi's letter from Stans to his friend Gessner and was published first in 1807. It is reprinted in De Guimps, *Pestalozzi*, 152.
24. Pestalozzi, *How Gertrude Teaches Her Children*, 46.
25. De Guimps, *Pestalozzi*, 165.
26. Charles Mayo, "Preface," to Elizabeth Mayo, *Lessons on Objects: As Given to Children between the Ages of Six and Eight in a Pestalozzian School at Cheam Surrey*, 16th ed. (London: Seeley, Jackson, and Halliday, 1859), v–x.
27. Hermann Krüsi, "'My Educational Recollections' Translated and Excerpted by His Son Hermann Krüsi," in *Studies in Education: A Series of Ten Numbers Devoted to Child Study and the History of Education*, ed. Earl Barnes (Stanford, CA: Stanford University, 1897), 230–239, 273–280: 274. These two accounts may be different translations of the same text.
28. John Ramsauer, "A Short Sketch of My Educational Life," in Barnard, *Pestalozzi*, 85.
29. As opposed to a novelistic, narrative sequel to *Leonard and Gertrude*, *How Gertrude Teaches Her Children* contains a series of letters Pestalozzi wrote on his methods around 1800 to his friend Gessner. The letters begin with the details of his experiment at Stans and Bergdorf and the move outward explaining different aspects of his theories and methods. The text was later republished with modifications.
30. In many ways this is a "chicken and egg" issue. Was Pestalozzi attracted to experience-based learning because of his difficulty with abstraction, or did his experiences as a teacher lead him to resist static pedagogical platitudes? Either way, his writing is clearly related to his pedagogy. To understand his ideas and their limitations, one had to experience his schools. Scholars frequently bemoan their inability to pin down any one aspect of Pestalozzi's philosophy. For most Anglophone historians of education, however, this inscrutability has led to a more simplistic and often instrumental interpretation of his writings, as opposed to analysis of the relationship between his philosophy and his style.
31. Carl von Raumer in Barnard, *Pestalozzi*, 94–95.
32. Pestalozzi, *How Gertrude Teaches Her Children*, 140.
33. Johannes Buss in Barnard, *Pestalozzi*, 200.
34. While this seems basic, Pestalozzi abstracts many different themes from this general conclusion. Nineteenth-century English and American educators, would create a way to talk about his theories that moves gradually from observation to volition, a distillation that seems to encompass many of the thinker's observations. A detailed discussion of these variations is not useful for the purposes of his study, but interested readers may wish to turn to Pestalozzi's original text to see how he developed his ideas and built and rebuilt

them through experience. Pestalozzi, "The Method," in *How Gertrude Teaches Her Children*, 309–336: 316.

35. Dieter Jedan, *Johann Heinrich Pestalozzi and the Pestalozzian Method of Language Teaching* (Bern: Peter Lang, 1981), 66.

36. Carl von Raumer in Barnard, *Pestalozzi*, 115–116.

37. Jedan, *Pestalozzi*, 38, 50–52; Clive Ashwin, "Pestalozzi and the Origins of Pedagogical Drawing," *British Journal of Education Studies* 24, no. 2 (June 1981):138–151; Johann Heinrich Pestalozzi, *A.B.C. der Anschauung oder Anschauungslehre der Massverhältnisse* (Zürich u. Bern: Gessner, 1803).

38. Charles Mayo, *Memoir of Pestalozzi: Being the Substance of a Lecture Delivered at the Royal Institution, Albemarle-Street, May, 1826* (London: Printed for J. A. Hessey, 93, Fleet Street, 1828), 20.

39. Carl von Raumer in Barnard, *Pestalozzi*, 86.

40. Silber, *Pestalozzi*, 206.

41. Silber, *Pestalozzi*, 207–208; Jedan, *Pestalozzi*, 54–67.

42. Silber, *Pestalozzi*, 217–218.

43. See, for example, Horace Mann's discussion of "exercises in thinking" in his "Seventh Annual Report of the Board of Education" in *The Common School Journal* 6, no. 9 (May 1, 1844):139–144.

44. John A. Griscom, *Year in Europe: Comprising a Journal of Observations in 1818 and 1819*, vol. 1 (New York: Collins and Hannay, 1824), 290.

45. Mayo, *Memoir of Pestalozzi*, 1.

46. Barnard, *Pestalozzi*, 94–95.

47. Silber, *Pestalozzi*, 324.

48. Silber, *Pestalozzi*, 301.

49. Mayo, *Pestalozzi*, 20.

50. As far as I can determine, there is no additional information available for her prior to 1822. After noting her birth, this is also when her *Dictionary of National Biography* entry begins. She never married and I have not yet been able to locate papers for her. There is more documentation for her career at the Home and Colonial Schools as she seems to have basically run the institution for many years and her publications were translated into many languages and went through dozens of editions. In a letter she wrote to E. A. Sheldon in 1863 she described herself, "I have been an amateur laborer in the cause of education forty years." Mayo to Sheldon, December 18 (ca. 1862–1863), E. A. Sheldon Papers, Box 1, Folder 56, Penfield Library, SUNY–Oswego. She lived and worked with her mother Elizabeth (Knowlys) Mayo (d. 1837) and was even buried in her grave, number 951 in Kensel Green Cemetery. Charles Herbart Mayo, *A Genealogical Account of the Mayo and Elton Families of the Counties of Wilts and Hereford* (London: Privately Printed by Charles Whittingham and Co., Ciswick Press, 1882), 79–81.

51. Introduction II, "Lear in Sicily Notes," Edward Lear Homepage, http://www.nonsenselit. org/Lear/LiS/Lis_notes.html#NOTEN, accessed, July 18, 2010.

52. Mayo, *Lessons on Objects* (1859), ix–x.

53. Elizabeth Mayo, *Lessons on Objects; as Given to Children between the Ages of Six and Eight, in a Pestalozzian School, at Cheam, Surrey* (London: R. B. Seeley and W. Burnside, 1837), 222.

54. Educational specimen box, mahogany, for the education of children, assembled in England, ca. 1850. Victoria and Albert Museum, B.5:1 to 5-2009.

55. Mayo, *Lessons on Objects* (1837), 1–2, 15–16.

56. Mayo, *Lessons on Objects* (1837), 64–65.

57. For more on infant schools in England, see Nanette Whitbread, *The Evolution of the Nursery Infant-School, 1800–1970* (London: Routledge & Kegan Paul, 1972). Earlier in the century, the infant school movement is often associated with Robert Owen and Samuel Wilderspin. For a discussion of how their work related to that of the Home and Colonial School Society, see Philip McCann and Francis A. Young, *Samuel Wilderspin and the Infant School Movement* (London: Croom Helm, 1982). When American abolitionist and woman's rights activist Lucretia Mott visited an infant school in England in July 1840 she noted, "Went to an infant school, taught by Pestalozzi with an owl: children very attentive." Lucretia Coffin Mott,

"Diary of Lucretia Coffin Mott," in *James and Lucretia Mott: Life and Letters*, ed. Anna Davis (Boston, MA: Houghton, Mifflin 1884), 566.

58. The school, often referred to under the general name of Home and Colonial School Society or the Home and Colonial Schools, closed in the early twentieth century.

59. Margaret E. M. Jones, "A Brief Account of the Home and Colonial Training Institution and of the Pestalozzian System, as Taught and Practiced in Their Schools, Extracted from the *Quarterly Paper of the Society*, for January 1862" (London: Groombridge and Sons, n.d.).

60. Mayo, *Mayo and Elton Genealogy*, 79–80.

61. Reynolds, *Quarterly* (1849), 194.

62. See, for example, J. Weitbrecht, *Object Lessons or Infant School Teacher's Manual* translated from Mayo's *Manual for Infant Schools* as *Skishu Sltikhah*, 1852, from a *Descriptive Catalogue of Bengali Works* (Calcutta: J. Long, Sanders Cones and Co, 1855), 41. The title would likely be spelled today "Shishu Shikah," which translates to "children's learning" or "children's education." Thanks to Rifat Hasan for help with translation. Sengupta, "Colonial Pedagogy," 108–111, 113–115.

63. It is interesting to consider whether the perceived needs of Indian students may have shaped the practice's implementation in England. For example, Jana Tschurenev has argued that the monitorial system of education was actually a hybrid of English and Indian pedagogical practices. Jana Tschurenev, "Diffusing Useful Knowledge: The Monitorial System of Education in Madras, London and Bengal, 1789–1840," *Paedagogica Historica* 44 (June 2008): 245–264.

64. Mayo, *Lessons on Objects* (1859), 76–77.

65. Parna Sengupta, "Colonial Pedagogy," 96–97.

66. Mayo, *Lessons on Objects* (1859), 83.

67. *Information on Common Objects for the Use of Infant and Juvenile Schools and Nursery Governesses* (London: Published for the Home and Colonial Infant School Society by Darton and Clark, 1845), iv.

68. Elizabeth Mayo, *Model Lessons for Infant School, Teachers and Nursery Governess Prepared for the Home and Colonial School Society* (London: R. B. Seeley and Burnside, 1838), iv–v.

69. Mayo, *Lessons on Objects* (1859), 202.

70. Charles Mayo and Elizabeth Mayo, *Practical Remarks on Infant Education for the Use of Schools and Private Families*, 4th ed. (London: Home and Colonial School Society, 1849), n.p.

71. Adam Smith, *The Theory of Moral Sentiments* (Philadelphia: A. Finley, 1817), 4–5.

72. John Frost, *Lessons on Common Things for the Use of Schools and Families* (Philadelphia: Lippincott, 1857).

73. Frost credits "Dr. Mayo" instead of Elizabeth Mayo as author of the book. Lucille Schultz has an excellent chapter on what she calls the "Pestalozzi-Mayo-Frost Connection" in her book, *The Young Composers: Compositions Beginnings in Nineteenth-Century Schools* (Carbondale: Southern Illinois University Press, 1989), 56–84.

74. Dorothea Dix, *Conversations on Common Things; Or, Guide to Knowledge with Questions* (Boston: Monroe and Francis, 1828), frontispiece; Thomas J. Brown, *Dorothea Dix: New England Reformer* (Cambridge, MA: Harvard University Press, 1998), 19–22.

75. This was intended to extend the argument made in the *Essay Concerning Human Understanding* and was published posthumously. Lawrence Cremin, *American Education: The Colonial Experience, 1607–1783* (New York: Harper Torchbooks, 1970), 361; John Locke, *Of the Conduct of the Understanding*, ed. F. W. Garforth, Classics in Education Series—No. 31 (New York: Teachers College Press, 1966), Section 19. For example, this translation of the quote appears in *The Works of Vicesimus Knox, D.D.* Vol. 4, *Liberal Education: Tract on the Degradation of Grammar Schools* (London: Printed for J. Mawman, 1824), 42.

76. Dorothea Dix, *Conversations*, 14–15.

77. Dix even opens her book with a comparison to Mrs. Trimmer's work. See *An Easy Introduction to the Knowledge of Nature. Adapted to the Capacities of Children. By Mrs. Trimmer. Revised, Corrected, and Greatly Augmented; and Adapted to the United States of America* (Boston: Printed by Manning and Loring, for David West, 1796).

78. Seth Lerer, *Children's Literature: A Reader's History, from Aesop to Harry Potter* (Chicago: University of Chicago Press, 2008), 105.

79. James Currie, "Subjects and Methods of Early Education," in *Object Teaching and Oral Lessons on Social Science and Common Things with Various Illustrations of the Principles and Practice of*

Primary Education as Adopted by the Model and Training Schools of Great Britain, Republished from Barnard's American Journal of Education, ed. Henry Barnard (New York: F. C. Brownell, 1860), 229–293: 237.

80. Carl Kaestle, *Pillars of the Republic: Common Schools and American Society, 1780–1860* (New York: Hill and Wang, 1983), 62–75; William J. Reese, *America's Public Schools: From the Common School to "No Child Left Behind"* (Baltimore, MD: Johns Hopkins University Press, 2005), 10–21.

81. Clearly, Rousseau's ideas would also be part of this intellectual mix, but there is less evidence American parents read Rousseau and works based on Rousseau in the same way they read and responded to Locke's writings and writings based on his work. Karin Calvert, *Children in the House: The Material Culture of Early Childhood 1600–1900* (Boston: Northeastern, 1992), 60.

82. Cremin, *American Education: The Colonial Experience*, 365–371.

83. Lawrence Cremin in Samuel F. Pickering, *John Locke and Children's Books in Eighteenth-Century England* (Knoxville: University of Tennessee Press, 1981), 9.

84. Eliza Lucas Pinckney, *The Letterbook of Eliza Lucas Pinckney*, ed. Elise Pinckney (Columbia: University of South Carolina Press, 1997), 19, 47–48.

85. Harriott Horry Ravenel, *Eliza Pinckney* (New York: Charles Scribner's Sons, 1896), 113.

86. Locke, *Thoughts Concerning Education*, section 150.

87. Ravenel, *Eliza Pinckney*, 114. These blocks were simply one type of "rational amusement" that came to be popular throughout the eighteenth century. Seth Lerer described toys John Newberry created to go along with his books to fulfill the desire for these kinds of toys. He notes that some books were designed with letters that could be cut out and pasted on blocks to teach children how to read. See Lerer, *Children's Literature*, 107.

88. Calvert, *Children in the House*, 59–60.

89. In fact, these two bodies of texts are linked as the metaphor of family was used to describe America's relationship with England.

90. Kaestle, *Pillars of the Republic*, 34–35.

91. Kaestle, *Pillars of the Republic*, 17–18.

92. In her letter she also pairs her reading of Locke with that of Richard Stark, an Irish clergyman and scholar. He wrote on both religious subjects and natural philosophy, penning a book on how to teach chemistry. The chemistry text is supposed to contain modern theory. It is not clear to which book she refers, though the religious text was published in the United States.

93. Undated letter in Box 1 of Letters to the Heaths, 1826–1879, MS Am 59, Houghton Library, Harvard University.

94. Elizabeth Smith and H. M. Bowlder, *Fragments, in Prose and Verse* (London: T. Cadell and W. Davies, 1818), 193–201.

95. Joseph Neef, *Sketch of a Plan and Method of Education: Founded on an Analysis of the Human Faculties and Natural Reason Suitable for the Offspring of a Free People, and for all Rational Beings* (Philadelphia, 1808), 6.

96. Gerald Gutek, *Joseph Neef, The Americanization of the Pestalozzianism* (University: University of Alabama Press, 1978).

97. For an account of Alcott's Temple School see Megan Marshall, *The Peabody Sisters: Three Women Who Ignited American Romanticism* (Boston: Houghton Mifflin, 2005), 293–326. It is interesting to note that around the same time, Comenius's seventeenth-century *Orbis Pictus* was republished in America, suggesting a renewed interest in the role of sense perception in literacy.

98. For many period critics and some historians of education, Pestalozzi's religious and philosophical views about children's goodness and spiritual potential were much more meaningful than his classroom teaching innovations, as developed and spread by students like Charles Mayo. This emphasis, in some ways, has been viewed as a more "authentic" reading of Pestalozzi's significance. I believe this has contributed to the dearth of scholarship on object lessons that some scholars have argued is a corruption of Pestalozzi's views as opposed to a particular kind of adaptation. See, for example, Jackie E. M. Latham, "Pestalozzi and James Pierrepont Greaves: A Shared Educational Philosophy," *History of Education* 31, no. 1 (2002): 59–70.

99. Lowell Mason, *Manual of the Boston Academy of Music for Instruction in the Elements of Vocal Music, on the System of Pestalozzi* (Boston: Hendee, 1834), 10.

100. Warren Colburn, *First Lessons on Arithmetic on the Plan of Pestalozzi: With Some Improvements* (Boston: Cummings and Hilliard, 1822).

101. *The Thirteenth Annual Report of the Superintendent of Public Instruction of the State of California, for the Year 1863* (Sacramento: O. M. Clayes, State Printer, 1863), 34.

102. For example, a teachers' institute was held in Worcester on April 19, 1854 that included Agassiz, Mason, and Guyot. *Teachers Institute in Worcester*, [Worcester, MA, 1854], Collections of the American Antiquarian Society, Worcester, MA. Kaestle described how one schoolteacher noted that the institute he attended affected his teaching for the entire school year. Kaestle, *Pillars of the Republic*, 129.

103. Molly Rogers, *Delia's Tears: Race, Science, and Photography in Nineteenth-Century America* (New Haven, CT: Yale University Press, 2010), 94–95; Lucille M. Schultz, *The Young Composers: Composition's Beginnings in Nineteenth-Century Schools* (Carbondale: Southern Illinois University Press, 1999), 81–82.

104. Hermann Krüsi, "The Life and Character of Pestalozzi," in *Prize Essay and Lectures Delivered before the American Institute of Instruction, New Haven, Connecticut, August 1853* (Boston: Ticknor, Reed and Fields, 1854), 27–52. The lecture was published in and became the basis for Krüsi's later biography of Pestalozzi. Hermann Krüsi, *Recollections of My Life*, ed. Mary Sheldon Alling (New York: Grafton Press, 1907), 130.

105. Krüsi also describes his changing views on slavery. True to his methods, Krüsi appreciated Harriet Beecher Stowe's "masterly exposition" of the horrors of slavery in *Uncle Tom's Cabin* because it drew readers into sympathy with the enslaved. But he walked out of a "one-sided and egotistic" lecture given by John Brown. It was only after Harper's Ferry that Krüsi began to feel sympathetically toward the reformer and noted discussing his example at anti-slavery meetings. Krüsi, *Recollections*, 158–161.

Chapter 2

1. *Sixth Annual Report of the Board of Education of the City of Oswego for the Year Ending March 31, 1859* (Oswego: Tarbell, 1859), 4–5.

2. Sheldon's *Autobiography* is a published book that includes excerpts from his diary, his own account of his life, and his correspondence and the reminiscences of friends, family, and former students. The text was heavily edited by his daughter and granddaughter. There is also an archive that includes an edited draft of this autobiography as well as transcripts of many of the documents that were mined for this book. It contains information gathered for the sesquicentennial of the Oswego Normal School, 1911, the year in which the *Autobiography* was published. Since the original letters no longer exists, the twenty-seven folders of this collection are one of the best sources on Sheldon's life and the history of the school. I use *Autobiography* to refer to the published volume. Edward Austin Sheldon and Mary Sheldon Barnes, *Autobiography of Edward Austin Sheldon* (New York: Ives-Butler, 1911), 116.

3. There were many possibilities for traveling from Oswego to Toronto. Sheldon likely took the daily steam-powered ferry that carried passengers across the lake. John Disturnell, *A Trip through the Lakes of North America* (New York: J. Disturnell, 1857), 231.

4. Sheldon, *Autobiography*, 117.

5. *The Educational Museum and the School of Art and Design for Upper Canada* (Toronto: Department of Public Instruction for Upper Canada, 1858).

6. J. Lynne Teather, *The Royal Ontario Museum: A Prehistory, 1830–1914* (Toronto: Canadian University Press, 2005), 71–73. It is difficult to trace exactly what Sheldon purchased in Toronto. Those records do not seem to survive. His purchase is not listed in the Annual Report of the Oswego School Department; perhaps, as he would later do with Miss Jones's appointment, he chose to keep some of his more experimental expenses out of the city's budget. In 1860 the school board did approve the purchase of "Object Lessons" from three businesses, including object lessons from a local dry goods store, the preparation of "natural object lessons" from a factory, and frames for pictures of natural history lessons. *Seventh Annual Report of the Board of Education of the City of Oswego for the Year Ending March 31, 1860* (Oswego: Tarbell, 1860), 14–17; *Oswego City Directory*, 1859. In 1861 and 1862, the Annual Reports included small purchases from the Department of Public Instruction UC

(Upper Canada), suggesting that Sheldon continued to purchase supplies from the Toronto depository.

7. Many educators connected to what would become the Oswego Normal School have written narrative accounts of the Oswego System that eulogize Sheldon and celebrate the history of this school, dubbed by one author as the "Fountainhead of Teacher Education." Oswego is usually included in general histories of American common and normal schools; however, many accounts of the school have relied heavily on laudatory anniversary publications as well as on Sheldon's *Autobiography*. While I certainly draw on the narrative accounts of these writers, my analysis builds on my own primary research into the records of the school and town and on larger national trends. Three books in this tradition are State University College of Education (Oswego, NY), *Historical Sketches Relating to the First Quarter Century of the State Normal and Training School at Oswego, N. Y.* (New York: Oliphant, 1888); Andrew Philip Hollis, *The Contribution of the Oswego Normal School to Educational Progress in the United States* (Boston: D. C. Heath, 1898); Dorothy Rogers, *Oswego: Fountainhead of Teacher Education: A Century in the Sheldon Tradition* (New York: Appleton-Century-Crofts, 1961). The best treatment of object-based learning in this period may be found in William Reese's article, "The Origins of Progressive Education," *History of Education Quarterly*, 41, no. 1 (March 2001): vi, 1–24.

8. It is possible that A. J. Downing's belief in the power of the built environment to shape an individual may have influenced Sheldon's later turn to object lessons. See, for example, A. J. Downing and Alexander Anderson, "On the Real Meaning of Architecture," in *The Architecture of Country Houses* (New York: D. Appleton, 1850).

9. Henry Reed Stiles, *The Stiles Family in America: Genealogies of the Connecticut Family* (Jersey City, NJ: Doan & Pilson, 1895), 283.

10. Manuscript of E.A. Sheldon Autobiography Files, page 362, Box 1, Folder 3, E.A. Sheldon Papers, Penfield Library, SUNY–Oswego.

11. Sheldon, *Autobiography*, 92–93.

12. Louisa Plumb Andrews, E. A. Sheldon Autobiography Files, page 3, Box 1, Folder 6, E. A. Sheldon Papers, Penfield Library, SUNY–Oswego.

13. Janet Shepherd, "Mayo, Elizabeth (1793–1865)," *Oxford Dictionary of National Biography*, Oxford University Press, 2004, http://www.oxforddnb.com/view/article/18455, accessed 7 April 2008.

14. He wrote in his annual report for that year, "Something, it is true, is now being done in this direction and teachers in these departments have regular and daily exercises in object lessons; but for the want of proper facilities much less is accomplished than could be desired." The curriculum had included "object lessons" since 1856. *Sixth Annual Report of the Board of Education of the City of Oswego for the Year Ending March 31, 1859* (Oswego: Tarbell, 1859), 25. It should be noted that class size for teachers was around forty students per class. In 1859, the average class size was forty-five. Each teacher would have an average of eighty-three registered pupils. Due to poor attendance, the daily number was around forty-five. This group would sometimes be divided in half for exercises and sometimes a second teacher might share the group. *Annual Report*, 1859, 5.

15. In his informative 1925 dissertation, which was later republished, Ned Dearborn argued that there was no difference between E. A. Sheldon's system and that of the Mayos. He referred to the two systems interchangeably. Sheldon did adopt much of the Mayos' pedagogy, but his system was more specific in that he offered clear ways of applying their pedagogy across the curriculum, in the classroom. Ned Dearborn, *Oswego Movement in American Education* (New York: Arno Press, 1969), 42–61.

16. Sheldon, *Autobiography*, 115.

17. The Oswego school system was divided into four sections: primary school, junior school, senior school, and high school; each of these was divided into three grades, A, B, and C. Students started in class C of the primary school, moving through B and A after the successful passage of exams, before graduating into the junior school. Class C through A was roughly for children from ages six to twelve, and they were to enter a given year according to their previous education and ability. Each school year was divided into three terms, of equal length, which started each year on April 1 and continued for forty weeks. S. S. Greene, *A Report on Object*

Teaching Made at the Meeting of the National Teachers' Association (Boston: Massachusetts Teachers' Association, 1865), 25–26.

18. *Seventh Annual Report of the Board of Education of the City of Oswego for the Year Ending March 31, 1860* (Oswego: Tarbell, 1860), 14–17.

19. "President Sheldon's Annual Address, July 23, 1861," *New York Teacher* 11, no. 1 (October 1861): 17–22: 22.

20. This lesson appears in Elizabeth Mayo's 1859 *Lessons on Objects*, likely, the edition Sheldon was using in Oswego. He would later offer his own revision on this lesson. Elizabeth Mayo, *Lessons on Objects, as Given to Children between the Ages of Six and Eight, in a Pestalozzian School, at Cheam, Surrey*, 16th ed. (London: Seeley, Jackson and Halliday, 1859), 10; E. A. Sheldon, Margaret E. M. Jones, and Hermann Krüsi, *A Manual of Elementary Instruction for the Use of Public and Private Schools and Normal Classes* (New York Charles Scribner, 1862), 112–113.

21. Letter from E. A. Sheldon in the *Educational Papers of the Home and Colonial Schools* 2, no. 1 (January 1860), 58–59; Sheldon, *Autobiography*, 135.

22. E. A. Sheldon, "Oswego Training School for Primary Teachers on Pestalozzian Principles," January 23, 1862 (College Activities, Scrapbooks and Clippings, Box 2, Folder 121), Penfield Library, SUNY–Oswego.

23. See Box 1, Folder 43, E. A. Sheldon Papers, Penfield Library, SUNY–Oswego, and Sheldon, Jones, and Krüsi, *Manual of Elementary Instruction* (1862).

24. From Mary V. Lee to E. A. Sheldon, Box 6, Folder 13, series II: Correspondence, August 30, 1881, Mary Sheldon Barnes Papers, Sophia Smith Collection, Smith College, Northampton, MA; Sheldon, preface to *Manual of Elementary Instruction* (New York: Charles Scribner, 1862), 5–10. Jones's sister noted, "Perhaps for her own happiness she has been too sensitive. Unkindness might vex and annoy others it deeply wounded her." This observation suggests the possibility that Jones may have misread her colleagues' responses to her work in Oswego, though Lee's letter appears to be quite explicit in its description of Jones's treatment. Bessie Coghlan, "M.E.M Jones," in State University College of Education, *Historical Sketches Relating to the First Quarter Century of the State Normal and Training School at Oswego, N. Y.* (Oswego: R. J. Oliphant, 1888). 132–134.

25. From Mary V. Lee to E. A. Sheldon, Box 6, Folder 13, series II: Correspondence, August 30, 1881, Mary Sheldon Barnes Papers, Sophia Smith Collection, Smith College, Northampton, MA; Sheldon, preface to *Manual of Elementary Instruction* (New York: Charles Scribner, 1862), 5–10.

26. "To My Dear Schoolteacher, 1856." Cotsen Children's Library, Princeton University (Manuscripts 23064).

27. S. W. Seton, "Report," in *Annual Report of the New York City Board of Education, 1856*, 62.

28. Seton, "Report," 50–51.

29. "Multiplication Table Tree," ca. 1850, American Antiquarian Society, Worcester, MA.

30. Elizabeth Mayo and E. A. Sheldon, *Lessons on Objects* (New York: Charles Scribner and Sons, 1863), 214–222.

31. Correspondence of Mrs. Louisa Plumb Andrews, likely recorded for the 1911 sesquicentennial of the school. E. A. Sheldon Autobiography Files [marked omitted], pages 4–5, Box 1, Folder 6, Penfield Library, SUNY–Oswego. Louisa went on to spend twelve years teaching in the Oswego schools; State University College of Education, *Historical Sketches of Oswego*, 236.

32. "The Educational Convention," *Commercial Times*, Wednesday, February 12, 1862, n.p. The use of the reading metaphor in terms of object study is a favored twenty-first-century material culture metaphor. Scholars talk about reading objects as texts, yet as the Oswego method and contemporary scholarship suggests, the same objects may be both legible and illegible. Plus the reading metaphor emphasizes what can be verbally described as opposed to what may be sensed or experienced in other ways, a problem for any academic field based on nontextual research. Bjørnar Olsen, "Material Culture after Text: Re-Membering Things," *Norwegian Archaeological Review* 36, no. 2 (2003): 87–104.

33. Hyland Kirk, *A History of the New York State Teachers Association* (New York: Kellogg, 1883), 39–41.

34. *Proceedings of the Educational Convention, Held at Oswego, N. Y., February 11, 12, and 13, 1862, to Examine into a System of Primary Instruction by Object Lessons* (New York: Harper & Brothers, 1862) 3.

35. *Proceedings*, 9.

36. *Proceedings*, 10.

37. Sheldon, Jones, and Krüsi, *Manual of Elementary Instruction* (1862), frontispiece.

38. *Programme of Exercises for Educational Meeting to Be Held at Oswego, Feb. 11 1862*, E. A. Sheldon Papers, Box 2, Folder 39, Penfield Library, SUNY–Oswego.

39. *Proceedings*, 13.

40. *Proceedings*, 25–26.

41. Hill makes a point of distinguishing between the development of reasoning ability and the development of imagination, an important distinction. Thomas Hill, *True Order of Studies* (New York: G. P. Putnam's Sons, 1875).

42. H. B. Wilbur, "The Natural Order of the Development of the Human Faculties," *New York Teacher*, 4, no. 1 (October 1861): 1–29.

43. This quotation is from Wilbur's definition of idiocy in *The First Annual Report of the New York Asylum for Idiots* (1852). Trent explains that Wilbur draws directly on Seguin's definition of idiocy here. James W. Trent, *Inventing the Feeble Mind: A History of Mental Retardation in the United States* (Berkeley: University of California Press, 1994), 17.

44. Wilbur, "The Natural Order of the Development of the Human Faculties," pp. 8–10.

45. Elizabeth Prentiss, *Little Susy's Little Servants/By Her Aunt Susan* (New-York: Anson D. F. Randolf, 1857).

46. H. B. Wilbur, "Object Teaching," *American Journal of Education* 30 (March 1865): 188–208, 199.

47. Wilbur, "Object Teaching," 199.

48. Wilbur, "Object Teaching," 199.

49. Mary P. Winsor, *Reading the Shape of Nature: Comparative Zoology at the Agassiz Museum* (Chicago: University of Chicago Press, 1991), 12–15.

50. "Education to Be," *Continental Monthly* 1, no. 6 (June 1862): 673.

51. Jones to Sheldon, n.d. (ca. 1862–3), E. A. Sheldon Papers, Box 1, Folder 55, Special Collections of Penfield Library, State University of New York at Oswego, Oswego, NY.

52. Mayo to Sheldon, December 18 (ca. 1862–3), E. A. Sheldon Papers, Box 1, Folder 56, Special Collections of Penfield Library, SUNY at Oswego, Oswego, NY.

53. "Strictures on Dr. Wilbur's Address" in *New York Teacher* 12, no. 3 (February 1863): 155–166 [new series].

54. This organization was founded in 1857 and later became the National Educational Association. Zalmon Richards, "Historical Sketch of the National Educational Association," in National Education Association of the United States, William Torrey Harris, and Zalmon Richards, *History of the National Educational Association of the United States* (Washington, DC: National Educational Association, 1892), 16–31.

55. Greene, *A Report on Object Teaching*, 11.

56. Greene, *Report on Object Teaching*, 16.

57. Greene, *Report on Object Teaching*, 31.

58. *Sixth Annual Report of the Board of Education of the City of Oswego for the Year Ending March 31, 1859* (Oswego: Tarbell, 1859), 46; *Tenth Annual Report of the Board of Education of the City of Oswego for the Year Ending March 31, 1863* (Oswego: Commercial Times Print, 1863), 48.

59. *Eighth Annual Report of the Board of Education of the City of Oswego for the Year Ending March 31, 1861* (Oswego: Times Steam Press, 1861), 18.

60. E. A. Sheldon, Margaret E. M. Jones, and Hermann Krüsi, *A Manual of Elementary Instruction*, 6th ed. (New York: Charles Scribner, 1870), 27–40.

61. Correspondence of Mrs. Otis Plumb Andrew and Jenny Stickney Lansing, recorded for the 1911 sesquicentennial of the school. Autobiography file, Box 1, Folders 6, page 3 and 16, page 3, E. A. Sheldon Papers, Penfield Library, SUNY–Oswego. Stickney helped found the City Training School in Boston. Andrew Philip Hollis, *The Contribution of the Oswego Normal School to Educational Progress in the United States* (Boston: D. C. Heath, 1898), 47–48.

62. Mary Orr File, Student Papers, Special Collections of Penfield Library, SUNY at Oswego, Oswego, NY.

63. Sheldon's training school started the process of becoming a New York State Normal School in 1863 and eventually would become SUNY–Oswego. For more on the history of this school, see Dorothy Rogers, *Fountainhead*, 1961. Even as object lessons spread throughout the United States, they fell out of favor in Oswego. In what Sheldon's daughter Mary Sheldon Barnes remembered as "the big fight," in 1872 the Oswego Board of Education discontinued object teaching. One newspaper that supported the curricular change reported that nine out of ten families considered it a "mischievous, expensive and a cruel humbug." Sheldon, *Autobiography*, 221–225.

64. Christine A. Ogren, *The American State Normal School* (New York: Palgrave Macmillan, 2005), 34–37.

65. "Local Intelligence, Board of Education, Interesting Debate on the Question of Teaching Special Subjects in the Schools Unequal Appropriation of the School Moneys" (September 19, 1862). *New York Times* (1857-Current file), p. 2.

66. *California State Teachers' Institutional Educational Convention, Proceedings of the California State Teachers' Institute and Educational Convention in Session in the City of San Francisco from May 4th–9th, 1863* (Sacramento, 1863) Appendix B.

67. From Bloomington Anniversary Week—State University, *Chicago Tribune*, June, 27, 1862, 2.

68. "Reform in the Public Schools. Favorable Impressions of a New Jersey Visitor to the Schools of Cincinnati," *Cincinnati Daily Gazette*, July 13, 1877, 3.

69. "Lady Teachers' Association," *Cincinnati Daily Gazette*, November 20, 1873, 7.

70. Charlotte L. Forten Grimké, *The Journal of Charlotte L. Forten* (New York: Dryden Press, 1953), 191–198 (July 26, 1863).

71. *Fourth Semi-Annual Report of the Superintendent of Public Schools of the City of Boston, March 1862* (Boston: J. E. Farwell, 1862), 84.

72. *Seventh Annual Report of the Superintendent of Public Schools of the City of Boston, September 1863* (Boston: J. E. Farwell, 1863), 17–18.

73. *Eleventh Annual Report of the Superintendent of Public Schools of the City of Boston, September 1865* (Boston: J. E. Farwell, 1866), 26.

74. *Eleventh Annual Report of the Superintendent of Public Schools of the City of Boston, September 1865* (Boston: J. E. Farwell, 1866), 15–17, 36–37. Philbrick's concerns are unfolding within an educational culture that comes to emphasize written tests as opposed to public examinations, which would have allowed for a more thorough assessment of object lessons in the classroom; William J. Reese, *Testing Wars in the Public Schools: A Forgotten History* (Cambridge, MA: Harvard University Press, 2013), 170–177.

75. *Thirty-First Semi-Annual Report of the Superintendent of Public Schools of the City of Boston, March 1877* (Boston: Rockwell and Churchill, 1877), 69–70.

76. A variation of lessons on forms was central to the kindergarten movement, known as Froebel's second gift. It comprised a wooden sphere, cylinder, and cube. It is supposed to teach the concept of unity, as the sphere may fit inside the cylinder and the cylinder may fit inside the cube. See Norman Brosterman and Kiyoshi Togashi, *Inventing Kindergarten* (New York: Harry N. Abrams, 1997), 46–49.

77. For example, these short lessons were advocated at Oswego (see Table 2.1).

78. "Our Common Schools," *Harpers Weekly*, February 26, 1870, 141–142.

79. I was able to work with a set of these forms and solids at the Huntington Library in California. J. W. Schermerhorn, *New Forms and Solids for Object Teaching containing sixty-four Pieces— there being 48 plane forms, fifteen solids, and a six-inch rule, among which are several NEW Forms and Solids, not included in any other set.* Korzenik Art Education Ephemera Collection, Box 77, Set 01, Huntington Library, San Marino, California.

80. This was just one of many companies that sold this type of product, which had been in the market for decades by 1870. See J. A. Bancroft, *Illustrated Catalogue of School Merchandise* (Philadelphia: J. A. Bancroft, n.d.), 12; Holbrook's Mathematical Forms, 1859, National Museum of American History.

81. Fanny Rothkopf—1877–1881, "Class III" Notebook, Archives of the Alumni Association of Hunter College, 1872–2005, Box 99, Folder 4, Archives & Special Collections, Hunter College Libraries, Hunter College of the City University of New York, New York City.

82. *Proceedings of the California State Teachers' Institute and Educational Convention, 1863* (Sacramento: 1863), Appendix B.

83. *Fourth Biennial Report of the Superintendent of Public Instruction of the State of California for the School Years 1871 and 1872* (Sacramento, 1871–72), 247.

84. For example, Gustavo F. J. Ciriliano, *Oswego en el Normalismo Argentino* (Buenos Aires: Editorial Nueva Generación, 2003) described the influence of Oswego on Argentina, and "Pestalozzi to Japan: Switzerland to New York to Tokyo, 1875–1878" (in *The History of Modern Japanese Education: Constructing the National School System*, by Benjamin Duke [New Brunswick, NJ: Rutgers University Press, 2009], 182–297) looks at how these methods traveled to Japan.

85. Andrew Philip Hollis, *The Contribution of the Oswego Normal School to Educational Progress in the United States* (Boston: D. C. Heath, 1898), 109.

86. Shaw was a philanthropist particularly devoted to educational causes like kindergarten and industrial training. Charles W. Eliot described her passion for education and educational reform quite clearly in her memorial, noting her interest "in concrete teaching, in training the senses" as well as training in observation and reasoning, an approach in sympathy with object-based pedagogical reforms. Charles W. Eliot, "Opening Address," in *Pauline Agassiz Shaw: Tributes Paid Her Memory at the Memorial Service Held on Easter Sunday April 8, 1917, at Faneuil Hall*, Boston (Boston: 1917), 29.

87. Mary Alling-Aber, *An Experiment in Education, Also the Ideas Which Inspired It and Were Inspired by It* (New York: Harper & Brothers, 1897) 41.

88. Samuel Eliot Morison, *One Boy's Boston, 1887–1901* (Boston: Houghton Mifflin, 1962), 44.

89. Mary R. Alling, *The Children's Own Work* (Boston: Industrial Home Press, 1883), 7; Mary Alling-Aber, *An Experiment in Education, also, the Ideas Which Inspired It and Were Inspired by It* (New York: Harper & Brothers, 1897), 4.

90. Alling, *The Children's Own Work*, 27–29.

91. Alling, *The Children's Own Work*, 39–40.

92. Alling-Aber, *An Experiment in Education*, 25–28.

93. Ella Flagg Young, *Some Types of Modern Educational Theory, Contributions to Education Number VI* (Chicago: University of Chicago Press, 1902), 23.

94. In 1885, Mary Sheldon married Earl Barnes, her former student. The pair collaborated on several writing projects. I refer to her as Sheldon Barnes to differentiate her from her father, though she spent more than a decade working as an academic prior to her marriage. For more on Mary Sheldon Barnes, see Frances E. Monteverde, "Considering the Source: Mary Sheldon Barnes," in *Bending the Future to Their Will: Civic Women, Social Education, and Democracy*, ed. Margaret Smith Crocco and O. L. Davis Jr. (Lanham: Rowman & Littlefield, 1999), 17–46. After Michigan, Sheldon Barnes studied at Cambridge and taught at Wellesley, Stanford, and Oswego.

95. Mary Sheldon Barnes to Frances and Edward A. Sheldon, September 28, 1871, in Mary Sheldon Barnes Papers, Box 2, Folder 1, Sophia Smith Collection, Smith College, Northampton, MA.

96. Mary Sheldon Barnes to Frances and Edward A. Sheldon, October 10, 1871, in Mary Sheldon Barnes Papers, Box 2, Folder 1, Sophia Smith Collection, Smith College, Northampton, MA.

97. Mary Sheldon Barnes to Edward A. Sheldon, February 6, 1872, in Mary Sheldon Barnes Papers, Box 2, Folder 1, Sophia Smith Collection, Smith College, Northampton, MA.

98. Monteverde, "Considering the Source," 26–27.

99. Mary Sheldon Barnes, *Studies in American History* (Boston: D.C. Heath, 1893), 384–385.

100. *How Shall I Teach History?* (Boston: D. C. Heath, 1889), 36, cited in Stuart A. McAninch, "The Educational Theory of Mary Sheldon Barnes: Inquiry Learning as Indoctrination in History Education," *Educational Theory* 40, no. 1 (Winter 1990): 45–52: 49.

101. Stuart A. McAninch criticized Sheldon Barnes for her treatment of race in *Studies in American History*. He rightly notes that she does not include sources related to lynching or racism and

expresses a fear of labor radicalism. McAninch, "The Educational Theory of Mary Sheldon Barnes," 49–52.

102. Sheldon Barnes, *Studies in American History*, iii.

103. Mary Sheldon Barnes, *Studies in General History* (Boston: D.C. Heath, 1901), vii.

104. Elizabeth Mayo, *Lessons on Shells* (London: R. B. Seeley and W. Burnside, 1832), 5n1.

105. "Nature an Educator," ca. 1860, Mary Sheldon Barnes Papers, Box 9, Folder 21, Sophia Smith Collections, Smith College Archives.

106. Mayo, *Lessons on Objects* (1859), 1–2.

107. Karen Halttunen, *Confidence Men and Painted Women: A Study of Middle-Class Culture in America, 1830–1870* (New Haven, CT: Yale University Press, 1982); James W. Cook, *The Arts of Deception: Playing with Fraud in the Age of Barnum* (Cambridge, MA: Harvard University Press, 2001); Michael Leja, *Looking Askance: Skepticism and American Art from Eakins to Duchamp* (Berkeley: University of California Press, 2004).

108. Warren Burton, *The Culture of the Observing Faculties* (New York: Harper & Brothers, 1865), 21.

109. Warren Burton, *Helps to Education in the Homes of Our Country* (Boston: Crosby and Nicholas, 1863), 274.

110. Drew Gilpin Faust, *This Republic of Suffering: Death and the American Civil War* (New York: Vintage Civil War Library, 2008).

Chapter 3

1. Beard became known for his pedagogical illustrations used in Sunday school "Chalk Talks" and was very concerned with the religious education of children through images. He was quite familiar with the contents of an ideal classroom. Thelma S. Rohrer, "Beard, Frank," *American National Biography Online*, February 2000, accessed November 27, 2009, http://www.anb.org.ezp-prod1.hul.harvard.edu/articles/17/17-00055.html.

2. "The Object Lesson," *Schermerhorn's Monthly*, January 1876, 1–9, and February 1876, 71–74.

3. "The Object Lesson," *Schermerhorn's Monthly*, January 1876, 1–2.

4. The word "empathy: is not used in English until the early twentieth century. However, it best approximates the fellow feeling this pedagogy encouraged between viewers and those depicted in visual sources. The German word *Einfühlung*, which was used in the period under consideration, referenced one's ability to understand things on a deeper level, "to 'feel into' works of art or into nature." Karsten Stueber, "Empathy," *The Stanford Encyclopedia of Philosophy* (Summer 2008 Edition), Edward N. Zalta, ed., http://plato.stanford.edu/archives/sum2008/entries/empathy/.

5. Sarah Trimmer, whose conversations with children, like those of Maria Edgeworth and Mrs. Marcet, led children to knowledge through looking and talking and created a series of books with both biblical and historical pictures for children. These pictures were available either for display on nursery walls or to be bound in a book. Sarah Trimmer, "A Series of Prints of English History Designed as Ornaments for Those Apartments in which Children Receive the First Rudiments of Their Education." London: Printed and Sold by John Marshall, at no. 4 Aldermary Church-Yard, in Bow-Lane, and No. 17, Queen-street, Cheapside, 1792. Cotsen Children's Library, Department of Rare Books and Special Collections, Princeton University Library, Princeton, NJ.

6. Irene Whaley and Tessa Rose Chester, *A History of Children's Book Illustration* (London: John Murray with the Victoria and Albert Museum, 1988).

7. William J. Reese, *America's Public Schools: From the Common School to "No Child Left Behind"* (Baltimore, MD: Johns Hopkins University Press, 2005), 28–30.

8. In the collections of the National Museum of American History and the American Antiquarian Society. See David Morgan, *Protestants and Pictures: Religion, Visual Culture and the Age of American Mass Production* (New York: Oxford University Press, 1999), and Pat Crain, *The Story of A* (Stanford, CA: Stanford University Press, 2000).

9. "Buffalo" Drawn on Stone & Printed by Childs & Inman. From a sketch from life by T. R. Peale. Published by Am. S. S. Union. Collection of American Antiquarian Society.

10. In this case, Gale is linking his beauty to her ability to feel sympathy for the boy. Journal from Greene Street School, January 2, 1838, page 14, Gale Family Papers, Collection of the American Antiquarian Society. Paula Kopacz, who published an edited edition of Anna Gale's diary in *Studies in American Renaissance* (1996) explains that the "cannibal" is likely Peter the Wild Boy.

11. Hermann Krüsi, Pestalozzi's assistant, described the use of these pictures of familiar objects to instruct children. Hermann Krüsi, "'My Educational Recollections' translated and excerpted by his son Hermann Krüsi," in *Studies in Education: A Series of Ten Numbers Devoted to Child Study and the History of Education*, ed. Earl Barnes (Stanford, CA: Stanford University, 1897), 230–239, 273–280: 274.

12. Massimiano Bruno, "Images of Science in the Classroom: Wall Charts and Science Education, 1850–1920," in *Visual Cultures of Science*, ed. L. Pauwels (Hanover, NH: University Press of New England, 2006), 90–117. For a history of these collections of images in books or boxes, see Anke te Heesen, *The World in a Box: The Story of an Eighteenth-Century Picture Encyclopedia*, trans. Ann M. Hentschel (Chicago: University of Chicago Press, 2002).

13. *Bilder zum ersten Anschauungs-Unterricht* (Esslingen: Schrieber, n.d., ca. 1850), 1. Euro 19Q 44901 Cotsen Children's Library, Princeton University.

14. C. F. A. Lehrer, *The Picture-Book of Elementary Ideas*, trans. Madame de Chatelain. (Stuttgart: K. Thienemann [Jul. Hoffmann], [ca. 1865]), Cotsen Children's Library, Princeton University.

15. This is a common trope and also appears in Johann Siegmund Stoy's eighteenth-century *Bilder-Akademie für die Jugend*. See Heesen, *The World in a Box*, Tableau A; William Darton and Thomas Bewick, *The Rational Exhibition for Children* (London: Darton and Harvey, 1800).

16. "Wheat" No. 1 from Oliver and Boyd's Object-Lesson Cards, English 19 Oversize Folio 26556, Cotsen Children's Library, Princeton University Library, Princeton, New Jersey. An earlier version of this analysis appeared as "On an Object Lesson, or Don't Eat the Evidence," *Journal of the History of Childhood and Youth* 3, no. 1 (Winter 2010): 6–12.

17. A series of object lessons on the Great Exhibition entitled *Fireside Facts from the Great Exhibition* used a wide array of lessons to teach children about categories of objects and their natural histories and uses. *Fireside Facts from the Great Exhibition Being an Amusing Series of Object Lessons on the Food and Clothing of All Nations in the Year 1851* (London: Houlston and Stoneman, 1851).

18. See Carla Yanni, "Nature as Natural Resource: The Edinburgh Museum of Science and Art," in *Nature's Museums: Victorian Science and the Architecture of Display* (Baltimore: Johns Hopkins University Press, 1999), 91–110.

19. "To Teachers" introductory card for Vegetable Kingdom in Oliver and Boyd's Object-Lesson Cards, English 19 Oversize Folio 26556, Cotsen Children's Library, Princeton University Library, Princeton, New Jersey.

20. Shirley Wajda, "'And a Little Child Shall Lead Them': American Children's Cabinets of Curiosities," in Leah Dilworth, *Acts of Possession: Collecting in America* (New Brunswick, NJ: Rutgers University Press, 2003), 44.

21. "Suggestions to Teachers" introductory card in Bancroft Brothers Object-Lesson Cards, Original Artwork 26700, Cotsen Children's Library, Princeton University Library, Princeton University.

22. *Sixty-Ninth Semi-Annual Conference of the Church of Latter-Day Saints* (Deseret News Company, 1898), 58.

23. Lucille Schultz, "Pestalozzi's Mark on Nineteenth-Century Composition Instruction: Ideas Not in Words, but in Things," *Rhetoric Review* 14, no. 1 (Fall 1995): 23–43.

24. *Forty-Fifth Annual Report of the Trustees of the Perkins Institution and Massachusetts Asylum for the Blind*, October 1876 (Boston: Albert J. Wright, State Printer, 1977), 57–58.

25. Johanna Drucker, "Harnett, Haberle, and Peto: Visuality and Artifice among the Proto-Modern Americans," *Art Bulletin* 74, no. 1 (March 1992): 37–50; John Haberle, *A Bachelor's Drawer 1890–94*, oil on canvas, 20 x 36 in., Metropolitan Museum of Art, Purchase, Henry R. Luce Gift, 1970, 1970.193. Perhaps Haberle's work reflected the education he received in 1860s New Haven, when object teaching was included in the curriculum. In 1861 New Haven lists object teaching as part of the curriculum for students ranging in age from five to nine,

which Haberle would have been at that time, as well as for older students. *Annual Report of the Board of Education for the New Haven City School District for the Year Ending September 1, 1861* (New Haven: E. Hayes, 1861), 19–21.

26. Elizabeth Mayo, *Lessons on Shells* (London: R. B. Seeley and W. Burnside, 1832), n.p.

27. *The Home and Colonial School Society's Manual, For Infant Schools and Nurseries, Prepared at the Desire of the Committee by Miss Rebecca Sunter, Late Mistress of the Model Infant School, under the superintendence of Miss Mayo* (London: The Society, Groombridge and Sons, 1856), 90.

28. The HCS version is at the Cotsen Children's Library. The two ASSU sets are at Winterthur and the American Antiquarian Society. They are inscribed 1852 and 1859, respectively.

29. Pictures lessons on scripture prints followed a similar format. For example, a Home and Colonial Schools lesson on a scripture print of Cain's murder of Abel follows the same conventions. After examining the picture to determine why the children think Cain looks angry and what happened in the story, the children are told the Bible story and are challenged to apply the lesson to their own lives. They are told "to guard against anger. How this may be done. When struck not to strike again; when called bad names, not to call names in return. In whose sight would such a spirit be pleasing?" From "E. C. Tufnell's Report, Answers to Examination Questions, by Students of the Home and Colonial Infant and Juvenile School Society," *Minutes of the Committee of Council, 1846* (1847) 45, 579–581, published in Anne Digby and Peter Searby, *Children, School and Society in Nineteenth-Century England* (London: Macmillan, 1981), 79–80.

30. Sheldon, Jones, and Krüsi, *Manual of Elementary Instruction* (1862), 389–391.

31. *Home and Colonial School Society's Manual*, 90.

32. *Home and Colonial School Society's Manual*, 193–194.

33. For more on this in the context of children and cruelty to animals, see Katherine C. Grier, *Pets in America: A History* (Chapel Hill: University of North Carolina Press, 2006). She explicitly addresses the scene in this lithograph in relation to kindness to animals. It might be a point of comparison here to note that Calkins mentions the study of natural history as a way to teach children to be kinder to animals. This suggests a fascinating point of cultural tension. Natural history study was dependent on the collection (and death) of specimens. This issue comes up frequently, particularly later in the century, as object lessons gradually morph into nature study.

34. Sheldon, Jones, and Krüsi, *Manual of Elementary Instruction* (1862), 384–391.

35. *Annual Report of the State Normal and Training School at Oswego for the Year Ending September 30, 1871* (Albany: the Argus Company, 1871), 76–78. I have not been able to locate the print or painting at the center of this lesson. Any suggestions would be appreciated.

36. *Seventh Annual Report of the Board of Education of the City of Oswego for the Year Ending March 31, 1860* (Oswego: Tarbell, 1860), 23.

37. J. M. Ives, "The Four Seasons of Life: Old Age 'The Season of Rest,'" drawn by Parsons & Atwater (New York: Currier and Ives, ca. 1868), Library of Congress, Washington, DC.

38. Nancy Finlay, ed., *Picturing Victorian America: Prints by the Kellogg Brothers of Hartford, Connecticut, 1830–1880* (Middletown, CT: Wesleyan University and the Connecticut Historical Society, 2009), 34–35.

39. Elizabeth Johns, *American Genre Painting: The Politics of Everyday Life* (New Haven, CT: Yale University Press, 1991), xii–xiii.

40. N. A. Calkins, *Principles of Education; And Design of Prang's Aids for Object-Teaching* (Boston: Prang, 1877), 4.

41. Claire Strom, "Calkins, Norman Allison," *American National Biography Online*, February 2000, accessed December 22, 2006, http://www.anb.org/articles/09/09-00144.html; Norman A. Calkins, Obituary, December 25, 1895, *New York Times*. Thomas Hunter, who founded the New York City Normal School, which became Hunter College appears to have had a sort of rivalry with Calkins. Hunter credited him with introducing object lessons but criticized Calkins for doing little good because teachers did not fully adopt his methods. Thomas Hunter, *The Autobiography of Thomas Hunter* (New York: Knickerbocker Press, 1931), 363.

42. Object-lesson pedagogy is closely related to the nature study movement. Sally Gregory Kohlstedt, *Teaching Children Science: Hands-on Nature Study in North America, 1890–1930* (Chicago: University of Chicago Press, 2010).

43. N. A. Calkins, *A Classified List of Object Teaching Aids for Home and School* (New York: J. W. Schermerhorn, 1872).

44. Calkins, *A Classified List*, 35.

45. Mary P. Winsor, *Reading the Shape of Nature: Comparative Zoology at the Agassiz Museum* (Chicago: University of Chicago Press, 1991), 14; Joel Asaph Allen and American Museum of Natural History, *Autobiographical Notes and a Bibliography of the Scientific Publications of Joel Asaph Allen* (New York: American Museum of Natural History, 1916), 8–9.

46. N. A. Calkins, *A Manual to Accompany Prang's Natural History Series* (Boston: Prang, 1873?), 6.

47. Calkins, *A Classified List*, 43.

48. The decision to start with a single example parallels Louis Agassiz's desire to have a synoptic room in the Museum of Comparative Zoology at Harvard. He planned to introduce visitors to categories of specimens, as opposed to overwhelming them with an array of scientifically ordered examples. Winsor, *Reading the Shape of Nature*, 124.

49. N. A. Calkins, *Prang's Natural History Series, for Schools and Families: Animals and Plants Represented in Their Natural Colors, and Arranged for Instruction with Object Lessons* (Boston: Prang, ca. 1872–73), original cards archived at American Antiquarian Society, Worcester, MA.

50. Calkins, *Manual*, 6.

51. N. A. Calkins, *Plan of Instruction Embodied in Prang's Natural History Series, for Schools and Families: Animals and Plants Represented in their Natural Colors, and Arranged for in Instruction with Object Lessons* (Boston: Prang and Co, 1872–3), n.p.

52. N. A. Calkins, *A Manual to Accompany Prang's Natural History Series* (Boston: Prang, 1873?), 5.

53. Prang also published a series of small, postage stamp–size prints of animal, insect, and plant life that are numbered. They are in the Archives of American Art in the Mary Margaret Sittig research material collection on Louis Prang, 1870–1970. I have not been able to locate a key, but I have found another set of the images pasted into a children's scrapbook on object teaching called *Books with Words and Pictures for Home, Kindergarten and School* (New York: Bible House, ca. 1878), n.p., Joseph Downs Collection, Winterthur Museum.

54. It is unclear exactly how popular this series may have been. As was common, Calkins published several ringing endorsements from teachers and superintendents in New York, Massachusetts, Connecticut, Illinois, and Cincinnati, including Sheldon at Oswego, along with his series. "How Prang's Natural History Are Received" in Calkins, *Manual*, 1873: Part II, 23–25. This mode of instruction influenced other pedagogical projects, suggesting that it may have had a broader impact. Children's games reflected this desire to instruct via comparison, study, and classification. For example, *Avilude or the Game of Birds*, published in 1893, required all of these skills. The game consisted of sixty-four cards divided into eight groups, like "Honey Eaters" or the "Pigeon Tribe," each of which contains pairs that represent an engraving and a description of a particular bird. The game proceeded as children matched pictures of birds to their descriptions. West & Lee, Worcester Mass, 1893, Joseph Downs Collection, Winterthur Museum.

55. Zoology; Subject of Lesson: Mammalia, Perkins Institution, ca. 1893 (Samuel P. Hayes Research Library, Perkins School for the Blind, Watertown, MA, AG13_05_0031c).

56. N. A. Calkins, *Principles of Education; and Design of Prang's Aids for Object-Teaching* (Boston: Prang, 1877), 5.

57. Calkins, *Principles of Education*, 5.

58. J. M. Mancini looks at these antiquated images as a way to address "social and economic change," by consciously deemphasizing the mechanization of shoemaking. This is a fair interpretation; however, it does not consider the larger pedagogical context of these images. JoAnne Marie Mancini, *Pre-Modernism: Art-World Change and American Culture from the Civil War to the Armory Show* (Princeton, NJ: Princeton University Press, 2005), 83.

59. *Capital*, Volume 1, Section 4, "The Fetishism of Commodities and the Secret Thereof," from *The Marx-Engels Reader*, ed., Robert Tucker (New York: Norton, 1978), 319–329.
60. Calkins, *Principles of Education*, 17.
61. Calkins, *Principles of Education*, 22.
62. Calkins, *Principles of Education*, 66.
63. This categorization is still the way connoisseurs explain traditional printmaking processes. Bamber Gascoigne prefers the terms relief, intaglio, and planographic. *How to Identify Prints* (New York: Thames & Hudson, 2004).
64. Calkins, *Principles of Education*, 44–48.
65. Calkins, *Principles of Education*, 66.
66. Ann-Sophie Lehmann addresses a similar problem in her work on "Showing Making" in relation to the creation of images as "materially constructed artifacts." The object-lesson approach of Calkins and Prang suggests a further elaboration of the analysis she offers in that their images also suggest that pictures can show more abstract forms of thinking and reasoning, beyond solving the specific material creative problems addressed in the craft or making process illustrated or embodied in the images. Ann-Sophie Lehmann, "Showing Making: On Visual Documentation and Creative Practice," *Journal of Modern Craft* 5, no. 1 (March 2012): 9–24.
67. Critics of object lessons attacked this aspect of the pedagogy as unnecessary, arguing that children did not need to be taught things they saw every day. For more on the debate surrounding object lessons in the classroom, see Oswego, NY, Board of Education, *Proceedings of the Educational Convention, Held at Oswego, NY, February 11, 12 and 13, 1862 to Examine into a System of Primary Instruction by Object Lessons* (New York: Harper & Brothers, 1862).
68. National Society for Promoting the Education of the Poor in the Principles of the Established Church, *Manuals for Teachers—No. 1: The Cultivation of the Senses* (Philadelphia: Eldredge & Brother, 1879), 71–72.
69. Elizabeth Mayo, *Lessons on Objects, as Given to Children between the Ages of Six and Eight, in a Pestalozzian School, at Cheam, Surrey*, 16th ed. (London: Seeley, Jackson, and Halliday, 1859), 1–2.
70. *Books with Words and Pictures for Home, Kindergarten and School*, Joseph Downs Collection, Winterthur Museum.

Chapter 4

1. Frances Benjamin Johnson, "Louis Firetail (Sioux, Crow Creek), wearing tribal clothing, in American history class, Hampton Institute, Hampton, Virginia," 1899, Library of Congress, Prints & Photographs Division, LC-DIG-ppmsca-12031.
2. H. B. Frissell confirmed Johnston's appointment on November 15, 1899, and thanked her for the final proofs on January 24, 1900. Because the photographs include a lesson on Thanksgiving, which was November 30, 1899, I believe they were taken around that time. H. B. Frissell to F. B. Johnston, November 15, 1899, and January 24, 1900, container 7 (microfilm reel 5), Frances Benjamin Johnston Papers, Library of Congress.
3. For a thorough historiography of the photographs, see Sarah Bassnett, "From Public Relations to Art: Exhibiting Frances Benjamin Johnston's Hampton Institute Photographs," *History of Photography* 32, no. 2 (Summer 2008): 152–168; Carrie Mae Weems, Vivian Patterson, Denise Ramzy, Katherine Fogg, Williams College Museum of Art, and Hood Museum of Art, *Carrie Mae Weems: The Hampton Project; Hampton Project, Before and After* (New York: Aperture, in association with Williams College Museum of Art, Williamstown, MA, 2000); Laura Wexler, "Black and White and Color: The Hampton Album," in *Tender Violence: Domestic Visions in an Age of U.S. Imperialism* (Chapel Hill: University of North Carolina Press, 2000), 127–176; Shawn Michael Smith, "Photographing the 'American Negro': Nation, Race, and Photography at the Paris Exposition of 1900," in *American Archives: Gender, Race and Class in Visual Culture* (Princeton, NJ: Princeton University Press, 1999), 156–186; Frances Benjamin Johnston,

Lincoln Kirstein, and the Museum of Modern Art, *Hampton Album* (New York: Museum of Modern Art, 1966).

4. The Library of Congress Prints and Photographs Division houses a huge collection of Johnston photographs including scores of Hampton that have not been digitized or, as far as I have been able to determine, published.

5. "Hampton Normal and Agricultural Institute: Report of Special Committee," *American Missionary Extra* (August 1869), 2.

6. In some ways, the kind of education I am describing might seem similar to John Dewey's progressive "learning by doing" ideology. Chronologically, however, object lessons are the appropriate context for Armstrong's curriculum. Donald Generals has argued that Booker T. Washington, Hampton's most famous graduate and teacher, was a progressive educator who should be ranked along with Dewey in his linking of activity and learning. This chapter complements Generals's argument by claiming that looking backward for the origins of this kind of activity toward Armstrong and object lessons offers another and possibly more compelling context for this type of pedagogy. Donald Generals, "Booker T. Washington and Progressive Education: An Experimentalist Approach to Curriculum Development and Reform," *Journal of Negro Education* 69, no. 3 (Summer 2000): 215–234; William Reese, "The Origins of Progressive Education," *History of Education Quarterly* 41, no. 1 (Spring 2001): vi, 1–24.

7. Andrew Phillip Hollis even notes that the South was behind the North in terms of its education for white children because of the association of progressive methods with schools for African American students. Andrew Phillip Hollis, *The Contribution of the Oswego Normal School to Educational Progress in the United States* (Boston: D. C. Heath, 1898), 68–69.

8. Manuscript diary of Ingraham, a teacher in Hawaii in the 1850s, Saturday, May 24, 1856, p. 32, Huntington Library, San Marino, CA.

9. Robert Engs, *Educating the Disenfranchised and Disinherited: Samuel Chapman Armstrong and Hampton Institute, 1839–1893* (Knoxville: University of Tennessee Press, 1999), 18.

10. Engs, *Educating the Disenfranchised*, 80; *Memories of Old Hampton* (Hampton, VA: Institute Press, 1909), 4.

11. M. F. Armstrong, Helen W. Ludlow, and Thomas Fenner, *Hampton and Its Students by Two of Its Teachers* (New York: G. P. Putman's Sons, 1874), 59.

12. Hollis, *The Contribution of the Oswego Normal School*, 65.

13. "Report of President Hopkins, of Williams College, Mass., Mr. Hyde, of the Board of Agriculture, Mass., Secretary Northrup, of the Board of Education, Conn., and General Garfield, M.C., upon the Hampton Normal and Agricultural Institute" (1870; reprinted from the *American Missionary* of August 1869), 9.

14. Mark M. Smith, *How Race Is Made: Slavery, Segregation, and the Senses* (Chapel Hill: University of North Carolina Press, 2006), 12.

15. For example, Pratt describes this in *Battlefield and Classroom: Four Decades with the American Indian, 1867–1904*, ed. Richard Henry Pratt and Robert Marshall Utley (Norman: University of Oklahoma Press, 2004), 180–183; for more on the ledger drawings from Fort Marion, see Janet C. Berlo et al., *Plains Indian Drawings, 1865–1935: Pages from a Visual History* (New York: Harry Abrams, 1996); Janet C. Berlo and Ruth B. Phillips, *Native North American Art* (Oxford: Oxford University Press, 1998), 122–130. After Hampton, Pratt went on to found the Carlisle Indian School in Pennsylvania, leading to the broad expansion of the boarding school concept for native students under the Department of the Interior. Frederick E. Hoxie, *A Final Promise: The Campaign to Assimilate the Indians, 1880–1920* (Lincoln: University of Nebraska Press, 1984), 56–58.

16. Ludlow, who also edited the *Southern Workman* and several other publications about Hampton, had lived in Oswego, New York. She came to Hampton in 1872 as part of the American Missionary Association. There is no record that she attended the Oswego Normal School, but she was surely familiar with the goals of object lessons that came to define her hometown's national reputation starting in the early 1860s. The extent to which her language was informed by a possible connection to Sheldon and the Oswego Normal School is unclear. It appears that Helen's father was the abolitionist Reverend Henry G. Ludlow and her brother was Fitz Hugh Ludlow, author of *The Hasheesh Eater*. According to notes in the Mary

Sheldon Barnes Papers it appears that Ludlow's uncle may have worked with E. A. Sheldon to found a new Congregational Church in Oswego. Hampton Institute and Helen W. Ludlow, *Ten Years Work for the Indians* (Hampton, VA: Hampton Institute, 1888), 30; notes for E. A. Sheldon, *Autobiography*, pages 98–100, Mary Sheldon Barnes Papers, Box 9, Folder 10, Sophia Smith Collection, Smith College, Northampton, MA.

17. In addition to the emphasis on the assumed perceptive abilities of Native American students, many students needed to master the English language before moving into the Normal course. Object lessons were particularly well adapted for language study. Michael C. Coleman, *American Indian Children at School, 1850–1930* (Jackson: University Press of Mississippi, 1993), 105–126.

18. For example, Harriet Beecher Stowe visited the classroom at Fort Marion in 1877 (her Florida home was nearby) and described the walls of their schoolroom, "Large spelling cards adorned one side of the wall, containing various pictures and object-lessons adapted to the earliest stages of learning." Pratt, *Battlefield and Classroom*, 156. Further research is required to determine how elementary object lessons were used for older African American students in "colored schools" in the North. This is difficult to do because those schools are not always age-graded, which may be an important clue to solving this mystery. The *Harper's Weekly* engraving of a "Colored School," Figure 2.4, appears to be teaching slightly older children simple lessons on forms.

19. In an exhaustive study of Hampton records, he cites numerous examples in which black students are referred to as "demonstrative" and "cheerful" while "Indian students are "reserved, sensitive and self-conscious." Furthermore, he explains that black students were viewed as being able to help civilize the newly arrived native students, giving the black students a chance to be philanthropic. Donal Lindsey, *Indians at Hampton Institute, 1877–1923* (Urbana: University of Illinois Press, 1995), 88–112.

20. Jeanne Zeidler and Mary Lou Hultgren, "'Things African Prove to Be a Favorite Theme': The African Collection at the Hampton University," in *ART/Artifact* (New York: Prestel, 1988), 97–152: 97.

21. *Catalogue of the Hampton Normal and Agricultural Institute, for the Academic Year 1875–6* (Hampton, VA: Normal School Steam Press, 1876), 24.

22. Cora Folsom to H. B. Frissell, January 1, 1911, Hampton Museum Correspondence, Hampton University Archives; Lindsey, *Indians at Hampton Institute*, 177–178.

23. Cora Folsom, "Report on the Hampton Museum, 1905," Hampton University Archives.

24. While Hampton requested "co-operation" in providing apparatus necessary in the study of Physical Sciences and natural history, they listed a wide range of philosophical apparatus used in instruction. *Catalogue of the Hampton Normal and Agricultural Institute, Hampton Virginia, for the Academic Year 1875-1876* (Hampton, Virginia: Normal School Steam Press, 1876) 24, 43; *Catalogue of the Hampton Normal and Agricultural Institute, Hampton Virginia, for the Academic Year 1897-1898* (Hampton, Virginia: Printed on the Institute Press, 1898), 22.

25. *Hampton Normal and Agricultural Institute Annual Reports for the Academical and Fiscal Year Ending June 30, 1886* (Hampton, VA: Normal School Steam Press Print, 1886) 18.

26. *Southern Workman* 7, no. 7 (July 1878): 50.

27. Hampton Institute and Ludlow, *Ten Years Work for the Indians*, 30.

28. Ludlow also mentions Dr. Peet's Language Lessons designed for the instruction of deaf mutes as useful for teaching Native American students. This is another variation of object-lesson pedagogy, which had been adapted for language instruction. *Hampton Normal and Agricultural Institute, Annual Reports for the Academical and Fiscal Year Ending June 30, 1882* (Hampton, VA: Normal School Steam Press Print, 1882), 36–38.

29. Collections of the Quincy Historical Society, Quincy, Massachusetts.

30. *Southern Workman* 8, no. 6 (June 1879): 67.

31. W. E. B. Du Bois, *Souls of Black Folk* (New York: Penguin Books, 1996), 54.

32. Caroline F. Putnam, "A Freedman's School in Virginia," *Harper's Weekly* 12, no. 2 (December 1874): 1015; Edward T. James et al., *Notable American Women, 1607–1950: A Biographical Dictionary*, vol. 1 (Cambridge, MA: Harvard University Press, 1971), s.v. "Holley, Sallie."

33. The reading done here was not necessarily reading as an individual relationship with a book but as a performative, public act. This is also how news was spread at Hampton in the early years. News stories would be cut out of various publications and posted on the wall for students to read and to be seen reading.

34. James et al., *Notable American Women*, 347.

35. This origin story is repeated in many newspaper articles on Kitchen Gardens as well as in the introduction to most editions to her manual. See Emily Huntington, *The Kitchen Garden, Or, Object lessons in Household Work* (New York: Schermerhorn, 1893), 9–10.

36. Unlike the Normal School, the Butler/Whittier School served the local community and did not intend to train all of its pupils for a career in teaching. In some cases younger native students (under fourteen) who were able to speak English might be sent to the school as well. Elizabeth Hyde, "Of the Butler School," *Hampton Normal and Agricultural Institute, Annual reports for the Academical and Fiscal Year Ending June 30, 1883* (Hampton, VA: Normal School Steam Press Print, 1883), 33; Lindsey, *Indians at Hampton Institute*, 118–119.

37. Barbara Beatty, *Preschool Education in America: The Culture of Young Children from the Colonial Era to the Present* (New Haven, CT: Yale University Press, 1995), 54.

38. Elizabeth Peabody and Mrs. Horace Mann, *The Moral Culture of Infancy and Kindergarten Guide* (Boston: T. O. H. P. Burnham, 1863); Norman Brosterman and Kiyoshi Togashi, *Inventing Kindergarten* (New York: Harry Abrams, 1997).

39. The formal Kitchen Garden curriculum was modified several times from the 1870s through the 1910s. I have analyzed three printed versions of the manual, 1883, 1893, and 1912, two manuscript lesson books, and numerous newspaper and magazine accounts. The Kitchen Garden Association, *Advanced Lessons in Kitchen Garden* (New York: Schermerhorn, 1883); Emily Huntington and Frédéric Vors, *The Kitchen Garden of Object Lessons in Household Work* (New York: Schermerhorn, 1893); Mabel Louise Keech, *Training the Little Homemaker by Kitchengarden Methods* (Philadelphia: J. B. Lippincott, 1912); manuscript notebooks kept by New York City Kitchen Garden teacher Kate Van Santvoord Olcott in 1878 and 1881. (These manuscripts are available online from the Milbank Memorial Library, Teachers' College, Columbia University.)

40. Huntington and Vors, *Kitchen Garden*, 20.

41. Huntington and Vors, *Kitchen Garden*, 96.

42. Brosterman and Togashi, *Inventing Kindergarten*, 74, 88.

43. Huntington and Vors, *Kitchen Garden*, 117–118, 110–111.

44. Olive Thorne, "Little Housemaids," *St. Nicholas Magazine* 6, no. 6 (April 1879): 403.

45. "The Kitchen-Garden: How Housework Is Taught by Object Lesson in Several Cities," *New York Times*, March 18, 1880. One newspaper account suggested that the concept had made it to Calcutta, India. "The Work of the Kitchen Garden," *New York Times*, April 20, 1881.

46. "The Kitchen Garden: How Housework Is taught by Object lesson in Several Cities," *New York Times*, March 18, 1880.

47. Elizabeth Hyde's report on "The Butler School" in *Hampton Normal and Agricultural Institute, Annual Reports for the Academical and Fiscal Year Ending June 30, 1886* (Hampton, VA: Normal School Steam Press Print, 1886), 26–27.

48. Elizabeth Hyde's report in *Hampton Normal and Agricultural Institute, Annual Reports for the Academical and Fiscal Year Ending June 30, 1883* (Hampton, VA: Normal School Steam Press Print, 1883), 33.

49. Helen Ludlow, "The Evolution of the Whittier Primary School," *Southern Workman* 35, no. 5 (May 1906): 290.

50. See, for example, "Ironing Song March," *St. Nicholas Magazine* 10, no. 5 (1883): 364.

51. Beatty briefly mentioned a Kitchen Garden at Hampton as late as 1907. Beatty, *Preschool Education in America*, 108.

52. Booker T. Washington, *Up from Slavery* (New York: Doubleday, 1901), 50–53.

53. Francis Greenwood Peabody, *Education for Life* (New York: Doubleday, Page, 1918).

54. James D. Anderson, *The Education of Blacks in the South, 1860–1935* (Chapel Hill: University of North Carolina Press, 1988), 34.

55. Engs, *Educating the Disenfranchised*, 79–80.

56. Hampton Institute and Ludlow, *Ten Years Work for the Indians*, 24–25. Hampton discontinued its Indian program in 1922. In 1912 government funding was cut, in large part due to the racist rhetoric of southern white political leaders about the comingling of the races at the school as well as to the school's decision to refocus on the needs of its African American population. Donal Lindsey provides a nuanced treatment of this period of the school's history; Lindsey, *Indians at Hampton Institute*, 247–271.

57. E. A. Sheldon, "The Mental Effect of Manual Training," a speech given by Edward Austin Sheldon at the New York State Teachers' Association held at Watkins Glen, NY, July 4, 5, and 6, 1888, Container 1, Folder 40, Edward Austin Sheldon Papers, Penfield Library, SUNY–Oswego. I believe this view of manual training may be linked to the Arts and Crafts Movement, particularly as object-lesson pedagogues frequently linked hand, heart, and mind, a theme often raised within the Arts and Crafts Movement. For the Arts and Crafts movement in the United States, see Wendy Kaplan, "America: The Quest for Democratic Design," in *The Arts & Crafts Movement in Europe & America: Design for the Modern World*, ed. Wendy Kaplan, Alan Crawford, Los Angeles County Museum of Art, Delaware Art Museum, and Cleveland Museum of Art (New York: Thames & Hudson in association with the Los Angeles County Museum of Art, 2004), 246–283.

58. At the same time, these images seem to flatten the difference between the bodies of the students and the tools they employ as workers. Most images do not focus on them as individual workers. Shawn Michael Smith suggests that the African American male students pictured may have felt unsafe staring directly at Frances Benjamin Johnston because of her race and gender. Smith, "Photographing the 'American Negro,' " 170.

59. S. C. Armstrong, "Work and Duty in the East," in *The American Missionary* 36 (1882): 378–380.

60. "The Work of Hampton Institute," *New York Times*, April 29, 1900.

61. Armstrong's curriculum was certainly racist in its application. As Anderson notes, "Routine and repetitive manual labor activities were developed to screen and condition students to serve as missionaries of the Hampton idea." Anderson, *The Education of Blacks in the South*, 47.

62. One could also make the case here that Washington's famous statement—"In all things that are purely social we can be as separate as the fingers, yet one as the hand in all things essential to mutual progress" from the Atlanta Exposition in 1895—was a rhetorical object lesson similar in emphasis to "object lessons on the human body." For example, N. A. Calkins offered a lesson on the hand: "Hand and Its Parts.—Talk about the hand and its uses for *holding, throwing, catching, lifting, pulling,* and *feeling*; about using one hand more than the other; about the parts of the hand—the back of the hand, where the knuckles are; the palm of the hand, inside; of the fingers, naming each; of the thumb, showing how it can touch each of the fingers." Norman A. Calkins, *Primary Object Lessons, for Training the Senses and Developing the Faculties of Children*, 40th ed. (New York: Harper's, 1898), 416; Robert J. Norrell, *Up from History: The Life of Booker T Washington* (Cambridge, MA: Belknap Press of Harvard University Press, 2009), 121–126.

63. Booker T. Washington, Louis R. Harlan, and Norman Barton Wood, *The Booker T. Washington Papers*, vol. 3, *1889–1895* (Urbana: University of Illinois Press, 1972), 201, 218, and 285.

64. *Hampton Normal and Agricultural Institute, Annual Reports for the Academical and Fiscal Year Ending June 30, 1896* (Hampton, VA: Normal School Steam Press, 1897), 13.

65. Jane Simonsen discusses this in *Making Home Work: Domesticity and Native American Assimilation in the American West, 1860–1919* (Chapel Hill: University of North Carolina Press, 2006). She described ways in which Native American homes were transformed into "object lessons," documenting their progress, but does not connect this to the pedagogical strategy of object lessons.

66. This concept is not quite the same as the trope of the New Negro, though they are clearly related. While individuals identified in books like Washington's *A New Negro for a New Century* as "new negroes" could certainly be viewed as object lessons, the emphasis is on the identification of a group made up of successful individuals versus a call for an argument about those individuals made through observation. Henry Louis Gates Jr., "The Trope of the New Negro and the Reconstruction of the Image of the Black," *Representations* 24 (Autumn 1988): 129–155.

67. R. H. Pratt, "List of names, age, tribe, etc., of Indian boys and girls at Hampton Normal and Agricultural Institute, Virginia, plaster casts of whose heads were taken by Clark Mills, Esq., March, 1879," *Proceedings of the United States National Museum* 2 (1879): 211.

68. Mary Sheldon Barnes and Earl Barnes, *Studies in American History* (Boston: D. C. Heath, 1893), 384–385.

69. For analysis of these before and after photographs, see Wexler, "Black and White and Color."

70. Frances Benjamin Johnston, photographer, Louis Firetail Sioux, Crow Creek, wearing tribal clothing, in American history class, Hampton Institute, Hampton, Virginia. Hampton Virginia, 1899 [or 1900], photograph, retrieved from the Library of Congress, https://www. loc.gov/item/98502982/, accessed May 23, 2017.

71. Lindsey, *Indians at Hampton Institute*, 100.

72. "Social Life at the School," *Southern Workman* (June 1892): 101.

73. "Justice to the Indians," *Independent*, May 11, 1882, 17. This is but one of many cases in which the term was used this way. For example, an article titled "A Grand Object Lesson" detailed a parade in Philadelphia in which native students dressed as "a band of braves, mounted and in their war paint" were followed by native students from Hampton, Carlisle, and Lincoln wearing cadet uniforms and carrying slates. "A Grand Object Lesson," *Daily Inter Ocean*, September 22, 1887, 2. Buffalo Bill Cody further employed the metaphor in his Wild West Shows, advertising his Indian subjects as "Object Lessons."

74. While the General Allotment Act, commonly known as the Dawes Act (1887), would address this question, in 1884, the Indian Rights Association argued for a path that would allow some Indians to become citizens. Notably, students like those with Armstrong were ideal candidates, as noted in the 1884 book *The Indian before the Law* by Henry Pancoast, "Let every graduate of Hampton, Carlisle or any Government school be entitled to American citizenship" (Philadelphia, The Indian Rights Association, 1884), 25; Jill E. Martin, "'Neither Fish, Flesh, Fowl, nor Good Red Herring': The Citizenship Status of American Indians, 1830–1924," *Journal of the West* 29, no. 3 (1990): 75–87; Philip Deloria, *Playing Indian* (New Haven, CT: Yale University Press, 1998).

75. The author is deeply grateful to curator Emil Her Many Horses (Oglala Lakota) of the National Museum of the American Indian for taking the time to examine this photograph with me. Personal Meeting, July 24, 2009. Some of these items may still be at Hampton Institute. For comparison, note particularly the Lakota Sioux Eagle Feather Bonnet and Trailer. This example is stylistically similar to the one depicted and dated 1920–1930. Emma Hansen, Beatrice Medicine, and Buffalo Bill Historical Center, *Memory and Vision: Arts, Cultures, and Lives of Plains Indians People* (Seattle: University of Washington Press, 2007), 166–167. Firetail's shirt (sometimes called a war shirt) is very similar to an example from the Yanktonai Sioux, from 1880–1900 and even appears to be made out of canvas instead of buckskin, which was a popular replacement. Firetail belonged to the Yankton division of the Crow Creek Sioux. Audrey Porsche, *Yutó'Keca* [Transitions: The Burdick Collection] (Bismarck: State Historical Society of North Dakota, 1987), 29.

76. "Indian Incidents," *Southern Workman* (May 1899): 189.

77. According to a museum exhibition catalog by Mary Lou Hultgren, Paulette Fairbanks Molin, Rayna Green, Virginia Foundation for the Humanities and Public Policy, and Hampton University, *To Lead and to Serve: American Indian Education at Hampton Institute 1878–1923*, the items are drawn from the museum's collections (Charlottesville: Virginia Foundation for the Humanities and Public Policy with Hampton University, 1989), 30. There is a photograph in the Frances Benjamin Johnston Collection at the Library of Congress of another young man wearing the same shirt (Lot 11051.5).

78. United States Office of Indian Affairs, *Annual Report of the Commissioner of Indian Affairs* (1900), 729.

79. "Mr. and Mrs. Louis Firetail, Crow Creek Reservation, SD," 1902 (Smithsonian Institution Negative Number 54,723 (National Anthropological Archives, copy of image at Hampton), *Southern Workman* 32, no. 4 (April 1903): 252. Firetail was also a carpenter's apprentice before he went to Hampton. Louis Firetail, Indian Student Record Collection, Hampton University Archives, Hampton, Virginia.

80. Hampton Normal and Agricultural Institute, *Twenty-Two Years' Work of the Hampton Normal and Agricultural Institute at Hampton, Virginia: Records of Negro and Indian Graduates and Ex-students* (Hampton, VA: Normal School Press, 1893), 491.

81. W. E. B. Du Bois, "Charts and graphs showing the condition of African Americans at the turn of the century exhibited at the Paris Exposition Universelle in 1900," LOT 11931 (M), Prints and Photographs, Library of Congress.

82. "Address of Grover Cleveland and Booker T. Washington Delivered at Carnegie Hall, New York, under the Auspices of the Presbyterian Church," March 3, 1894, Ohio Historical Center Archives Library.

Chapter 5

1. "A McKinley Tariff Object Lesson," Tin-Cleveland/Stevenson RSN 81698X05 and DiSalle 315264.3557, National Museum of American History, Smithsonian Institution.

2. Quentin R. Skrabec, *William McKinley: Apostle of Protectionism* (New York: Algora, 2008), 89, 97.

3. "A Tumble in American Tin; the Product of Laufman's Factory Falls Out of a Window," *New York Times*, June 19, 1891, p. 8.

4. "M'Kinleyized Tissue Paper; Jewelers Don't Like It: They Find It an Expensive Article," *New York Times*, July 10, 1891, p. 8.

5. "Tis the Rich Man's Tariff," *New York Times*, October 10, 1892, p. 5.

6. "The Carpet Industry," *New York Times*, November 11, 1891, p. 4.

7. "A Tariff Object Lesson," *Los Angeles Times*, March 18, 1892, p. 4.

8. See Miles Orvell, *The Real Thing: Imitation and Authenticity in American Culture, 1880–1940* (Chapel Hill: University of North Carolina Press, 1989); Bill Brown, *Sense of Things: The Object Matter of American Literature* (Chicago: University of Chicago Press, 2003); Beverly Gordon, *The Saturated World: Aesthetic Meaning, Intimate Objects, Women's Lives, 1890–1940* (Knoxville: University of Tennessee Press, 2006). I address the narrative potential of photographs of late nineteenth-century interiors elsewhere. S. A. Carter, "Picturing Rooms: Interior Photography, 1870–1900," *History of Photography* 34, no. 3 (2010): 251–267.

9. Stephen Conn, *Museums and American Intellectual Life 1876–1926* (Chicago: University of Chicago Press, 1998); David Jenkins, "Object Lessons and Ethnographic Displays: Museum Exhibitions and the Making of American Anthropology," *Comparative Studies in Society and History* 36, no. 2 (April 1994): 242–270; Robert Rydell, *All the World's a Fair* (Chicago: University of Chicago Press, 1985); Simon Bronner and Henry Francis du Pont Winterthur Museum, eds., *Consuming Visions: Accumulation and Display of Goods in America, 1880–1920* (New York: Norton, 1989).

10. *Tariff Acts of 1883, 1890, 1894 1897: Administrative Act of 1890. War Revenue Act of 1898. Porto Rican and Hawaiian Acts, 1900* (Washington, DC: Government Printing Office, 1890).

11. These lessons rarely engage in a treatment of a given item's exchange value, which was central to addressing the abstractability of material things in Marx's discussion of commodities. But the emphasis on an object's biography and on use value does not preclude understanding the subject of object lessons as commodity training. This fits closely with Appadurai's critique of Marx in that things may be understood as in a "commodity situation" that indicates their potential exchangeability "commodity context," even if the focus is not directly on exchange value. Karl Marx, "Capital, Volume 1, Section 3," in *The Marx-Engels Reader*, ed. Robert C. Tucker (New York: Norton, 1978), 312–316; Arjun Appadurai, *The Social Life of Things: Commodities in Cultural Perspectives* (Cambridge: Cambridge University Press, 2003), 13–16.

12. Elizabeth Mayo and E. A. Sheldon, *Lessons on Objects* (New York: Scribner, Armstrong, 1873), 208–209.

13. US Congress, Senate Committee on Finance, *(51) H.R. 9416, Act to Reduce the Revenue and Equalize Duties on Imports, and for Other Purposes* (Washington, DC, 1890), 81.

14. N. A. Calkins, *Classified List of Object Teaching Aids for Home and School* (New York: Schermerhorn, 1872), 33.

15. N. A. Calkins, *Manual for Teachers to Accompany Prang's Aids for Object Teaching* (Boston, 1877), 25, from University of Chicago "Pamphlets on Teaching."

16. "Rubber," from Bancroft Bros. & Co's Object-Lesson Cards, Original Artwork 26700, Cotsen Children's Library, Princeton University Library.

17. *A Few Suggestions with Brief Notes on Some of the Raw Products Which Enter into the Commerce of the World* (Philadelphia Commercial Museum, 1901), 8–9.

18. Philadelphia Commercial Museum Vegetable & Mineral Cabinets Courtesy of the Economic Herbarium of Oakes Ames (ECON), Harvard University Herbaria.

19. Here I am referring to Bill Brown's assertion that objects or things are determined through their relation to people in his essay "Thing Theory." I am arguing here that, in part, object lessons shaped these relationships. Bill Brown, "Thing Theory," in *Things* (Chicago: University of Chicago Press, 2004), 4.

20. Dorothy Ross, *G. Stanley Hall: The Psychologist as Prophet* (Chicago: University of Chicago Press, 1972), 125–130; Alice Boardman Smuts and Robert W. Smuts, *Science in the Service of Children, 1893–1935* (New Haven, CT: Yale University Press, 2006), 34–36.

21. Just like Mary Alling-Aber's Marlborough Street School, Hall's study was funded by Pauline Agassiz Shaw and examined a comparable, though less wealthy and socially exclusive, population. Shaw lent Hall four experienced kindergarten teachers, who interviewed four hundred children during their first weeks of primary school, three at a time, in the coatrooms of Boston school buildings. G. Stanley Hall, "The Contents of Children's Minds," *Princeton Review* (January–June 1883): 249–273.

22. G. Stanley Hall, "Contents of Children's Minds," 273.

23. Gail Bederman, *Manliness and Civilization: A Cultural History of Gender and Race in the United States, 1880–1917* (Chicago: University of Chicago Press, 1995), 92–94.

24. G. Stanley Hall, "Contents of Children's Minds," 256.

25. Jonathan Crary, *Techniques of the Observer: On Visions and Modernity in the Nineteenth Century* (Cambridge, MA: MIT Press, 1990), 102.

26. Louis Menand, *The Metaphysical Club: A Story of Ideas in America* (New York: Farrar, Straus, and Giroux, 2001), 324–325; Kurt Danziger, "Apperception," in *The Oxford Companion to the Mind*, ed. Richard L. Gregory (Oxford: Oxford University Press 1987), Oxford Reference Online, http://www.oxfordreference.com/views/ENTRY.html?subview=Main&entry=t159.e57.

27. M. E. Sadler, "Rooper, Thomas Godolphin (1847–1903)," rev. M. C. Curthoys, in *Oxford Dictionary of National Biography*, ed. H. C. G. Matthew and Brian Harrison (Oxford: Oxford University Press, 2004), http://www.oxforddnb.com/view/article/35822.

28. T. G. Rooper, *Apperception: Or the Essential Mental Operation in the Act of Learning, an Essay on "A Pot of Green Feathers"* (Syracuse, NY: C. W. Bardeen, 1891), v–vi, 38.

29. Rooper, *Apperception*, 6.

30. Rooper, *Apperception*, 25.

31. Rooper, *Apperception*, 5.

32. See, for example, John J. A'Becket, "Hofman's Object Lesson," *The Cosmopolitan; a Monthly Illustrated Magazine*, October 1, 1896, 618. In this tale the protagonist wrongly suspects his wife of flirting with another man who is then killed and decapitated. His preserved head is sent to their New York City home as an object lesson. Stories featuring shop bills transformed into specie are a common, gendered "object lesson" intended to teach women the value of money. See, for example, "An Object-lesson," *The Youth's Companion*, August 27, 1885, 344, and "A $5,000 Object Lesson," *Christian Advocate*, September 29, 1887, 630.

33. Ruth Hall, "An Object Lesson," *Prairie Farmer*, April 30, 1864, 314.

34. Tetia Moss, "Object Lessons," *Godey's Lady's Book and Magazine*, September 1874, 224.

35. These stories explicitly draw upon the idea of the object lessons as a metaphor for looking at the world in literature. Other texts that do not explicitly use this metaphor also rely on similar patterns of observation and visual evidence to drive their arguments. For example, the idea of the object lessons could be applied to the work of Theodore Dreiser (*Sister Carrie*) and Henry James ("The Real Thing," *The Golden Bowl*).

36. "In Many Gay Pictures: How Soap, Tobacco, Whisky and Beer Are Advertised," *Washington Post*, November 10, 1889, 16.

37. Robert Jay, *The Trade Card in Nineteenth-Century America* (Columbia: University of Missouri Press, 1987), 3. They fall out of favor by 1900. Jay attributes this to a combination of factors, but namely to changes in bulk mailing rates that made large, illustrated magazines and catalogs more affordable (99–103).

38. "Mrs. Potts' Cold Handle Sad Irons," ca. 1880s, Grossman Collection (Col 838), Cabinet 8, drawer 4, box 8, Winterthur Museum.

39. "Decker Bros. Grand, Upright, and Square Pianos," Decker Bros. (n.d.), New York, New York, United States, TC6550.0004.655, Baker Library, Harvard Business School, Historical Collections, http://via.lib.harvard.edu:80/via/deliver/deepLinkItem?recordId=olvwork88844&componentId=HBS.BAKER.TC:4304.

40. "Le Page's Liquid Glue," Russia Cement Company (n.d.), Gloucester, Massachusetts, United States, TC4060.0005:406, Baker Library, Harvard Business School, Historical Collections, http://via.lib.harvard.edu:80/via/deliver/deepLinkItem?recordId=olvwork80274&componentId=HBS.BAKER.TC:384.

41. Dave Cheadle and Russ Mascieri, *Victorian Trade Cards: Historical Reference and Value Guide* (Paducah, KY: Collector's Books, 1996), 219.

42. "Carter's Mucilage," Carter, Dinsmore & Co. (n.d.), Boston, Massachusetts, United States, TC4060.0001:406, Baker Library, Harvard Business School, Historical Collections, http://via.lib.harvard.edu:80/via/deliver/deepLinkItem?recordId=olvwork79576&componentId=HBS.BAKER.TC:1096.

43. "Carnrick's Soluble Food," Reed & Carnrick (n.d.), United States, TC4100.0004:41, Baker Library, Harvard Business School, Historical Collections, http://via.lib.harvard.edu/via/deliver/deepLinkItem?recordId=olvwork80329&componentId=HBS.BAKER.TC:99.

44. N. K. Fairbanks Company, "An Object Lesson," Box 2, Folder 17, Series: Soap, Warshaw Collection of Business Americana, 1838–1953, National Museum of American History, Washington, DC.

45. Less colorful newspaper advertisements also occasionally adopted the trope of the object lesson. Typically, it was not to illustrate a concept but to explain the wonders that awaited potential consumers in shops. These advertisements often promised that "object lessons" on bicycles, hats, or the latest fashions could be had in their stores. Department stores like Wanamaker's often produced newspaper advertisements mentioning object lessons like these.

46. "Two men who attract attention," ca. 1895, *Boston Sunday Journal*, March 31, 1895, from the N. W. Ayer Advertising Agency Records, "Hornby's Oatmeal: Book 156," Series 02, Box 40, Folder 1, National Museum of American History, Washington, DC.

47. John Dewey, *The School and Society* (Chicago: University of Chicago Press, 1900), 24–25.

48. Rebecca Harding Davis, "A Great Object-Lesson," *Independent*, July 30, 1903, 1778.

49. Rebecca Harding Davis, *Life in the Iron Mills*, ed. Cecelia Tichi (Boston: Bedford Books, 1998).

50. Elizabeth Mayo, *Lessons on Objects, as Given to Children between the Ages of Six and Eight, in a Pestalozzian School, at Cheam, Surrey*, 16th ed. (London: Seeley, Jackson, and Halliday, 1859), 1–2.

Epilogue

1. Varied examples of these approaches include Nancy Carlisle, Peter Harholdt, Colby College Museum of Art, and Society for the Preservation of New England Antiquities, *Cherished Possessions: A New England Legacy* (Boston: Society for the Preservation of New England Antiquities, in association with Antique Collectors' Club, 2003); Laurel Thatcher Ulrich, *The Age of Homespun: Objects and Stories in the Creation of an American Myth* (New York: Knopf, 2001); Richard L. Bushman, *The Refinement of America: Persons Houses Cities* (New York: Vintage Books, 1993); Henry Glassie, *Folk Housing in Middle Virginia: A Structural Analysis of Historic Artifacts* (Knoxville: University of Tennessee Press, 1975); Dell Upton, *Holy Things and Profane: Anglican Parish Churches in Colonial Virginia* (New York: Architectural History Foundation, and Cambridge, MA: MIT Press, 1986); Colleen McDannell, *Material Christianity: Religion and Popular Culture in America* (New Haven, CT: Yale University Press, 1995); Ken Ames, *Death in the Dining Room and Other Tales of Victorian Culture* (Philadelphia: Temple University Press, 1992); Ann Smart Martin, "Makers, Buyers, and Users: Consumerism as a Material Culture Framework," *Winterthur Portfolio* 28, no. 2–3 (Summer–Autumn 1993): 141–157; Robin Bernstein, "Material Culture and the Performance of Race," *Social Text 101* 27, no. 4 (Winter 2009): 67–94; Jules Prown and Kenneth Haltman, eds., *American Artifacts: Essays in Material Culture* (East Lansing: Michigan State University Press, 2000).

2. Charles Montgomery's method was published as "Some Remarks on the Practice and Science of Connoisseurship" in the *American Walpole Society Note Book* in 1961, 7–20 and reprinted by Thomas Schlereth in *Material Culture Studies in America: An Anthology* (Nashville, TN: American Association for State and Local History, 1982) 145–152; E. McClung Fleming, "Artifact Study: A Proposed Model" in *Winterthur Portfolio*, 9 (1974) 153–173; Jules David Prown, "Mind in Matter: An Introduction to Material Culture Theory and Method" in *Winterthur Portfolio* 17, no. 1 (Spring 1982): 1–19.

3. Susan Pearce provides a helpful appendix, "Models for Object Study," in her book *Museums, Objects, Collections: A Cultural Study* (Washington, DC: Smithsonian Institution Press, 1993) that includes Prown's and Fleming's methods as well as the approaches of Panofsky, Elliot, Batchelor, and her own method ("Thinking about Things"). I focus on Montgomery, Fleming, and Prown because of their similarity to object lessons and their central importance to the training of US students in material culture studies.

4. Jules D. Prown, "Reflections on Teaching American Art History," *Panorama: Journal of the Association of Historians of American Art* 2, no. 2 (Summer 2016), http://journalpanorama. org/reflections-on-teaching-american-art-history/, accessed August 23, 2016; Jules Prown, "Generations: Art, Ideas and Change," College Art Association, Chicago, February 11, 2010 (unpublished manuscript). The author is grateful to Jules Prown for sharing the text of this presentation with her.

5. Jules Prown, "The Truth of Material Culture? History or Fiction?" in *Art as Evidence: Writings on Art and Material Culture* (New Haven, CT: Yale University Press, 2001), 220–234. Though the course was defunct when Prown arrived in the 1950s, the Harvard Museum Course had long associated the university with object study and curatorial training. Sally Ann Duncan, "Harvard's 'Museum Course' and the Making of America's Museum Profession," *Archives of American Art Journal* 42, no. 1–2 (2002): 2–16. Writing in 1930, Harvard art history professor Langdon Warner argued for the importance of studying "the things well made by man" as opposed to just the titles, artists, and locations of fine art slides. He continued, "For the world is full of objects from shoes to sonnets." In many ways his argument that students consider the "essential" qualities of objects as opposed to their accidental qualities (like location) mirrors Elizabeth Mayo's object-lesson pedagogy. Langdon Warner, "On the Teaching of Fine Arts," from Paul J. Sachs, "Course materials for Fine Arts 15a: Museum Practices and Museum Problems, 1930–1931," Harvard University Archives, Harvard University, Cambridge, MA.

6. Jules Prown, "The Promise and Perils of Context," *Art as Evidence*, 249.

7. Educator N. A. Calkins provided the following object lesson on a chair in one of his manuals, "James. 'The seat is flat and horizontal.' George. 'It is lower at the back than in the front—it is not quite horizontal.' Lucy. 'The back is slanting.' Martha. 'The horizontal piece at the top of the back is flat.'" N. A. Calkins, *Primary Object Lessons for a Graduated Course of Development: A Manual for Teachers and Parents with Lessons for the Proper Training of the Faculties of Children* (New York: Harper & Brothers, 1861), 299–301.

8. At the Academy of Design in New York in 1886, Captain Pratt offered an object lesson on these kinds of items as produced by students at the Carlisle Indian School: "He brought on the platform some articles made by the students for the purpose, he said, of giving the audience an object lesson showing what Indians can do when educated and civilized." "The Academy of Design. Sixty-First Annual Exhibition," *New York Herald-Tribune*, April 3, 1886.

9. Before and after photographs of Native American students at Hampton and Carlisle often include images of students in interiors as a contrast to images of students in open, natural settings to document their move toward "civilization," a settled life in a house.

10. Frances Benjamin Johnston, "Conversation lesson, subject—the chair," March 15, 1901, Frances Benjamin Johnston Collection, LOT 12369, Library of Congress Prints and Photographs Division, Washington, DC.

11. In her chapter on Gay and Fletcher in *Making Home Work*, Jane Simonsen analyzes this image in detail. Gay assigned each chair in the photograph a figurative role based on nineteenth-century tropes: "Seat of War," "Survival of the Fittest," and "Arch of Triumph." Simonsen, "The Cook, the Photographer, and Her Majesty, the Allotting Agent: Unsettling Domesticity in E. Jane Gay's *Choup-nit-ki*." Jane E. Simonsen, *Making Home Work: Domesticity and Native*

American Assimilation in the American West, 1860–1919 (Chapel Hill: University of North Carolina Press, 2006), 111–149.

12. E. Jane Gay, "Three broken chairs outdoors, to each of which E. Jane Gay has assigned the characters of those in her story: The Cook, the Photographer and her Majesty," from the album *Choup-nit-ki, With the Nez Percés,* 1889–1892, Jane Gay Dodge papers, Schlesinger Library for the History of Women in America, Radcliffe Institute, Cambridge, Massachusetts.

13. I explore these ideas further in my short essay "Object Study as Interdisciplinary Exploration for the Twenty-First Century," in *Panorama: Journal of the Association of Historians of American Art* 2, no. 1 (Summer 2016), http://journalpanorama.org/sarah-anne-carter-the-chipstone-foundation/, accessed August 23, 2016. For more on the pedagogical value of the interdisciplinary demands of material culture, see Laurel Ulrich, Ivan Gaskell, Sara Schechner, Sarah Anne Carter, and Samantha Van Gerbig, *Tangible Things: Making History through Objects* (New York: Oxford University Press, 2015).

BIBLIOGRAPHIC ESSAY

Object Lessons in the Archives

I first stumbled on object lessons in Harvard's online library catalog. I was looking for books about American material culture and began noticing a range of books with "Object Lessons" in the title. I traced that to a subject heading called "object-teaching," and I found myself scrolling through a list of then-unfamiliar titles—*Lessons on Objects, Object Lessons, Object Teaching*, and on and on. I made my way to the Gutman Library at the Harvard Graduate School of Education and discovered a whole history of material-based education. My exploration of object lessons, the subject of this book, led me to rethink the material foundations of nineteenth-century American culture and the broader practice, both past and present, of reasoning from things.

This interdisciplinary project, about what I discovered was a mutable historic practice that transitioned from classroom reality to flexible metaphor, presented a range of research challenges. I had to first document the existence of a historic pedagogy to study, beyond the traces it left in textbooks. One major challenge in defining the term "object lesson" is that while its meaning changed over time, these changes happened gradually and unevenly. Different definitions existed simultaneously. From 1861 to 1913 it appears nearly twenty-seven thousand times in *Readex's America's Historical Newspapers* database, simultaneously referring to a formal mode of pedagogy, a general way of teaching with an object, and as a metaphor.[1] Similarly the practice was adopted at different times, in various formats, for different ages of students in school districts across the United States (and around the world). It was difficult to compare the application of the practice across school departments because in the mid-nineteenth century the common school movement progressed irregularly across the nation impacting cities and smaller communities in the northern, southern, and western states in uneven ways. After spending months digging archaeological "test pits" in the voluminous archives of Gutman Library Special Collections, I became convinced that object lessons were not just the subject of pedagogical discourse but had actually been in use or at least experimented with in the classrooms across the country. I found object lessons in curricula in public school reports at various moments from the 1860s to the 1880s for Atlanta, Georgia; Baltimore, Maryland; Boston, Massachusetts; Brooklyn, New York; Burlington, Vermont; Cleveland, Ohio; Chicago, Illinois; Denver, Colorado; Houston, Texas; Lawrence, Kansas; Louisville, Kentucky; Milwaukee, Wisconsin; San Francisco, California; and Yankton, South Dakota, among other places.[2] I further traced this phenomenon through archival collections across the United States, as detailed in my notes.

Apart from documenting the history of object lessons I had to define the term and decide what was and what was not an object lesson. While I primarily considered the formal five-step object lessons created by Elizabeth Mayo and adapted by her many followers, especially E. A. Sheldon, which moved from observation to composition, I also considered a wider range of material-based teaching practices. The term also referred to more general, less formal ways of teaching that involved objects. For example, a description of a simple "object lesson" to be used in a primary school began with a teacher holding up a book, asking children to identify the object and then following up with, "How do you know it is a book?" The lesson continued to examine the book for its parts, to consider how paper was made, and perhaps to discuss the things—other than books—that were made from paper like a bandbox, a letter, or a kite.[3] The object lesson referred not to the book, but to the entire classroom conversation organized around the book. Sometimes, the more general phrase "object teaching" could be used to refer to this type of lesson though there was not always a sharp difference between the two terms. The related phrase, "objective teaching," could refer to any sort of lesson that included material things, like an abacus or a spelling stick with movable letters, as opposed to a lesson on a discrete object. By the 1880s and 1890s, object lessons and related forms of object teaching came to be gradually transformed into other classroom activities like nature study. Similarly, I discovered that there were object lessons on visual sources, which I termed picture lessons. In these cases the images did not necessarily replace or transparently represent the objects or scenarios depicted, but the mode of representation was part of the lesson. Later in the century, particularly into the 1890s, photographs were sometimes included as ancillary to object-based lessons or to document a lesson in progress. All of these modes of teaching referred to different ways in which classroom instruction could be organized around material things.

Another semantic issue involves the difference between object lessons, or the earlier variation "lessons on objects," and "lessons on common things." While there is definite overlap—and at least one instance of the same book published under both of these titles—the term "common things" refers to a different genre of lessons. "Common things" typically included information that would be considered the "common knowledge" that would make one an educated and informed individual, whether about manufacturing, natural history, or geography as well as information about material things. This distinction may seem to index the contemporary shift toward "thing theory," an intellectual move often associated with the work of theorist and literary scholar Bill Brown. However, nineteenth-century usage, and therefore my analysis of it, does not necessarily map onto these current theoretical considerations. Object lessons could just as easily be offered on a pair of scissors—clearly a bounded object—or on a more thing-like substance such as camphor or a set of relationships centered on something more abstract like a material-based process in a textile mill.[4]

Since I started this project more than a decade ago, object lessons have gradually been receiving more scholarly attention, though they had been critically ignored for nearly a century. In part, the continued popularity of the object-lesson metaphor has occluded its history as an actual, specific classroom practice. When viewed as a historical turn of phrase, as a metaphor drawn from the nineteenth century, it seems to help explain what scholar Miles Orvell—echoing Edith Wharton's explanation of upper-class life in *Age of Innocence*—referred to as the "hieroglyphic world" of the Gilded Age.[5] The idea that there was an understood language of material things in the nineteenth-century United States—whether addressing cosmopolitan influences, the abundance of world's fairs (the Columbian Exhibition as "America's Great Object Lesson"), or material manifestations of race, class, gender, or authenticity—envelops the metaphor in a seemingly appropriate historical veneer without getting anywhere near the schoolrooms in which these lessons may have happened.[6]

Few historians of education have examined object lessons. Until the past few decades, many of the historians who wrote about this practice were "educationists" aimed at reforming the present as well as understanding the past. As historian and theorist of education Marc Depaepe has explained, in the nineteenth century, "History [of education] was used primarily for practical educational purposes, such as drawing inspiration and motivation from the examples of the past, as well as theoretical purposes, for example, by providing ideas and conceptions to be used as building blocks for a contemporary theory of education."[7] These presentist notions continue to affect how some view the history of education from the outside as well as how some within the field continue to select topics or frame their questions. Some early historians disagreed with the ways object teachers employed the theories of Johann Heinrich Pestalozzi as the intellectual foundation for their object lessons. Others saw only the poorly implemented aspects of the practice without considering the intellectual goals, ambitions, or potential for the practice to be successfully used in the classroom. It was easy for writers from Charles Dickens to local journalists to poke fun at inept teachers trying to teach children that it was a penny and *not* a hunk of coal that would burn a hole in one's pocket or violently "dissolving" lumps of gum camphor in alcohol with a knife.[8] John Dewey's dismissal of object lessons as pedagogically unsound—especially when compared to his experience-based methods—may have further stymied research on object lessons.[9] I am not interested in assessing the success or perceived success of this practice as classroom pedagogy. Learning is difficult enough to assess in the contemporary classroom, let alone in the historic classroom. I would like to suggest that the importance of "object lessons" as a cultural phenomenon is not registered simply in its pedagogical utility but also in the ways this notion became embedded in American culture as rhetoric.

In most histories of education, the practice of object lessons has been little more than a blip on the way from the establishment of free common schools to full-blown progressive, child-centered learning. For example, William Reese's survey of the history of American public schools includes a helpful section contextualizing object lessons and Pestalozzi's ideas as a part of progressive education.[10] Authors have addressed specific pedagogical approaches to different subjects in the nineteenth-century classroom through the study of objects, maps, nature study, or student composition without considering the broader intellectual trajectory of object lessons.[11] Other historians have focused on the place of object lessons within specific schools or as applicable only to early child education.[12] At the same time, scholars in the growing field of childhood studies are just beginning to consider the role children and childhood have played in shaping American cultural life, particularly in terms of its material dimensions.[13] To date, historian Parna Sengupta's work on object lessons in colonial India best highlights some of the larger cultural issues packed into this pedagogical practice, particularly as related to the material dimensions of race and racism.[14] Her scholarship addresses some of the racial assumptions that are embedded in object lessons in the United States.

Object lessons have not been a central topic of inquiry for those who study American material culture, despite the fact that questions related to the practice are at the core of much scholarship on nineteenth-century American cultural life.[15] In aligned fields—visual culture and the history of making—scholars are beginning to unpack the intellectual value of the object lesson idea.[16] How do objects express meaning? How does an observer draw information from the study of material things or pictures? What may things reveal about culture, an individual, or a community? For example, in both object lessons and material culture methodology, particularly Jules Prown's method best articulated in the essay

"Mind in Matter: An Introduction to Material Culture Theory and Method," students are instructed to separate observing and experiencing objects from thinking about and reasoning from objects.[17] Furthermore, as a classroom practice, the object-lesson method directs teachers to ask questions about objects' origins and histories, a mode of inquiry that suggests the creation of both social and cultural biographies of things as commodities, which relates to the scholarship of Arjun Appadurai and Igor Kopytoff.[18] In these ways, object lessons may be considered a prehistory to contemporary material cultural methods. While it is not the sole purpose of this book, an important outcome will be to offer object lessons as a way of understanding the nineteenth-century material world.[19]

Notes

1. A search for "Object Lesson" in *Readex's America's Historical Newspapers Database*, 1861–1913, turned up 26,987 results on August 30, 2016.
2. Public School Reports Collection, Gutman Library Special Collections, Harvard Graduate School of Education.
3. "Object Lessons," *Connecticut Common School Journal and Annals of Education* 5, no. 12 (December 1858): 365.
4. Thing theory consciously considers the meanings of things in relation to human actors and considers things as items that may reject as well as invite discourse. This could be a useful way to think about the work of object lessons, which may be understood to transform mute, opaque things into legible objects, in the most general sense. Bill Brown, "Thing Theory," in *Things* (Chicago: University of Chicago Press, 2004), 1–16.
5. Miles Orvell, *The Real Thing: Imitation and Authenticity in American Culture, 1880–1940* (Chapel Hill: University of North Carolina Press, 1989).
6. Kristin Hoganson, "Cosmopolitan Domesticity: Importing the American Dream, 1865–1920," *American Historical Review* 107, no. 1 (2002): 55–83.
7. Marc Depaepe, "The Ten Commandments of Good Practices in History of Education Research." *Zeitschrift Für Pädagogische Historiographie* 15 (2010): 31–34.
8. Charles Dickens, "Object Teaching," *Massachusetts Teacher and Journal of Home and School Education* (July 1862): 258; Harriet Starr, "The Object Lesson," *Harper's Weekly* 11, no. 16 (1907): 1688.
9. For example, Dewey explained in *Democracy and Education* that "object lessons" aimed to teach a child about objects before allowing the child to use them, as opposed to his assumption that children learn through doing. John Dewey, *Democracy and Education* (Mineola, NY: Dover, 2004), 191. In *School and Society* he makes it clear that object lessons simply constitute another set of the "ready made material" presented for student consumption as opposed to an opportunity for individual development. John Dewey, *The Child and the Curriculum and the School and Society* (Chicago: University of Chicago Press, 1959),149.
10. William Reese, "The Origins of Progressive Education," *History of Education Quarterly*, 41, no. 1 (Spring 2001): 1–24: 3; Reese, *America's Public Schools: From the Common Schools to "No Child Left Behind"* (Baltimore: Johns Hopkins University Press, 2005).
11. See, for example, Martin Brückner, *The Geographic Revolution in Early America* (Chapel Hill: University of North Carolina Press, 2006); Peggy Aldrich Kidwell, Amy Ackerberg-Hastings, and David Lindsay Roberts, *Tools of American Mathematics Teaching, 1800–2000* (Baltimore, MD: Johns Hopkins University Press, 2008); Deborah Jean Warner, "Commodities for the Classroom: Apparatus for Science and Education in Antebellum America," *Annals of Science [Great Britain]* 45, no. 4 (1988): 387–397. Lucille Schultz's work on the history of writing composition argues for the importance of object lessons to the history

of writing pedagogy, without considering the larger place of object lessons in American culture. Lucille M. Schultz, *The Young Composers: Composition's Beginnings in Nineteenth-Century Schools* (Carbondale: Southern Illinois University Press, 1999). This connection would only enhance her analysis. Sally Kohlstedt has considered the ways object lessons may have fed into the nature study movement. Her focus is on the 1890s. Sally Gregory Kohlstedt, "Nature, not Books: Scientists and the Origins of the Nature Study Movement in the 1890s," *Isis* 96, no. 3 (September 2005): 324–352.

12. See, for example, Dorothy Rogers, *Oswego: Fountainhead of Teacher Education: A Century in the Sheldon Tradition* (New York: Appleton-Century-Crofts, 1961), and Barbara Beatty, *Preschool Education in America: The Culture of Young Children from the Colonial Era to the Present* (New Haven, CT: Yale University Press, 1995).

13. See, for example, Karen Sánchez-Eppler, *Dependent States: The Child's Part in Nineteenth-Century American Culture* (Chicago: University of Chicago Press, 2006); Steven Mintz, *Huck's Raft: A History of American Childhood* (Cambridge, MA: Belknap Press of Harvard University Press, 2004); Miriam Forman-Brunell, *Made to Play House: Dolls and the Commercialization of American Girlhood, 1830–1930* (New Haven, CT: Yale University Press, 1993); Karin Calvert, *Children in the House: The Material Culture of Early Childhood 1600–1900* (Boston: Northeastern University Press, 1992); Sharon Brookshaw's essay "The Material Culture of Children and Childhood," *Journal of Material Culture* 14, no. 3 (2009) 365–383, looks at ways that material evidence in British museums may be used to think about children's experiences as well as adult ideas about childhood. Scholars focusing on design have also started to consider the importance of designing for children: Marta Gutman and Ning de Coninck-Smith, *Designing Modern Childhoods: History, Space, and the Material Culture of Children* (Newark: Rutgers University Press, 2008), and Tanya Harrod, Juliet Kinchin, and Aidan O'Connor, *Century of the Child: Growing by Design 1900–2000* (New York: Museum of Modern Art, 2012).

14. Parna Sengupta, "An Object Lesson in Colonial Pedagogy," *Comparative Studies in Society and History* 45, no. 1 (2003): 96–121; Parna Sengupta, *Pedagogy for Religion: Missionary Education and the Fashioning of Hindus and Muslims in Bengal* (Berkeley: University of California Press, 2011). See also William J. Glover, "Objects, Models, and Exemplary Works: Educating Sentiment in Colonial India," *Journal of Asian Studies* 64, no. 3 (2005): 539–566, which links object lesson pedagogy to the development of model towns and settlements in the early twentieth century.

15. Cultural historians Simon Bronner and David Jenkins linked the practice to the development of nineteenth-century ethnographic museums, though with little emphasis on classroom practice. Because he does not consider pedagogical sources, Bronner places the pedagogy as an invention of the late nineteenth century. Simon Bronner and Henry Francis du Pont Winterthur Museum, eds., "Object Lessons: The Work of Ethnological Museums and Collections," in *Consuming Visions: Accumulation and Display of Goods in America, 1880–1920* (New York: Norton, 1989); David Jenkins, "Object Lessons and Ethnographic Displays: Museum Exhibitions and the Making of American Anthropology," *Comparative Studies in Society and History* 36, no. 2 (1994): 242–270.

16. Canadian scholar Karen Stanworth makes the intriguing argument that Ryerson's Education Museum in Canada employed object lessons to develop prescribed ways of understanding social order and citizenship through engagement with visual culture. She seems to be persuaded by the critics of object lessons who argued that the pedagogy was another form of prescribed, rote learning. Karen Stanworth, *Visibly Canadian: Imaging Collective Identity in the Canadas, 1820–1910* (Montreal: McGill-Queen's University Press, 2014), 76–100. On October 3, 2015, I took part in a symposium at the Henry Moore Institute in Leeds, England, entitled *Object Lessons: Sculpture and the Production of Knowledge*, in conjunction with the exhibition *Object Lessons* (September 30, 2015–January 3, 2016). Organized by Rebecca Wade, the exhibition included the Cabinet of Educational Specimens from the Victoria and Albert Museum (B.5:1 to 5-2009). As part of this symposium I was introduced to the work of Ann-Sophie Lehmann from the University of Groningen who presented "The Original Object Lesson: On the Past and Present of Material Literacy" and argued that there is a through line from historic object lessons to contemporary museum material collections.

She published a version of her talk here: Ann-Sophie Lehmann "Objektstunden: Vom Materialwissen zur Materialbildung" in *Materialität: Herausforderungen für die Sozial- und Kulturwissenschaften*, ed. H. Kalthoff, T. Cress, and T. Röhl (Paderborn: Wilhelm Fink, 2016), 171–194.

17. Jules Prown, "Mind in Matter: An Introduction to Material Culture Theory and Method," *Winterthur Portfolio* 17, no. 1 (Spring 1982): 1–19.

18. Arjun Appadurai, "Introduction: Commodities and the Politics of Value" and Igor Kopytoff, "The Cultural Biography of Things: Commoditization as Process," in Appadurai, *The Social Life of Things: Commodities in Cultural Perspective*, ed. Arjun Appadurai (Cambridge: Cambridge University Press, 2003), 3–64.

19. For example, scholars like thing theorist Bill Brown mention object lessons as a way to find meaning in things, without considering the actual classroom practice or mechanism through which these lessons moved from physical object to language. Bill Brown, *A Sense of Things: The Object Matter of American Literature* (Chicago: University of Chicago Press, 2003).

SELECTED BIBLIOGRAPHY

Manuscript, Rare Book, and Museum Collections

This list includes key repositories and, where appropriate, the major collections consulted in those repositories. Full citations for specific manuscripts, objects, prints, and photographs are provided throughout the text in notes and are not listed here.

American Antiquarian Society, Worcester, MA

Archives of American Art, Washington, DC
   Mary Margaret Sittig research material on Louis Prang, 1870–1970

British Library, London, England

California Historical Society, San Francisco, CA
   Photography Collection

Cotsen Children's Library, Princeton University Libraries, Princeton, NJ

Hampton University, Hampton, VA
   Hampton Institute Archives
   University Museum Archives

Harvard University Libraries, Cambridge, MA
   Baker Library, Harvard Business School
     Economic Botany Collections
     Education
       Historic Textbook Collections
       School Report Collection
     Ernst Mayer Library, Museum of Comparative Zoology
     Gutman Library Special Collections, Harvard Graduate School of
     Harvard College Archives
     Houghton Library
       A. Bronson Alcott Papers
       Letters to the Heaths, 1826–1879

Hunter College Archives, New York, NY
   New York City Normal School Student Files

Huntington Library, San Marino, CA
   Diana Korzenik Collection

Houston Metropolitan Research Center

Library of Congress, Washington, DC
    Charts and graphs showing the condition of African Americans at the turn of the century
        exhibited at the Paris Exposition Universelle in 1900 [Prints and Photograph Division]
    Frances Benjamin Johnston Collection [Prints and Photograph Division]
    Frances Benjamin Johnston Papers

National Anthropological Archives, Washington, DC
    Photographic collections

National Museum of American History, Washington, DC
    Division of Home and Community Life
        Warshaw Collection of Business Ephemera
    N. W. Ayer Advertising Agency Records
        Division of Political History

National Museum of the American Indian, Washington, DC

Newberry Library, Chicago, IL

New-York Historical Society, New York, NY
    Records of the New York City Public Schools

Penfield Library, Archives and Special Collections, State University of New York-Oswego, Oswego, NY
    E. A. Sheldon Papers
    University Clipping Files

Oswego Historical Society, Oswego, NY

Samuel P. Hayes Research Library, Perkins School for the Blind, Watertown, MA

Princeton Historical Society, Princeton, NJ

Quincy Historical Society, Quincy, MA

Schlesinger Library for the History of Women in America, Radcliffe Institute, Cambridge, MA

Smithsonian American Art Museum/Archives of American Art, Washington, DC

Sophia Smith Collections, Smith College, Northampton, MA
    Mary Sheldon Barnes Papers

Winterthur Museum and Library and the Joseph Downs Collection, Winterthur, DE
    Grossman Collection
    Museum Collections

Periodicals

American Educational Monthly
American Journal of Education
American Missionary
Chicago Tribune
Christian Advocate
Cincinnati Daily Gazette
Commercial Times (Oswego, NY)
Common School Journal (Boston)
Connecticut Common School Journal and Annals of Education
Continental Monthly
Cosmopolitan, a Monthly Illustrated Magazine

Daily Inter-Ocean (Chicago)
Godey's Lady's Book and Magazine
Harper's Monthly
Harper's Weekly
The Independent (New York)
Los Angeles Times
Massachusetts Teacher and Journal of Home and School Education
New York Teacher
New York Times
Prairie Farmer (Chicago)
Quarterly Education Magazine and Record of the Home and Colonial School Society
Schermerhorn's Monthly (New York)
Southern Workman
St. Nicholas Magazine
Washington Post
Youth's Companion

Annual Reports and Proceedings

Annual Report of the Board of Commissioners of Public Schools to the Mayor and City Council of Baltimore (MD)
Annual Report of the Board of Education for Denver, Col.
Annual Report of the Board of Education for the Atlanta (GA) Public Schools
Annual Report of the Board of Education for the Cleveland (OH) Public Schools
Annual Report of the Board of Education for the Department of Public Instruction for the City of Lawrence (KS)
Annual Report of the Board of Education for the Department of Public Instruction for the City of Topeka (KS)
Annual Report of the Board of Education of the City of Oswego (NY)
Annual Report of the Board of Education of the City of Yankton, Dakota Territory
Annual Report of the Board of School Commissioners Milwaukee (WI)
Annual Report of the Board of Trustees of the Male High School, Female High School and Public Schools of Louisville (KY)
Annual Report of the Board of Trustees of the Public Schools of the City of Washington (DC)
Annual Report of the City Superintendent of Schools in Brooklyn (NY)
Annual Report of the Commissioner of Indian Affairs
Annual Reports of the Hampton Normal and Agricultural Institute
Annual Report of the Massachusetts Board of Education
Annual Report of the New York City (NY) Board of Education
Annual Report of the State Commissioner of Common Schools to the State of Ohio
Annual Report of the State Normal and Training School at Oswego (NY)
Annual Report of the Superintendent of Common Schools of San Francisco, California
Annual Report of the Superintendent of Public Schools of Burlington, Vermont
Annual Report of the Superintendent of Public Instruction of the City of Chicago (IL)
Annual Report of the Superintendent of Public Instruction of the State of California
Annual Report of the Superintendent of Public Instruction of the State of Kansas
Biennial Report of the Superintendent of Public Instruction of the State of Colorado
Catalogue of the Hampton Normal and Agricultural Institute
Journal of the Board of Education of the City of New York
Manual of the Rutland (VT) Graded Schools
Proceedings of the California State Educational Convention
Proceedings of the United States National Museum
Report of the Chief Superintendent pf the Public Schools of the City of New Orleans (LA)
Semi-Annual Report of the Superintendent of Public Schools of the City of Boston (MA)

Printed Sources

Allen, Joel Asaph, and American Museum of Natural History. *Autobiographical Notes and a Bibliography of the Scientific Publications of Joel Asaph Allen.* New York: American Museum of Natural History, 1916.

Alling, Mary R. *The Children's Own Work.* Boston: Industrial Home Press, 1883–84.

Alling-Aber, Mary Rose. *An Experiment in Education, also, the Ideas Which Inspired It and Were Inspired by It.* New York: Harper & Brothers, 1897.

Ames, Kenneth L. *Death in the Dining Room and Other Tales of Victorian Culture.* American Civilization. Philadelphia: Temple University Press, 1992.

Anderson, James D. *The Education of Blacks in the South, 1860–1935.* Chapel Hill: University of North Carolina Press, 1988.

Appadurai, Arjun, ed. *The Social Life of Things: Commodities in Cultural Perspective.* Cambridge: Cambridge University Press, 2003.

Armitage, Kevin C. *The Nature Study Movement: The Forgotten Popularizer of America's Conservation Ethic.* Lawrence: University of Kansas Press, 2009.

Armstrong, M. F., Helen W. Ludlow, and Thomas P. Fenner. *Hampton and Its Students.* New York: G. P. Putnam's Sons, 1874.

Armstrong League of Hampton Workers. *Memories of Old Hampton.* Hampton, VA: Institute Press, 1909.

Ashwin, Clive. "Pestalozzi and the Origins of Pedagogical Drawing." *British Journal of Educational Studies* 29, no. 2 (June 1981): 138–151.

Barnard, Henry, ed. *Object Teaching, and Oral Lessons on Social Science and Common Things, with various Illustrations of the Principles and Practice of Primary Education, as Adopted in the Model and Training Schools of Great Britain. Republished from Barnard's American Journal of Education.* New York: F. C. Brownell, 1860.

Barnard, Henry. *Pestalozzi and Pestalozzianism. Life, Educational Principles, and Methods of John Henry Pestalozzi; with Biographical Sketches of Several of His Assistants and Disciples.* Papers for the Teacher. [6th Ser.]. New York: F. C. Brownell, 1862.

Barnes, Earl, ed. *Studies in Education: A Series of Ten Numbers Devoted to Child Study and the History of Education.* Stanford, CA: Stanford University, 1897.

Bassnett, Sarah. "From Public Relations to Art: Exhibiting Frances Benjamin Johnston's Hampton Institute Photographs." *History of Photography* 32, no. 2 (Summer 2008): 152–168.

Beatty, Barbara. *Preschool Education in America: The Culture of Young Children from the Colonial Era to the Present.* New Haven, CT: Yale University Press, 1995.

Bederman, Gail. *Manliness and Civilization: A Cultural History of Gender and Race in the United States, 1880–1917.* Chicago: University of Chicago Press, 1995.

Benzaquén, Adriana Silvia. "Locke's Children." *Journal of the History of Childhood and Youth* 4, no. 3 (Fall 2011): 382–402.

Berch, Bettina. *The Woman behind the Lens: The Life and Work of Frances Benjamin Johnston, 1864–1952.* Charlottesville: University Press of Virginia, 2000.

Berlo, Janet Catherine, American Federation of Arts, and Drawing Center, eds. *Plains Indian Drawings, 1865–1935: Pages from a Visual History.* New York: Harry N. Abrams, 1996.

Berlo, Janet Catherine, and Ruth B. Phillips. *Native North American Art.* Oxford History of Art. Oxford: Oxford University Press, 1998.

Bernstein, Robin. "Material Culture and the Performance of Race." *Social Text* 101, no. 4 (Winter 2009): 67–94.

Bernstein, Robin. *Racial Innocence: Performing American Childhood and Race from Slavery to Civil Rights.* New York: New York University Press, 2011.

Bronner, Simon J., and Henry Francis du Pont Winterthur Museum, eds. *Consuming Visions: Accumulation and Display of Goods in America, 1880–1920.* Winterthur Book. New York: Norton, 1989.

Brookshaw, Sharon. "The Material Culture of Children and Childhood." *Journal of Material Culture* 14, no. 3 (2009): 365–383.

Brosterman, Norman, and Kiyoshi Togashi. *Inventing Kindergarten.* New York: Harry N. Abrams, 1997.

Brown, Bill. *A Sense of Things: The Object Matter of American Literature.* Chicago: University of Chicago Press, 2003.

Brown, Bill. *Things.* Chicago: University of Chicago Press, 2004.

Brown, Thomas J. *Dorothea Dix: New England Reformer.* Harvard Historical Studies, 127. Cambridge, MA: Harvard University Press, 1998.

Brückner, Martin. *The Geographic Revolution in Early America: Maps, Literacy, and National Identity.* Chapel Hill: Published for the Omohundro Institute of Early American History and Culture by University of North Carolina Press, 2006.

Buckelew, Sarah F. *Practical Work in the School Room. Part I, A Transcript of the Object Lessons on the Human Body: Given in Primary Department, Grammar School no. 49, New York City.* New York: A. Lovell, 1885.

Burton, Warren. *The Culture of the Observing Faculties in the Family and the School: Or, Things about Home, and How to Make Them Instructive to the Young.* New York: Harper & Brothers, 1865.

Bushman, Richard L. *The Refinement of America: Persons, Houses, Cities.* New York: Vintage Books, 1993.

Calkins, Norman A. *Classified List of Object Teaching Aids for Home and School.* New York: Schermerhorn, 1872.

Calkins, Norman A. *Manual of Object-Teaching: With Illustrative Lessons in Methods and the Science of Education.* New York: Harper, 1882.

Calkins, Norman A. *A Manual to Accompany Prang's Natural History Series for Schools and Families. Animals and Plants Represented in Their Natural Colors and Arranged for Instruction with Object Lessons.* Boston: Prang, 1873.

Calkins, Norman A. *Plan of Instruction Embodied in Prang's Natural History Series, for Schools and Families: Animals and Plants Represented in their Natural Colors, and Arranged for in Instruction with Object Lessons.* Boston: Prang and Co, 1872–73.

Calkins, Norman A. *Primary Object Lessons for a Graduated Course of Development: A Manual for Teachers and Parents.* New York: Harper & Brothers, 1861.

Calkins, Norman A. *Primary Object Lessons, for Training the Senses and Developing the Faculties of Children.* 40th ed., rev ed. New York: American Book Company, 1898.

Calkins, Norman A. *Principles of Education; And Design of Prang's Aids for Object-Teaching.* Boston: Prang, 1877.

Calvert, Karin Lee Fishbeck. *Children in the House: The Material Culture of Early Childhood, 1600–1900.* Boston: Northeastern University Press, 1992.

Caplan, Ralph. *By Design: Why There Are No Locks on the Bathroom Doors in the Hotel Louis XIV, and Other Object Lessons.* New York: McGraw-Hill, 1984.

Carlisle, Nancy Camilla. *Cherished Possessions: A New England Legacy.* Photography by Peter Harholdt. Boston: Society for the Preservation of New England Antiquities, in association with Antique Collectors' Club, 2003.

Carr, Jean Ferguson, Stephen L. Carr, and Lucille M. Schultz. *Archives of Instruction: Nineteenth-Century Rhetorics, Readers, and Composition Books in the United States.* Studies in Writing & Rhetoric. Carbondale: Southern Illinois University Press, 2005.

Cheadle, Dave, and Russ Mascieri. *Victorian Trade Cards: Historical Reference and Value Guide.* Paducah, KY: Collector Books, 1996.

Cirigliano, Gustavo F. J., and Alexander F. Beattie. *Oswego En El Normalismo Argentino.* Buenos Aires: Editorial Nueva Generación, 2003.

Cohen, Michael David. *Reconstructing the Campus: Higher Education and the American Civil War.* Charlottesville: University of Virginia Press, 2012.

Colburn, Warren. *First Lessons in Arithmetic on the Plan of Pestalozzi: With Some Improvements.* 2nd ed. Boston: Cummings and Hilliard, 1822.

Coleman, Michael C. *American Indian Children at School, 1850–1930.* Jackson: University Press of Mississippi, 1993.

Conn, Steven. *Do Museums Still Need Objects?* Philadelphia: University of Pennsylvania Press, 2010.

Conn, Steven. *Museums and American Intellectual Life, 1876–1926.* Chicago: University of Chicago Press, 1998.

Cook, James W. *The Arts of Deception: Playing with Fraud in the Age of Barnum.* Cambridge, MA: Harvard University Press, 2001.

Crain, Patricia. *The Story of A: The Alphabetization of America from the New England Primer to the Scarlet Letter.* Stanford, CA: Stanford University Press, 2000.

Crary, Jonathan. *Techniques of the Observer: On Vision and Modernity in the Nineteenth Century.* Cambridge, MA: MIT Press, 1990.

Cremin, Lawrence Arthur. *American Education: The Colonial Experience, 1607–1783.* New York: Harper & Row, 1970.

Cremin, Lawrence Arthur. *American Education: The National Experience, 1783–1876.* New York: Harper & Row, 1980.

Crocco, Margaret, and O. L. Davis, eds. *"Bending the Future to their Will": Civic Women, Social Education, and Democracy.* Lanham, MD: Rowman & Littlefield, 1999.

Danto, Arthur Coleman, Center for African Art, Buffalo Museum of Science, Virginia Museum of Fine Arts, and Henry Art Gallery. *Art/Artifact: African Art in Anthropology Collections.* New York: Center for African Art, 1988.

Daston, Lorraine, ed. *Things that Talk: Object Lessons from Art and Science.* New York: Zone Books, 2004.

Davis, Rebecca Harding. *Life in the Iron Mills.* Edited by Cecelia Tichi. Bedford Cultural Editions. Boston: Bedford Books, 1998.

Dearborn, Ned Harland. *The Oswego Movement in American Education.* Contributions to Education, no. 183. New York: Teachers College, Columbia University, 1969. Originally published in 1925.

Deloria, Philip Joseph. *Playing Indian.* Yale Historical Publications. New Haven, CT: Yale University Press, 1998.

Depaepe, Marc. "The Ten Commandments of Good Practices in History of Education Research." *Zeitschrift Für Pädagogische Historiographie* 15 (2010): 31–34.

Dewey, John. *The Child and the Curriculum and the School and Society.* Chicago: University of Chicago Press, 1959.

Dewey, John. *Democracy and Education.* Mineola, NY: Dover, 2004.

Dewey, John. *The School and Society.* Chicago: University of Chicago Press, 1900.

Digby, Anne and Peter Searby. *Children, School, and Society in Nineteenth-Century England.* London: Macmillan, 1981.

Dilworth, Leah, ed. *Acts of Possession: Collecting in America.* New Brunswick, NJ: Rutgers University Press, 2003.

Disturnell, John. *A Trip through the Lakes of North America: Embracing a Full Description of the St. Lawrence River, Together with All the Principal Places on its Banks, from Its Source to Its Mouth; Commerce of the Lakes, etc.; Forming Altogether a Complete Guide for the Pleasure Traveler and Emigrant; with Maps and Embellishments.* New York: J. Disturnell, 1857.

Dix, Dorothea Lynde. *Conversations on Common Things; or, Guide to Knowledge: With Questions: For the Use of Schools.* Boston: Munroe and Francis, 1828.

Downing, A. J., and Alexander Anderson. *The Architecture of Country Houses; Including Designs for Cottages, Farm Houses, and Villas, with Remarks on Interiors, Furniture, and the Best Modes of Warming and Ventilating. with Three Hundred and Twenty Illustrations.* New York: D. Appleton, 1850.

Drucker, Johanna. "Harnett, Haberle, and Peto: Visuality and Artifice among the Proto-Modern Americans." *Art Bulletin* 74, no. 1 (March 1992): 37–50.

Du Bois, W. E. B. *The Souls of Black Folk.* Penguin Twentieth-Century Classics. New York: Penguin Books, 1996.

Duke, Benjamin. *The History of Modern Japanese Education: Constructing the National School System*. New Brunswick, NJ: Rutgers University Press, 2009.

Duncan, Sally Ann. "Harvard's 'Museum Course' and the Making of America's Museum Profession." *Archives of American Art Journal* 42, no. 1–2 (2002): 2–16.

The Educational Museum and the School of Art and Design for Upper Canada. Toronto: Department of Public instruction for Upper Canada, 1858.

Eliot, Charles W. *Pauline Agassiz Shaw: Tributes Paid Her Memory at the Memorial Service Held on Easter Sunday April 8, 1917 at Faneuil Hall, Boston*. Boston, 1917.

Engs, Robert Francis. *Educating the Disfranchised and Disinherited: Samuel Chapman Armstrong and Hampton Institute: 1839–1893*. Knoxville: University of Tennessee Press, 1999.

Faust, Drew Gilpin. *This Republic of Suffering: Death and the American Civil War*. New York: Alfred A. Knopf, 2008.

Fireside Facts from the Great Exhibition Being an Amusing Series of Object Lessons on the Food and Clothing of all Nations in the Year 1851. London: Houlston and Stoulman, 65 Paternoster Row, 1851.

Fleming, E. McClung. "Artifact Study: A Proposed Model." *Winterthur Portfolio* 9, (1974): 153–173.

Forman-Brunell, Miriam. *Made to Play House: Dolls and the Commercialization of American Girlhood, 1830–1930*. New Haven, CT: Yale University Press, 1993.

Gascoigne, Bamber. *How to Identify Prints: A Complete Guide to Manual and Mechanical Processes from Woodcut to Inkjet*. 2nd ed. New York: Thames & Hudson, 2004.

Gates, Henry Louis. "The Trope of the New Negro and the Reconstruction of the Image of the Black." *Representations* 24 (Autumn 1988): 129–155.

Generals, Donald. "Booker T. Washington and Progressive Education: An Experimentalist Approach to Curriculum Development and Reform." *Journal of Negro Education* 69, no. 3 (Summer 2000): 215–234.

Glassie, Henry H. *Folk Housing in Middle Virginia: A Structural Analysis of Historic Artifacts*. Knoxville: University of Tennessee Press, 1975.

Glover, William J. "Objects, Models, and Exemplary Works: Educating Sentiment in Colonial India," *Journal of Asian Studies* 64, no. 3 (2005): 539–566.

Gordon, Beverly. *The Saturated World: Aesthetic Meaning, Intimate Objects, Women's Lives, 1890–1940*. Knoxville: University of Tennessee Press, 2006.

Greene, S. S. *A Report on Object Teaching Made at the Meeting of the National Teachers' Association*. Boston: Massachusetts Teachers' Association, 1865.

Grier, Katherine C. *Pets in America: A History*. Chapel Hill: University of North Carolina Press, 2006.

Griscom, John A. *Year in Europe: Comprising a Journal of Observations in 1818 and 1819*. Vol. I. New York: Collins and Hannay, 1824.

De Guimps, Roger. *Pestalozzi, His Life and Work*. Translated from the second French edition by J. Russell. New York: D. Appleton, 1892.

Gutman, Marta, and Ning de Coninck-Smith. *Designing Modern Childhoods: History, Space, and the Material Culture of Children*. Newark, NJ: Rutgers University Press, 2008.

Gutek, Gerald Lee. *Joseph Neef: The Americanization of Pestalozzianism*. University: University of Alabama Press, 1978.

Hall, G. Stanley, "The Contents of Children's Minds." *Princeton Review* (January–June 1883): 249–273.

Halttunen, Karen. *Confidence Men and Painted Women: A Study of Middle-Class Culture in America, 1830–1870*. Yale Historical Publications. Miscellany, 129. New Haven, CT: Yale University Press, 1982.

Hampton Institute and Helen W. Ludlow. *Ten Years' Work for Indians at the Hampton Normal and Agricultural Institute, at Hampton, Virginia*. Hampton, VA: Hampton Institute, 1888.

Hampton Normal and Agricultural Institute. *Twenty-Two Years' Work of the Hampton Normal and Agricultural Institute at Hampton, Virginia: Records of Negro and Indian Graduates and Ex-Students*. Hampton, VA: Normal School Press, 1893.

Hansen, Emma I., Beatrice Medicine, and Buffalo Bill Historical Center. *Memory and Vision: Arts, Cultures, and Lives of Plains Indian People*. Seattle: Buffalo Bill Historical Center, in association with University of Washington Press, 2007.

Harrod, Tanya, Juliet Kinchin, and Aidan O'Connor. *Century of the Child: Growing by Design 1900–2000*. New York: Museum of Modern Art, 2012.

Heesen, Anke te. *The World in a Box: The Story of an Eighteenth-Century Picture Encyclopedia*. Translated by Ann M. Hentschel. Chicago: University of Chicago Press, 2002. Published in German as *Der Weltkasten: Die Geschichte einer Bildenzyklopädie aus dem 18. Jahrhundert*. Göttingen: Wallstein Verlag, 1997.

Hill, Thomas. *The True Order of Studies*. New York: G. P. Putnam's Sons, 1875.

Hollis, Andrew Phillip. *The Contribution of the Oswego Normal School to Educational Progress in the United States*. Boston: D. C. Heath, 1898.

Hoganson, Kristin. "Cosmopolitan Domesticity: Importing the American Dream, 1865–1920." *American Historical Review* 107, no. 1 (2002): 55–83.

The Home and Colonial School Society's Manual for Infant Schools and Nurseries, Prepared at the Desire of the Committee by Miss Rebecca Sunter, Late Mistress of the Model Infant School, under the Superintendence of Miss Mayo. London: The Society, Groombridge and Sons, 1856.

Hoxie, Frederick E. *A Final Promise: The Campaign to Assimilate the Indians, 1880–1920*. Lincoln: University of Nebraska Press, 1984.

Hultgren, Mary Lou, Paulette Fairbanks Molin, Rayna Green, Virginia Foundation for the Humanities and Public Policy, and Hampton University. *To Lead and to Serve: American Indian Education at Hampton Institute, 1878–1923*. Charlottesville: Virginia Foundation for the Humanities and Public Policy in cooperation with Hampton University, 1989.

Hunter, Thomas. *The Autobiography of Thomas Hunter*. New York: Knickerbocker Press, 1931.

Huntington, Emily. *How to Teach Kitchen Garden; or, Object Lessons in Household Work*. New York: Doubleday, Page & Co., 1903.

Huntington, Emily, and Frédéric Vors. *The Kitchen Garden; or, Object Lessons in Household Work: Including Songs, Plays, Exercises, and Games, Illustrating Household Occupations*. New York: Schermerhorn, 1893.

Information on Common Objects for the Use of Infant and Juvenile Schools and Nursery Governesses. London: Published for the Home and Colonial Infant School Society by Darton and Clark, 1845.

Irmscher, Christopher. *Louis Agassiz: Creator of American Science*. Boston: Houghton Mifflin Harcourt, 2013.

Jay, Robert. *The Trade Card in Nineteenth-Century America*. Columbia: University of Missouri Press, 1987.

Jedan, Dieter. *Johann Heinrich Pestalozzi and the Pestalozzian Method of Language Teaching*. Stanford German Studies. Vol. 16. Bern: P. Lang, 1981.

Jenkins, David. "Object Lessons and Ethnographic Displays: Museum Exhibitions and the Making of American Anthropology." *Comparative Studies in Society and History* 36, no. 2 (April 1994): 242–270.

Johns, Elizabeth. *American Genre Painting: The Politics of Everyday Life*. New Haven, CT: Yale University Press, 1991.

Johnston, Frances Benjamin, Lincoln Kirstein, and Museum of Modern Art. *The Hampton Album; 44 Photographs from an Album of Hampton Institute*. New York: Museum of Modern Art; distributed by Doubleday, Garden City, NY, 1966.

Kaestle, Carl F., and Eric Foner. *Pillars of the Republic: Common Schools and American Society, 1780–1860*. American Century Series. New York: Hill and Wang, 1983.

Kaplan, Wendy, Alan Crawford, Los Angeles County Museum of Art, Delaware Art Museum, and Cleveland Museum of Art. *The Arts & Crafts Movement in Europe & America: Design for the Modern World*. New York: Thames & Hudson in association with the Los Angeles County Museum of Art, 2004.

Keech, Mabel Louise. *Training the Little Home Maker*. Philadelphia: J. B. Lippincott, 1912.

Kidwell, Peggy Aldrich, Amy Ackerberg-Hastings, and David Lindsay Roberts. *Tools of American Mathematics Teaching, 1800–2000*. Johns Hopkins Studies in the History of Mathematics. Baltimore, MD: Johns Hopkins University Press, 2008.

The Kitchen Garden Association. *Advanced Lessons in Kitchen Garden.* New York: Schermerhorn, 1883.

Knox, Vicesimus. *The Works of Vicesimus Knox, D.D.: With a Biographical Preface.* London: J. Mawman, 1824.

Kohlstedt, Sally Gregory. "Nature, not Books: Scientists and the Origins of the Nature Study Movement in the 1890s." *Isis* 96, no. 3 (September 2005): 324–352.

Kohlstedt, Sally Gregory. "Parlors, Primers, and Public Schooling: Education for Science in Nineteenth-Century America." *Isis* 81, no. 3 (September 1990): 424–445.

Kohlstedt, Sally Gregor. *Teaching Children Science: Hands-on Nature Study in North America, 1890–1920.* Chicago: University of Chicago Press, 2010.

Kriegel, Lara. *Grand Designs: Labor, Empire, and the Museum in Victorian Culture.* Durham, NC: Duke University Press, 2007.

Kirk, Hyland. *A History of the New York State Teachers Association.* New York: Kellogg, 1883.

Krüsi, Hermann. *Recollections of My Life.* Edited by Mary Sheldon Alling. New York: Grafton Press, 1907.

Lake, W. J. *The Book of Object Lessons; a Teacher's Manual.* London, 1857.

Lanning, Robert. "On Developing 'Representations from Presentations': Observing the Laws of the Natural and Social Worlds." *Journal of Historical Sociology* 4, no. 4 (1991): 359–379.

Latham, Jackie. "Pestalozzi and James Pierrepont Greaves: A Shared Educational Philosophy." *History of Education* 31, no. 1 (2002): 59–70.

Lears, T. J. Jackson. *Fables of Abundance: A Cultural History of Advertising in America.* New York: Basic Books, 1994.

Lehmann, Ann-Sophie. "Objektstunden: Vom Materialwissen zur Materialbildung." In *Materialität: Herausforderungen für die Sozial- und Kulturwissenschaften,* ed. H. Kalthoff, T. Cress, and T. Röhl, 171–194. Paderborn: Wilhelm Fink, 2016.

Lehmann, Ann-Sophie. "Showing Making: On Visual Documentation and Creative Practice." *Journal of Modern Craft* 5, no. 1 (March 2012): 9–24.

Leja, Michael. *Looking Askance: Skepticism and American Art from Eakins to Duchamp.* Berkeley: University of California Press, 2004.

Lerer, Seth. *Children's Literature: A Reader's History, from Aesop to Harry Potter.* Chicago: University of Chicago Press, 2008.

Lindsey, Donal F. *Indians at Hampton Institute, 1877–1923.* Blacks in the New World. Urbana: University of Illinois Press, 1995.

Locke, John. *An Essay Concerning Human Understanding.* 24th ed. London: W. Baynes, 1817.

Locke, John. "An Essay Concerning Human Understanding" (1689). In *The Philosophical Works and Selected Correspondence of John Locke* [electronic resource]. Charlottesville, VA: InteLex Corporation, 1995.

MacMullen, Edith Nye. *In the Cause of True Education: Henry Barnard & Nineteenth-Century School Reform.* New Haven, CT: Yale University Press, 1991.

Mancini, JoAnne Marie. *Pre-Modernism: Art-World Change and American Culture from the Civil War to the Armory Show.* Princeton, NJ: Princeton University Press, 2005.

Mann, Mary Tyler Peabody, and Elizabeth Palmer Peabody. *Moral Culture of Infancy, and Kindergarten Guide.* Boston: T.O.H.P Burnham, 1863.

Marshall, Megan. *The Peabody Sisters: Three Women Who Ignited American Romanticism.* Boston: Houghton Mifflin, 2005.

Marten, James. *The Children's Civil War.* Chapel Hill: University of North Carolina Press, 1998.

Martin, Ann Smart. "Makers, Buyers, and Users: Consumerism as a Material Culture Framework." *Winterthur Portfolio* 28, no. 2/3 (Summer–Autumn, 1993): 141–157.

Martin, Jill F. "'Neither Fish, Flesh, Fowl, nor Good Red Herring:' The Citizenship Status of American Indians, 1830–1924." *Journal of the West* 29, no. 3 (1990): 75–87.

Mason, Lowell. *Manual of the Boston Academy of Music for Instruction in the Elements of Vocal Music, on the System of Pestalozzi.* Boston: Hendee, 1834.

Mayo, Charles. *Memoir of Pestalozzi: Being the Substance of a Lecture Delivered at the Royal Institution, Albemarle-Street, May, 1826.* London: Printed for J. A. Hessey, 93 Fleet Street, 1828.

Mayo, Charles, and Elizabeth Mayo. *Practical Remarks on Infant Education: For the Use of Schools and Private Families.* 3rd rev. and enl. ed. London: Published for the Home and Colonial Infant School Society by R.B. Seeley and W. Burnside, 1841.

Mayo, Charles Herbart. *A Genealogical Account of the Mayo and Elton Families of the Counties of Wilts and Hereford.* London: Privately Printed by Charles Whittingham, Ciswick Press, 1882.

Mayo, Elizabeth. *Lessons on Objects, as Given to Children between the Ages of Five and Eight in a Pestalozzian School at Cheam, Surrey.* London: Seeley & Burnside, 1832.

Mayo, Elizabeth. *Lessons on Objects, as Given to Children between the Ages of Six and Eight, in a Pestalozzian School, at Cheam, Surrey.* 16th ed. London: Seeley, Jackson, and Halliday, 1859.

Mayo, Elizabeth. *Lessons on Shells.* London: R. B. Seeley and W. Burnside, 1832.

Mayo, Elizabeth. *Lessons on Shells, as Given in a Pestalozzian School, at Cheam, Surrey.* New York: P. Hill, 1833.

Mayo, Elizabeth. *Model Lessons for Infant School Teachers and Governesses. Prepared for the Home and Colonial Infant School Society.* 3rd ed. London: Seeley, Burnside, and Seeley, 1846.

Mayo, Elizabeth, and John Frost. *Lessons on Common Things; For the Use of Schools and Families. On the Basis of Dr. Mayo's Lessons on Objects.* Philadelphia: J. B. Lippincott, 1857.

Mayo, Elizabeth, and E. A. Sheldon. *Lessons on Objects, Graduated Series: Designed for Children between the Ages of Six and Fourteen Years: Containing also Information on Common Objects.* New York: C. Scribner, 1863.

Mayo, Elizabeth, and E. A. Sheldon. *Lessons on Objects, Graduated Series: Designed for Children between the Ages of Six and Fourteen Years: Containing also Information on Common Objects.* New York: C. Scribner, 1869.

Mayo, Elizabeth, and E. A. Sheldon. *Lessons on Objects, Graduated Series: Designed for Children between the Ages of Six and Fourteen Years: Containing also Information on Common Objects.* New York: Scribner, Armstrong, 1873.

McAninch, Stuart A. "The Educational Theory of Mary Sheldon Barnes: Inquiry Learning as Indoctrination in History Education." *Educational Theory* 40 (1990): 45–52.

McCallum, E. L. *Object Lessons: How to Do Things with Fetishism.* SUNY Series in Psychoanalysis and Culture. Albany: State University of New York Press, 1999.

McCann, Phillip, and Francis A. Young. *Samuel Wilderspin and the Infant School Movement.* London: Croom Helm, 1982.

McDannell, Colleen. *Material Christianity: Religion and Popular Culture in America.* New Haven, CT: Yale University Press, 1995.

Menand, Louis. *The Metaphysical Club: A Story of Ideas in America.* New York: Farrar, Straus and Giroux, 2001.

Messerli, Jonathan. *Horace Mann; a Biography.* New York, Knopf: 1972.

Mintz, Steven. *Huck's Raft: A History of American Childhood.* Cambridge, MA: Belknap Press of Harvard University Press, 2004.

Mitchell, Sue, and Scottish Museums Council, eds. *Object Lessons: The Role of Museums in Education.* Edinburgh: Her Majesty's Stationery Office, 1996.

Model Lessons for Infant School Teachers and Nursery Governesses Prepared for the Home and Colonial Infant School Society. London: R. B. Seeley, 1838.

Morgan, David. *Protestants and Pictures: Religion, Visual Culture and the Age of American Mass Production.* New York: Oxford University Press, 1999.

Morison, Samuel Eliot. *One Boy's Boston, 1887–1901.* Boston: Houghton Mifflin, 1962.

National Education Association of the United States, William Torrey Harris, and Zalmon Richards. *History of the National Educational Association of the United States; its Organization and Functions.* Washington, DC: National Educational Association, 1892.

Neef, Joseph. *Sketch of a Plan and Method of Education: Founded on an Analysis of the Human Faculties and Natural Reason Suitable for the Offspring of a Few People and for all Rational Beings*. Philadelphia: n.p., 1808.

Norrell, Robert J. *Up from History: The Life of Booker T. Washington*. Cambridge, MA: Belknap Press of Harvard University Press, 2009.

Ogren, Christine A. *The American State Normal School: An Instrument of Great Good*. New York: Palgrave Macmillan, 2005.

Olsen, Bjørnar. "Material Culture after Text: Re-Membering Things." *Norwegian Archaeological Review* 36, no. 2 (2003): 87–104.

Orvell, Miles. *The Real Thing: Imitation and Authenticity in American Culture, 1880–1940*. Chapel Hill: University of North Carolina Press, 1989.

Oswego, New York, Board of Education. *Proceedings of the Educational Convention, Held at Oswego, N. Y., February 11, 12, and 13, 1862, to Examine into a System of Primary Instruction*. New York: Harper & Brothers, 1862.

Pancoast, Henry Spackman. *The Indian before the Law*. Indian Rights Association. Publications. 1st Ser. Philadelphia: Indian Rights Association, 1884.

Pauwels, L., ed. *Visual Cultures of Science: Rethinking Representational Practices in Knowledge Building and Science Communication*. Interfaces, Studies in Visual Culture. Hanover, NH: University Press of New England, 2006.

Peabody, Francis Greenwood. *Education for Life; the Story of Hampton Institute, Told in Connection with the Fiftieth Anniversary of the Foundation of the School*. Garden City, NY: Doubleday, Page, 1918.

Pearce, Susan M. *Museums, Objects, and Collections: A Cultural Study*. Washington, DC: Smithsonian Institution Press, 1993.

Pestalozzi, Johann Heinrich. *ABC Der Anschauung, Oder, Anschauungs-Lehre Der Massverhältnisse*. Zurich: In Commission bey Heinrich Gessner, Buchhändler; in der J. G. Cotta'schen Buchhandlung, 1803.

Pestalozzi, Johann Heinrich. *How Gertrude Teaches Her Children; an Attempt to Help Mothers to Teach Their Own Children and an Account of the Method*. Translated by Lucy E. Holland and Francis C. Turner, edited by Ebenezer Cooke. Syracuse, NY: C. W. Bardeen, 1898.

Pestalozzi, Johann Heinrich. *Pestalozzi's Leonard and Gertrude*. Translated by Eva Channing. Heath's Pedagogical Library, no. 6. Boston: D. C. Heath, 1903.

Pickering, Samuel F. *John Locke and Children's Books in Eighteenth-Century England*. Knoxville: University of Tennessee Press, 1981.

Pinckney, Eliza Lucas. *The Letterbook of Eliza Lucas Pinckney*. Edited by Elise Pinckney and Marvin R. Zahniser. Columbia: University of South Carolina Press, 1997.

Porsche, Audrey, and State Historical Society of North Dakota. *Yutō'Keca* [Transitions: the Burdick Collection]. Bismark: State Historical Society of North Dakota, 1987.

Pratt, Richard Henry, and Robert Marshall Utley, eds. *Battlefield and Classroom: Four Decades with the American Indian, 1867–1904*. Norman: University of Oklahoma Press, 2003.

Prentiss, Elizabeth. *Little Susy's Little Servants/By Her Aunt Susan*. New York: Anson D.F. Randolf, 683 Broadway, 1857.

Prochner, Larry. *A History of Early Childhood Education in Canada, Australia, and New Zealand*. Vancouver: University of British Columbia Press, 2009.

Prown, Jules David. *Art as Evidence: Writings on Art and Material Culture*. New Haven, CT: Yale University Press, 2001.

Prown, Jules David. "Mind in Matter: An Introduction to Material Culture Theory and Method." *Winterthur Portfolio* 17, no. 1 (Spring 1982): 1–19.

Prown, Jules David, and Kenneth Haltman, eds. *American Artifacts: Essays in Material Culture*. East Lansing: Michigan State University Press, 2000.

Ravenel, Harriott Horry. *Eliza Pinckney*. Women of Colonial and Revolutionary Times. New York: C. Scribner's Sons, 1896.

Reese, William J. *America's Public Schools: From the Common School to "No Child Left Behind."* The American Moment. Baltimore, MD: Johns Hopkins University Press, 2005.

Reese, William J. "The Origins of Progressive Education." *History of Education Quarterly* 41, no. 1 (March 2001): vi, 1–24.

Reese, William J. *Testing Wars in the Public Schools: A Forgotten History.* Cambridge, MA: Harvard University Press, 2013.

Ricks, George. *Object Lessons and How to Give them, Second Series for Intermediate and Grammar Schools.* Heath's Pedagogical Library. Boston: D.C. Heath, 1895.

Riskin, Jessica. *Science in the Age of Sensibility: The Sentimental Empiricists of the French Enlightenment.* Chicago: University of Chicago Press, 2002.

Rogers, Dorothy. *Oswego: Fountainhead of Teacher Education; a Century in the Sheldon Tradition.* New York: Appleton-Century-Crofts, 1961.

Rogers, Molly. *Delia's Tears: Race, Science, and Photography in Nineteenth-Century America.* New Haven, CT: Yale University Press, 2010.

Rooper, T. G. *Apperception: Or, the Essential Mental Operation in the Act of Learning. An Essay on "A Pot of Green Feathers."* Syracuse, NY: C. W. Bardeen, 1891.

Rose, Anna Christina. "'Personal Powers of the Child': Object Lessons and Languages of Agency in the Science of Childhood." *Journal of the History of Childhood and Youth* 4, no. 3 (Fall 2011): 369–381.

Rose, Jane Atteridge. "A Bibliography of Fiction and Non-Fiction by Rebecca Harding Davis." *American Literary Realism, 1870–1910* 22, no. 3 (Spring 1990): 67–86.

Ross, Dorothy. *G. Stanley Hall: The Psychologist as Prophet.* Chicago: University of Chicago Press, 1972.

Rousseau, Jean-Jacques. *Emile or on Education.* Translated and edited by Allan Bloom. New York: Basic Books, 1979.

Rydell, Robert W. *All the World's a Fair: Visions of Empire at American International Expositions, 1876–1916.* Chicago: University of Chicago Press, 1985.

Sánchez-Eppler, Karen. *Dependent States: The Child's Part in Nineteenth-Century American Culture.* Chicago: University of Chicago Press, 2005.

Schlereth, Thomas J. *Material Culture Studies in America: An Anthology.* Nashville, TN: American Association for State and Local History, 1982.

Schultz, Lucille M. *The Young Composers: Composition's Beginnings in Nineteenth-Century Schools.* Studies in Writing & Rhetoric. Carbondale: Southern Illinois University Press, 1999.

Sengupta, Parna. "An Object Lesson in Colonial Pedagogy." *Comparative Studies in Society and History* 45, no. 1 (January 2003): 96–121.

Sengupta, Parna. *Pedagogy for Religion: Missionary Education and the Fashioning of Hindus and Muslims in Bengal.* Berkeley: University of California Press, 2011.

Sheldon, E. A., and Mary Sheldon Barnes. *Autobiography of Edward Austin Sheldon.* New York: Ives-Butler, 1911.

Sheldon, E. A., Margaret E. M. Jones, and Hermann Krüsi. *A Manual of Elementary Instruction, for the Use of Public and Private Schools and Normal Classes: Containing a Graduated Course of Object Lessons for Training the Senses and Developing the Faculties of Children.* New York: C. Scribner, 1862.

Sheldon, E. A., Margaret E. M. Jones, and Hermann Krüsi. *A Manual of Elementary Instruction, for the Use of Public and Private Schools and Normal Classes: Containing a Graduated Course of Object Lessons for Training the Senses and Developing the Faculties of Children.* 6th ed., rev. and enl. ed. New York: Scribner, Armstrong, 1870.

Sheldon Barnes, Mary. *Studies in General History.* Boston: D. C. Heath, 1901.

Sheldon Barnes, Mary, and Earl Barnes. *Studies in American History.* Boston: D. C. Heath, 1893.

Silber, Kate. *Pestalozzi; the Man and His Work.* 3rd ed. New York: Schocken Books, 1973.

Simonsen, Jane E. *Making Home Work: Domesticity and Native American Assimilation in the American West, 1860–1919.* Gender and American Culture. Chapel Hill: University of North Carolina Press, 2006.

Simonsen, Jane E. "'Object Lessons': Domesticity and Display in Native American Assimilation." *American Studies* 43, no. 1 (2002): 75–99.

Skrabec, Quentin R. *William McKinley, Apostle of Protectionism.* New York: Algora, 2008.

Smith, Adam. *The Theory of Moral Sentiment, Or, an Essay Towards an Analysis of the Principles, by which Men Naturally Judge Concerning the Conduct and Character, First of their Neighbours, and Afterwards of Themselves; Essay Towards an Analysis of the Principles; Smith's Theory of Moral Sentiments.* Boston: Wells and Lilly, 1817.

Smith, Elizabeth, and H. M. Bowdler. *Fragments in Prose and Verse. with some Account of Her Life and Character; Miss Smith's Life.* Burlington, NJ: D. Allinson, 1811.

Smith, Mark. *Sensing the Past: Seeing, Hearing, Smelling, Tasting, and Touching in History.* Berkeley: University of California Press, 2007.

Smith, Mark M. *How Race Is Made: Slavery, Segregation, and the Senses.* Chapel Hill: University of North Carolina Press, 2006.

Smith, Shawn Michelle. *American Archives: Gender, Race, and Class in Visual Culture.* Princeton, NJ: Princeton University Press, 1999.

Smuts, Alice Boardman, and Robert W. Smuts. *Science in the Service of Children, 1893–1935.* New Haven, CT: Yale University Press, 2006.

Stanworth, Karen. *Visibly Canadian: Imaging Collective Identity in the Canadas, 1820–1910.* Montreal: McGill-Queen's University Press, 2014.

State University College of Education. *Historical Sketches Relating to the First Quarter Century of the State Normal and Training School at Oswego, N.Y.* Oswego, NY: R. J. Oliphant, 1888.

Stiles, Henry Reed. *The Stiles Family in America. Genealogies of the Connecticut Family. Descendants of John Stiles, of Windsor, Conn., and of Mr. Francis Stiles, of Windsor and Stratford, Conn., 1635–1894; also the Connecticut New Jersey Families, 1720–1894; and the Southern (Or Bermuda-Georgia) Family, 1635–1894. with Contributions to the Genealogies of some New York and Pennsylvania Families.* Jersey City, NJ: Doan & Pilson, 1895.

Teather, J. Lynne. *The Royal Ontario Museum: A Prehistory, 1830–1914.* Toronto: Canadian University Press, 2005.

Trent, James W. *Inventing the Feeble Mind: A History of Mental Retardation in the United States.* Medicine and Society, 6. Berkeley: University of California Press, 1994.

Tröhler, Daniel. *Johann Heinrich Pestalozzi.* Aufl ed. Bern: Haupt Verlag, 2008.

Tschurenev, Jana. "Diffusing Useful Knowledge: The Monitorial System of Education in Madras, London and Bengal, 1789–1840." *Paedagogica Historica* 44 (June 2008): 245–264.

Tucker, Robert C., Karl Marx, and Friedrich Engels, eds. *The Marx-Engels Reader.* 2nd ed. New York: W. W. Norton, 1978.

Ulrich, Laurel. *The Age of Homespun: Objects and Stories in the Creation of an American Myth.* 1st ed. New York: Alfred A. Knopf, 2001.

Upton, Dell. *Holy Things and Profane: Anglican Parish Churches in Colonial Virginia.* Architectural History Foundation Books, 10. New York: Architectural History Foundation and Cambridge, MA: MIT Press, 1986.

US Congress Senate Committee on Finance. *Act to Reduce the Revenue and Equalize Duties on Imports, and for Other Purposes,* Public Law (51) H.R. 9416. 1890.

Walker, J. *The Handy Book of Object Lessons: From a Teacher's Note Book.* Philadelphia: Lippincott, 1884.

Warner, Deborah Jean. "Commodities for the Classroom: Apparatus for Science and Education in Antebellum America." *Annals of Science [Great Britain]* 45, no. 4 (1988): 387–397.

Washington, Booker T. *Up from Slavery: An Autobiography.* Garden City, NY: Doubleday, 1901.

Washington, Booker T., Louis R. Harlan, and Raymond Smock. *The Booker T. Washington Papers.* Vol. 3. Edited by Louis R. Harlan. Urbana: University of Illinois Press, 1972.

Washington, Booker T., Fannie Barrier Williams, and Norman Barton Wood. *A New Negro for a New Century: An Accurate and Up-to-Date Record of the Upward Struggles of the Negro Race: The Spanish-American War, Causes of it: Vivid Descriptions of Fierce Battles: Superb Heroism and Daring Deeds of the Negro Soldier . . . Education, Industrial Schools, Colleges, Universities, and their Relationship to the Race Problem.* Chicago: American Publishing House, 1900.

Weems, Carrie Mae, Vivian Patterson, Frederick Rudolph, Denise Ramzy, Katherine Fogg, Williams College Museum of Art, and Hood Museum of Art. *Carrie Mae Weems: The Hampton Project; Hampton Project, Before and After*. New York: Aperture, in association with Williams College Museum of Art, Williamstown, MA, 2000.

Wexler, Laura. *Tender Violence: Domestic Visions in an Age of U.S. Imperialism*. Cultural Studies of the United States. Chapel Hill: University of North Carolina Press, 2000.

Whaley, Irene, and Tessa Rose Chester. *A History of Children's Book Illustration*. London: John Murray, 1988.

Whitbread, Nanette. *The Evolution of the Nursery-Infant School: A History of Infant and Nursery Education in Britain, 1800–1970*. Students Library of Education. London: Routledge and Kegan Paul, 1972.

Winsor, Mary P. *Reading the Shape of Nature: Comparative Zoology at the Agassiz Museum*. Science and Its Conceptual Foundations. Chicago: University of Chicago Press, 1991.

Yanni, Carla. *Nature's Museums: Victorian Science and the Architecture of Display*. Baltimore, MD: Johns Hopkins University Press, 1999.

Young, Ella Flagg. *Some Types of Modern Educational Theory*. Contributions to Education, no. 6. Chicago: University of Chicago Press, 1902.

Young, William A. *History of the Houston Public Schools 1836–1965*. Houston: Gulf School Research Development Association, 1968.

INDEX

Page references to tables, figures, and notes are indicated by *t*, *f*, *n*, respectively.
Color insert falls between pages 98 and 99.